THE POPPY

Also by Nicholas J. Saunders

Contested Objects (ed. with Paul Cornish)
Beyond the Dead Horizon (ed.)
Killing Time
Peoples of the Caribbean
Matters of Conflict (ed.)
Alexander's Tomb
Ancient Americas
Trench Art
Icons of Power (ed.)
Animal Spirits
People of the Jaguar

THE POPPY

A Cultural History
from Ancient Egypt
to Flanders Fields
to Afghanistan

Nicholas J. Saunders

ONEWORLD

A ONEWORLD BOOK

First published by Oneworld Publications 2013

Copyright © Nicholas J. Saunders 2013

The moral right of Nicholas J. Saunders to be identified
as the author of this work has been asserted by him in accordance with
the Copyright, Designs and Patents Act 1988

ISBN: 978-1-85168-705-3
Ebook ISBN: 978-1-78074-185-7

Cover design by David Wardle
Illustrations © Andrea Hill
Printed and bound by Bookwell, Finland

Oneworld Publications
10 Bloomsbury Street, London WC1B 3SR
England

Stay up to date with the latest books,
special offers, and exclusive content from
Oneworld with our monthly newsletter

Sign up on our website
www.oneworld-publications.com

For my father
Alan Geoffrey Saunders (1922–2010)
who gave me my first poppy

CONTENTS

ACKNOWLEDGEMENTS

THIS BOOK IS DEDICATED TO MY FATHER, WHO PASSED away as it was being written, and thus had no chance to read it.

The connection between war, memory, emotion and the Remembrance Poppy is visceral for me. I remember as a child standing on a cold winter morning in the late 1950s among the crowd gathered around Southampton's cenotaph, designed by Sir Edwin Lutyens. At its summit, out of sight, lay a recumbent First World War soldier, staring into the grey sky. As I fidgeted with the poppy Dad had given me, gigantic booms filled the air and made me jump – it was 11 a.m. on 11 November, and I've never forgotten it.. Dad had fought and been wounded in Italy during the Second World War, and was here to remember the many friends he had lost. I was too young to understand, yet I feel that, in a sense, this book began then, over fifty years ago, and that its completion is a small commemoration of my own father and all those who have died and suffered during the many wars of the twentieth and twenty-first centuries.

It is impossible to express adequately the gratitude I owe to those who have inspired and helped me with their advice, experience and insights over the years in which this book has taken shape. I am, however, especially grateful to Annette Becker, Barbara Bender, Franky Bostyn, James Brazier, Piet Chielens, Paul Cornish, Anna Baker Cresswell,

Dominiek Dendooven, Paul Gough, Tom Morgan, Stephen Mulqueen, Robin Ollington, Jeffrey Reznick, Rik Ryon, Tony Spagnoly, Lieven Stubbe, Gabriel Versavel, Patrice Warin and the late Marian Wenzel. I would like to express my thanks to Peter Tallack at The Science Factory and to all at Oneworld who have worked so hard to make this book possible – Marsha Filion, Ruth Deary, Jenny Page and Henry Jeffreys – and especially to Robin Dennis, my editor, whose expert eye has so improved the reading experience.

I owe a continuing debt to my wife, Pauline; my children, Roxanne and Alexander; my mother, Pat Saunders; and, ultimately, to my grand-fathers, Alfred William Saunders, of the King's Own Royal Regiment (Lancaster), and Matthew Inkerman Chorley, of the South Lancashire Regiment. Both fought in the Great War and survived. I like to think that they would be heartened to know that the generations for whose freedom they fought still wear the Remembrance Poppy, albeit in the bittersweet knowledge that young men and women are still fighting and dying in wars. The Remembrance Poppy is not a fading bloom for history's conflicts, but a reality that is perpetually rejuvenated by continuing sacrifice.

In Flanders Fields

In Flanders fields the poppies blow
Between the crosses, row on row,
That mark our place; and in the sky
The larks, still bravely singing, fly
Scarce heard amid the guns below.

We are the Dead. Short days ago
We lived, felt dawn, saw sunset glow,
Loved and were loved, and now we lie
In Flanders fields.

Take up our quarrel with the foe:
To you from failing hands we throw
The torch; be yours to hold it high.
If ye break faith with us who die
We shall not sleep, though poppies grow
In Flanders fields.

– John McCrae, 1915

THE POPPY

I

GENESIS

The Eurostar hurtles down the high-speed rail track that cuts through the French countryside from the port of Calais to the medieval city of Lille. For a moment, a scarlet blur fills the carriage windows, and is then pushed back by a fence of barbless wire. This is the largest war memorial the world has seen – a hundred million poppies straddling the railway and A1 motorway as they make their way south from the English Channel into the heart of northern France. Yet it is a figment of the imagination.

The memorial lives only as a proposal suggested in 1999 by Pascal Truffaut, a professor of architecture from Lille. His knowledge of the First World War and his professional expertise moved him to imagine something unique, something that would vividly commemorate the tens of thousands who died on the battlefield of the Somme in the summer of 1916, exactly the time of year when poppies appear. Crimson poppies would make a striking monument, Truffaut says, 'they should form a "river of blood", a permanent reminder of the sacrifice, and the horrors, of the war, for all the nations who were involved'.[1]

Truffaut's ribbon of red was planned to follow part of No Man's Land, the killing ground which divided the opposing Allied and German trenches. It was just to the north of here, at Ypres in Belgian Flanders, that John McCrae, a Canadian army doctor, wrote the poem 'In Flanders Fields' that ignited the passions of the postwar public and launched the very first Remembrance Poppy appeal. McCrae's poem has itself become the enduring memorial to the Great War.

It was May 1915. A few days earlier, the Germans had unleashed a choking fog of chlorine gas onto the Allied positions and McCrae had read the Order for the Burial of the Dead over the freshly dug grave of his friend Lieutenant Alexis Helmer. Blown to pieces by a bombardment just hours before, twenty-two-year-old Helmer was hurriedly buried in an impromptu battlefield cemetery, yards from the first-aid dugout where McCrae tended the wounded. At dawn the next day, McCrae gazed on the makeshift burials of those who had been killed, and noted the lively corn poppies that had sprung up between them. The scene played on his mind. Glancing occasionally at Helmer's grave, he immortalised the poppy in verse.

McCrae's poem caused a sensation on its publication. The corn poppy was rechristened the Flanders Poppy, and the image of its fragile blood-red petals rooted itself in the psyche of the English-speaking Allies as their emblem of remembrance. The poem and the poppies that inspired it were fused into one, a symbol used to raise money for the war effort, and later for postwar campaigns to honour the dead and to help those maimed by the war: the Remembrance Poppy.[2]

Tragic yet uplifting, lethal but comforting, the story of the Remembrance Poppy is international in spirit yet intimately personal. As a symbol the poppy has an ancient and fractured past, but this history has not prevented it from taking on new and contorted meanings in our modern commercial age. Over the last century, the flower became inseparable from our experience of countless conflicts, from the Great War through the Second World War to Iraq. Today it is embroiled in a new struggle – called until recently the 'War on Terror' – a seemingly unending state of conflict enlisting the men and women of our volunteer military, whether they are serving in the opium fields of Afghanistan or closer to home. The Remembrance Poppy is a touchstone for the issues and the aftermath of these wars – the value put on the sacrifice made by millions of dead, the place of pacifism, the importance of public remembrance, the billion-dollar trade in narcotics trafficking and the multi-billion-dollar business of war. The Remembrance Poppy is volatile, for ever entangled with people as they endure the chaos of war and then struggle to find some way to rebuild their lives once war has ended.

Of course, the poppy is also a real living thing. Around the world there are about 250 species of poppy, with 70 belonging to the genus *Papaver*, which takes its name from the Latin for 'poppy', and whose members characteristically ooze a creamy latex when cut.[3] These poppies range across the alkaline soils of Europe, North Africa and Central Asia. Poppy lives are brief, and they flourish in human company. The origins of the Remembrance Poppy are found in two of myriad species – the simple corn poppy and its powerful cousin, the opium poppy.

Despite the fact that the Remembrance Poppy itself was only conceived in the early part of the twentieth century, the red corn poppy and the pinkish-white opium poppy have had interwoven histories for centuries. They are the poppies of war. Both grow on sunlit, broken ground, and for millennia have inhabited the places where humans till the soil and bury their dead. The corn poppy (*Papaver rhoeas*) grew with abandon across Europe and the Middle East as trade wars gave way to the Crusades, which in turn gave way to the resource wars of nation states. The painkilling properties of opium have been highly valued as a powerful antidote to the traumas of battle throughout the ages. Long before the advent of modern medicine the opium poppy's (*Papaver somniferum*) juice and resin have been used to ease mental anguish and alleviate the pain of wounds. The opium poppy's soporific qualities brought temporary forgetfulness of suffering to those maimed and bereaved by conflict. Once John McCrae's poem claimed the corn poppy as the flower of remembrance, the fragile bloom was transformed. But while the Remembrance Poppy took on the corn poppy's appearance, its power to help individuals bear the pain of suffering and loss, and to continue with their lives despite it all, belong more to the realm of the opium poppy. Ancient traditions collided with modern events, and the two poppy species became one.

THE CORN POPPY'S AFFAIR with cultivated land is absolute. As long as the ground is broken, the scarlet flower will grow. Despite its apparent fragility, it is resilient, and possesses all the characteristics of a successful weed. It appears in late spring, as the warming land shrugs off the winter cold; it blooms in early summer, and its heavy, seed-filled pod weighs down the stem as the flower matures, bowing the four-petalled head. When ripe, the star-shaped top of the elongated oval pod explodes, casting thousands of black seeds to the wind, guaranteeing that new poppies sprout in the same fields year after year. The poppy contains a milky sap, whose alkaloid rhoeadine acts as a sedative, and has been used in folk medicine from ancient to modern times to make a mildly soporific tea. When crushed, the seeds yield nutritious oil, a tasty substitute for olive oil. Sunlight glimmers through its short-lived petals, which are silky to the touch and easily bruised. They provide the blush for a deep-red dye which is used to colour wine, though is too unstable for use on cloth.

Papaver somniferum means 'bringer of sleep', but the opium poppy is no less social than the corn poppy. It too seeks out the company of people, thriving on the churned earth, reappearing year after year. The similarities, however, end there. The opium poppy is more robust, stands a metre tall or more and appears in variegated hues, though white, pink and purple are the most common. Its capsule carries a resin loaded with alkaloids, of which morphine, thebaine and codeine are the most potent. The traditional method of harvesting is to score the immature capsule so that the sap leaks out and dries on the pod's outer surface. The sticky hardened resin is then scraped off and collected for use. The opium poppy is unique. Of the 27,000 different flowering plants in the world, only the opium poppy makes morphine.[4]

The opium poppy has a mysterious past, as no wild ancestor has been identified.[5] It has also enjoyed an elusive and unique relationship with humans for some eight thousand years because it is the only poppy species which has been domesticated as a crop.[6] Its origins may lie in Asia Minor (modern Turkey), or perhaps in the neighbouring Balkans, the heartland of early European agriculture. There are some early clues, however, from Western Europe.

In 1865, a charred poppy capsule was recovered from a waterlogged Neolithic village by Lake Pfäffikersee near Robenhausen in northern Switzerland. Dated to around 2500BCE,[7] the capsule appears to be from an intermediate species, a semi-wild opium poppy. Since that time, evidence of opium-poppy cultivation has been found by archaeologists in similar lakeside locations across Switzerland, from the Neolithic to the Bronze Age (c. 5500 to 800BCE).[8] At Egolzwil on the shores of former Lake Wauwil, in Lucerne, 6,000-year-old poppy-seed cakes and poppy heads have been excavated among clay hearths and pottery in well-preserved timber houses. The evidence suggests that poppies were more commonly grown here than wheat or barley.

Another major finding came in 1935, when fossilised ripe poppy capsules, later carbon dated to around 4000BCE, were discovered in the 'Cave of the Bats' in southern Spain. The capsules, along with locks of hair, were tucked inside woven grass baskets, which were laid among human skeletons – the earliest evidence to date of poppies being placed at a grave. It is likely this was a deliberate act, as the archaeologist Ralph Solecki discovered similar evidence from a far older site in Iraq. He found that pollen in a 6,000-year-old Neanderthal cave burial came from variously coloured flowers and appeared to have been placed purposefully around the skeletal remains.[9]

Remarkable evidence has recently come from La Marmotta by Lake Bracciano, a water-filled volcanic crater situated north-west of Rome. Since 1989, archaeologists have been excavating the remains of a large Neolithic town of wattle and daub houses supported on thousands of oak posts preserved in the sediments at the bottom of the lake. Inside a large thirty-two-foot-long building they discovered a statuette, carved from soapstone, of a voluptuous woman – a so-called 'Mother Goddess' figurine – which may indicate that the building served a religious purpose. They also found large quantities of well-preserved charred and uncharred opium-poppy seeds, pods and stigmatic discs (the 'cap' to the pod that contains the flower's reproductive stigma, which trap pollen). The seeds appear to be of a semi-wild variety, and so the poppies were most likely being cultivated near the village for their seeds and sap – and their painkilling effects. Dated to 5700BCE, they are the earliest samples of opium-poppy seeds found in a human settlement.[10]

For almost eight thousand years, the mildly narcotic corn poppy and the morphine-bearing opium poppy have grown alongside each other, united in their dependence on people. This enduring relationship, while still not fully understood, spanned humanity's transition from early agriculture to urban civilisation: these two poppies were ever present as medicine, religion, literature and art developed, and they can be traced through all these human endeavours.

HOW AND WHY did the humble corn poppy become a universal symbol of remembrance and memory? What made it so enduring that this symbolism has survived for millennia to be reborn on the last century's battlefields, from Flanders Fields to Helmand Province? Every year, eighty million red paper and plastic poppies are distributed around the world, carrying their message to remember and honour the dead. The lightest of petals bears the heaviest of burdens. Yet, each Remembrance Poppy should also remind us of a deep-rooted connection to the past, when the opium poppy floated the soul to the afterlife.

We disturb the earth for only a handful of reasons – to build somewhere to live, to grow plants for food and to bury our dead. Life and death flourish in the churning of soil, and it is in such places that poppies thrive – on the boundary between existence and extinction. From the wheat fields of antiquity to the battlefields of the Somme and Helmand, poppies have affected us as much as we have affected them. They have the power to enthral and repel, to beguile and repulse, a mirror held up to our imperfect humanity. Long before the twentieth century brought industrialised war to the world, the poppy haunted our imagination.

2

THE FLOWER OF FORGETFULNESS

Shielded from the sweltering heat of the Mesopotamian plain, in what is now southern Iraq, Sumerian scribes hunched over wet clay tablets in a cool room inside the walls of the city of Nippur. Here, in 3000 BCE, in the land between the Tigris and Euphrates rivers, one of these men etched two small images composed of vertical and horizontal arrow-shaped signs. Five thousand years later, in 1893, among the ancient city's crumbling ruins south of Baghdad, archaeologists uncovered thousands of their baked-clay tablets covered in the distinctive wedge-shaped signs of cuneiform, the world's first script.

They scrutinised tablets on law, politics and economics, slowly deciphering the pictographic signs. One of the tablets was recognised to have been inscribed by an anonymous Sumerian physician, who had committed his favourite remedies to the clay – creating the world's oldest-known list of medical prescriptions, dating back to 2100 BCE.[1] Professor Raymond Dougherty, a famous scholar of Near Eastern civilisations and curator of the Babylonian Collection at Yale University, had spent a lifetime studying inscriptions from ancient Mesopotamia when he turned to the document in 1927. As he scanned the clay, he pointed out an interesting combination of pictographic signs – *Hul* and *Gil*. *Hul*, he said, meant 'joy', and *Gil* represented several plants. Together, he mused, they might refer to a particular plant whose fruit could bring happiness or delight – in the form of opium.[2]

Almost a century later, however, scholars still dispute Dougherty's interpretation, since opium capsules and seeds have not yet been found by archaeologists in the field.[3] Still, it is likely that the Sumerians knew of the poppy's powerful mind-altering effects. Sumerian civilisation was born out of plant domestication, the annual flooding of the alluvium by the Tigris and Euphrates and the subsequent draining of marshes and channelling of the flood waters through a network of canals that had been built painstakingly – and with tremendous administrative control over the population – throughout southern Mesopotamia. Intensive, large-scale, year-round agriculture was ideal for refining newly domesticated species into food crops. It would also have been the perfect environment for poppies to take root. And while there is currently no archaeological evidence of poppy seeds or capsules, there is an intriguing association of the plant with one of ancient Sumer's major deities.

Nisaba was the sister of Ninsun, the mother of the Sumerian hero Gilgamesh, and, through her association with agricultural fertility, she has been identified as the goddess of the grain harvest. On a fragment of a carved-stone drinking vessel now in the State Museum in Berlin, she is depicted with poppy capsules sprouting from her shoulders.[4] Furthermore, Nisaba was the goddess of learning and the patron of Sumerian scribes, who often honoured her by ending their clay-tablet inscriptions with the phrase 'Nisaba be praised'.[5] The relationship between Sumerian agriculture, religion and an as yet unspecified poppy cultivar is clear in art if not yet in archaeology.

Dougherty for his part was not satisfied to take a single cuneiform sign on a single tablet as evidence of opium production in the region. Instead, he turned to a trove of ancient texts discovered in 1849 by the English archaeologist Sir Austen Henry Layard at Nineveh, in what is today northern Iraq, and taken to the British Museum soon afterwards. This extraordinary archive of two thousand tablets comprised the library of the Assyrian king Ashurbanipal, who ruled between 685 and 627BCE. The Assyrians rose to power around 2000BCE as the Sumerians declined, and unlike their predecessors, were an imperial civilisation whose territory stretched from Anatolia (modern Turkey) in the north to the Levant and Egypt in the south. The Assyrian cuneiform script appeared to have borrowed and incorporated many Sumerian signs. Searching through Ashurbanipal's royal library, Dougherty found example after example of the *Hul Gil* symbol.[6]

He was not the only researcher to trawl through the tablets in search of medicinal data. After their arrival in London, they had been studied by the British Museum's own Assyrian specialist and cuneiform expert Reginald Campbell Thompson (1876–1941), who would go on to excavate at Nineveh and Ur, and later teach T.E. Lawrence at Oxford. Thompson identified 250 vegetable narcotics which the Assyrians had used as medicines – opium among them. Royal physicians employed different parts of the opium-poppy plant for different purposes, and gave each a name: *săm araru* for the flower, *săm ukuš-rim* for the pods and *irrŭ* for the milky narcotic resin.[7] Thompson was convinced by the richly detailed catalogue in the Nineveh tablets that opium had been used for almost every medical condition: pregnancy, stomach troubles, eye problems, headaches, even inflammations and bruises.[8]

DECODING HUMANITY'S EARLY USE of the opium poppy leads us along the tangled paths of ancient languages, trying to discern the meanings of signs as they change over time and from one culture to another. It might seem that the physical remnants of art and architecture are more secure, yet art brings its own puzzles of interpretation. If one is unfamiliar with the ideas, beliefs and conventions that formed a piece of art, grasping its motifs and symbolism can be difficult. This is compounded when the writing system itself is pictographic, composed of miniature picture-signs that are half-way between art and language as we understand them.

Assyrian art epitomises the controversies. Around 880BCE, the king Ashurnasirpal II, who ruled from 883 to 859BCE, established his capital at Nimrud south of Nineveh on the River Tigris. It was here at his royal court that he initiated a new artistic tradition when he commanded his craftsmen to produce a suite of beautifully rendered bas-reliefs. Carved from gypsum and alabaster and then painted, these plaques stand over two metres tall and a metre wide and show imposing priests and terrifying winged and bird-headed supernatural creatures engaged in Assyrian rituals lost to the world of extinct religion and forgotten myth. Some of these ancient masterpieces depict realistic flowers, including a collection of stems crowned with round pods – the most compelling ancient images of the opium poppy.[9] Other plants include the blue lotus, a native of the River Nile that was a mild sedative used in ancient Egypt to promote health and for making perfumes. The blue lotus is also one of the flowers identified as among those eaten by the mythical Lotophagi (lotus eaters) in Homer's *Odyssey*, who were lulled into a state of contented apathy from dining on the narcotic bloom.

Fragments of another Assyrian bas-relief panel were uncovered between 1929 and 1934 from a courtyard of the royal city of Khorsabad, site of the capital of the monarch Sargon II, who reigned from 721 to

705BCE. As at Nimrud and Nineveh, these stone carvings recorded Assyrian religious belief, including what has been interpreted as a priest in the midst of an exorcism. He stands before 'a sacred tree', and, according to Yale medical historian Frederick Kilgour, 'it may be that the demons he is driving off are those of disease'. Most enticing, the priest by Kilgour's description 'holds in his left hand three mature poppy heads'.[10] Some have argued that these plants could be sacred pomegranates or revered pine cones,[11] or possibly motifs invented by the artists, but while a host of supernatural creatures climb across these sculptures, the Assyrian craftsmen appear to have been under royal orders to present plants with what we might call 'photographic accuracy'. Pomegranates are too big in proportion to their surroundings to be the plants shown here, and they do not hang from long stalks; furthermore, pine cones are clearly identifiable elsewhere on these monumental works of art. More convincing still is the usually ignored fact that the disputed poppy images from the ancient city of Nimrud show score lines on the round pod heads – lines that would be produced when harvesting raw opium.

The presence of the opium poppy on Assyrian sculptures is far from universally agreed, as these examples attest. The American botanist Abraham Krikorian has been vocal in his arguments against the existence of any physical evidence.[12] Yet scholarly caution does not imply that the Assyrians were unfamiliar with this narcotic flower, which blossomed all over their empire, an area which today includes the poppy-growing regions of Turkey and Iran. The empire's physicians and priests – often the distinction was slight – would have crafted tonics for the Assyrian public's medicinal and spiritual benefit, creating their recipes based on a close observation of human symptoms, a rigorous catalogue of supernatural belief and an intimate knowledge of the natural world – its plants, animals and minerals. A particular illness might be explained as punishment from a god or demon, and treatment involved placating the deity by prescribing a tonic to the patient: '[In] the evening a fever afflicted her and [at] dawn I gave [her] a plant to drink. Her temperature is normal [but] her feet are cold. Whereas before she coughed [she does not cough] now'.[13] The realistic approach to the portrayal of plants among Assyrian sculptors was most likely based on the need to identify powerful and potentially lethal species for their medicinal benefits; over time, the plants gained wider philosophical significance when it came to issues of life and death. The usefulness of the opium poppy would almost certainly have been noted in this commingling of body and spirit.

From its earliest cultivation the opium poppy was used to bridge the divide between pain and pleasure, between the living and the dead. The plant's milky sap relieved anguish, induced sleep and carried comfort and forgetfulness on its heavy, sweet scent. It was the stately herald of euphoria and the dreamworld.

EGYPT, A LAND WATERED by the Nile, animated by the breath of gods and haunted by evil spirits, became a unified kingdom under King Menes around 3150BCE. Its sacred temples and palaces – at Thebes, Memphis, Dendera and Abu Simbel – are a testament to the creative genius and skills of its people. The pivot of this universe was the pharaoh and the members of his court, whose earthly lives mirrored the cosmic paradise they believed they would inherit in the afterlife. According to Egyptian mythology, opium was regarded as a gift of the gods: Thoth, lord of letters, invention and wisdom, taught his mortal servants how to prepare it. In the Ebers Papyrus, a medical document from around 1550BCE, a spell to quell a headache fuses herbal exactness and religious cure as a divine example to humankind. 'Remedy which the goddess Isis prepared for the god Ra to drive out the pains that are in his head – berry of the coriander, berry [capsule] of the poppy plant, wormwood . . . juniper . . . [and] honey . . . When this remedy is used by him against all illnesses in the head and all sufferings and evils of any sort, he will become instantly well'.[14]

The Bronze Age (1600–1200BCE) saw an explosion of trade by land and sea, and the forging of new contacts between northern and southern Europe, North Africa and the Levant. The transmission of knowledge, the influence of art and the transactions of business brought Mesopotamia, the Levant, Turkey, Greece and Egypt into ever greater contact. The New Kingdom Dynasty of Egypt flourished during this period, and perhaps at this time the poppy itself, or ritual and medicinal potions containing it, first arrived on the banks of the Nile. It may have come as a gift along with diplomatic contacts that were crisscrossing the Middle East at the time, or via seafaring trade across the Mediterranean. Cyprus was at the crossroads of these seaborne routes.

Whether the gift of the gods or of the markets, sometime around 1500BCE vast quantities of miniature pottery vessels – their shape and form seemingly inspired by the poppy pod – appeared in Egypt and around the Levant. They appear to have originated in that trade hub, Cyprus, and would have been imported at great risk and expense – sea travel being a hazardous if profitable undertaking, as confirmed by the discovery of numerous Bronze Age shipwrecks that remain fully laden with their treasures. It was perhaps the contents and not the containers which held the real value: with the tallest standing a mere fifteen centimetres, they were clearly designed to hold liquids, and the shape of the vessels may have advertised their contents.[15] In 1968, the English archaeologist Robert Merrillees suggested that the pottery contained opium mixed with honey, or perhaps with wine or water.[16] Fascinating as this idea is, they may also have contained oils, ointments or perfumes.[17] Scientific analysis of residues found in these miniature jugs from Egyptian burials have been equivocal – a few indicate the possible presence of primitive opium, and one from Tel el-Ajjul in Israel did test positive for the drug,[18] but most reveal no traces.[19] There is no reason, however, why these containers could not have been reused or refilled with other liquids, or even valued enough to be buried with the dead.

Indeed, other aspects of the design of the vessels are evocative of poppies. Paintings on the jugs examined by Merrillees include parallel dark lines on the pod-like section that are tantalisingly akin to the incisions scored on a poppy capsule to release opium sap.[20] Equally attractive, though similarly speculative, is an explanation of why so many of these objects are found in child burials of the time. Across the world, opium has been used to quiet unruly children and calm those afflicted by illness or disease.

More generally, Egyptian art is a portal to the natural and supernatural worlds inhabited by the pharaoh, his family and the royal court. Egyptians were obsessed with amulets and charms, which were said to ward off evil and cure sickness and were used to express religious devotion. For this reason, amulets were placed with the dead in their tombs. These amulets were often made from precious metals and gemstones, each of which doubtless possessed its own symbolic powers. Some took on the appearance of the opium poppy, such as in the case of a reddish-brown carnelian necklace with beads shaped like poppy pods, belonging to the New Kingdom Dynasty of the Late Bronze Age, from around 1500 to 1200BCE.[21] Even more convincing is a pendant necklace found in 1882 in the so-called royal tomb at Amarna, the short-lived capital of the heretic pharaoh Akhenaton, who ruled between 1365 and 1350BCE. This extraordinary necklace features no fewer than fifty-three gold poppy-capsule-shaped beads, found strung alongside nine hollow gold pendants which resemble poppy husks.[22] It is tempting to imagine Akhenaten's dreamy new cult, which worshipped the *aten* sun disk, as somehow incorporating the soporific effects of opium.

More stunning jewellery, uncovered in 1908 near the ancient capital of Thebes, added fuel to the fiery archaeological debate about the prominence of the poppy symbol in Egyptian art. In the New Kingdom tomb of King Siptah, who reigned between 1197 and 1191BCE, and Queen Tauosrit, his stepmother, regent and briefly pharaoh in her own right from 1187 to 1185BCE, excavators found two exquisite golden earrings with 'hanging fruits' that seem to be modelled on the shape of opium-poppy pods, and whose scored surface could once again represent the harvesting method for opium resin.[23] The problem, as always, is interpretation. Are these poppies, pomegranates or an abstract symbol?[24] Is the scored design meant to replicate an actual object, or is it simply an artisan's fancy? On the side of the poppy as prototype was the curious discovery, in 1927, of a small statuette of a naked boy which was found alongside two mummified bodies in a poorly made wooden coffin in Saqqara, near Memphis. The figurine was wearing large carnelian earrings in the shape of a poppy pod, interpreted by archaeologists as a tribute dedicated by an elderly couple to a son who died before them – perhaps the earliest appearance of the poppy as a memorial to the dead.[25] In the spirit world of the Egyptians, it may be that the beneficence of opium accompanied the souls of the deceased, easing their afterlife in the same way as the food and drink that was buried with them would provide nourishment.

Opium poppies, like corn poppies, can have red petals, so it is often difficult to know exactly which species is being represented in art. For example, consider one of the most famous of Egyptian artefacts, the boy king Tutankhamun's 'winged scarab' pendant. Because of the circumstances of his early death in 1323 BCE – he is now thought to have succumbed to a wound inflicted while hunting or in battle, aged between eighteen and twenty – his tomb is filled with a number of prized items, including a beautiful amulet inlaid with semi-precious stones and coloured glass. In the centre lies a chalcedony scarab beetle enclosed in a gold frame to which poppy pods, papyrus and lotus flowers are attached.[26] Positioned beneath the scarab is an image of the ancient god Horus, who possessed a magical *udjat* eye as a symbol of protection, royal power, health and strength and who was manifested in the body of the living pharaoh.[27] The dual motif of the *udjat* eye and the poppy was also emblazoned on a magnificent golden bracelet which Tutankhamun was wearing on his right arm. Made from electrum, lapis lazuli and dark blue glass, the bracelet is decorated with a poppy, which is flanked at each end by two lotus buds. The poppy's exquisite petals are carved from translucent quartz and painted red; the stems are tied by a golden band.[28]

Yet an even more intriguing treasure greeted famed Egyptologist Howard Carter when he broke into the young king's tomb on 26 November 1922: a small golden sanctuary dedicated to Nekhbet, the vulture goddess, who also served as the royal emblem of Upper Egypt. The shrine is made of wood overlaid with gesso and covered with sheet gold, onto which scenes and inscriptions have been worked in intricate detail. One scene in a sequence shows Tutankhamun being addressed by his queen, Ankhesenamun. She says to him, 'Adoration in peace, receive the Great Enchantress, O Ruler, beloved of Amun!' In the second scene, the boy pharaoh sits on a cushion and his queen with her right hand pours water into a vessel of flowers; in her left hand she holds a lotus and a poppy.[29]

The poppy also appears in luminous wall paintings that depict the heavenly afterlife in carefully prepared sepulchres. In one notable example, corn poppies adorn the 'Palais de Hawata' at Hawarah in the

Fayyum. More unusually, they are also seen in the tomb of Princess Nzi-Khonsus, who died around 1100BCE. An astonishingly well-preserved 'poppy wreath' was resting on the princess's breast when her tomb was discovered in 1881. It has been interpreted as a symbol of beauty or commemoration – or perhaps both.[30]

Other tomb paintings give a sense for the ubiquity of flowers in palace gardens, where they would have been grown in arbours and alongside pools for decoration as well as for medicinal use. They have left their marks in tomb paintings at Thebes, and as bouquets on a finely carved ivory casket from the sepulchre of Tutankhamun, which now resides in the National Museum in Cairo – a scene which shows the boy king and his queen holding bunches of papyrus stems with lotus flowers and gilded poppies. Beneath the royal couple, two of their children are picking fresh poppies.[31]

EGYPTIANS INHABITED a distinctive landscape, which developed along the banks of the Nile from at least 4000BCE. The diversity of plants and animals which thrived in the rich alluvium – itself replenished by the great river's annual floods – contrasted with the stark and lifeless desert beyond. This physical world of astonishing extremes framed and shaped the Egyptian worldview, in particular the philosophy of life and death, and populated it with a host of gods, spirits and demons – many of whom took their appearance from real animals or were believed to possess qualities and powers derived from natural phenomena. Medicines were used to navigate between physical reality and spiritual belief. Typically, potions and spells incorporated plants, minerals and animal parts whose physical and psychological properties were intended to ward off the fiends who caused misfortune, illness and death. It made little difference if the effects of this sorcery were genuine or imagined. As in Sumeria and Assyria, it was the physicians and priests who possessed the overlapping knowledge of the natural world and of rituals and beliefs, and it is they who most likely knew best the effects of opium.

The herbal remedies prepared by the priests drew upon hundreds of plants, as recorded in the Ebers Papyrus, which was rediscovered in 1872. The fragile scroll runs to 110 pages and twenty metres, and lists seven hundred magical and medicinal formulae, to be used for such varied purposes as contraception, skin problems, dentistry, abscesses and broken bones.[32] The poppy appears in the Ebers Papyrus as *shepenn* or *shepenon*, a name which Saber Gabra, a curator in Egypt's National Museum in Cairo, believes was originally given to the corn poppy and then applied to the opium poppy, with the term *shepenn-dshr* referring to the red flower characteristic of the corn-poppy species.[33] It was the stronger opium poppy, Gabra believes, that was used in curing headaches and as a calming remedy. According to the Ebers Papyrus, Egyptian mothers spooned it to their unruly children: 'Capsules of poppy, and fly's dirt that is on the wall, are mixed, strained and taken for four days. [The infant] ceases immediately to cry'.[34] Hardly a surprising result, we might think today, for such a bizarre concoction of opium and wishful thinking. Similar remedies are still used in Egypt and North Africa, where an opium-poppy infusion remains a popular remedy to soothe a crying child and cure a cough.[35]

THE WORLD OF THE EGYPTIAN priests was not entirely cloistered. Though opium would eventually be grown by the Egyptians themselves, especially around Thebes, Alexandria and later Cairo, it was initially brought to the Nile by strangers from across the sea – by one of the Bronze Age's most precocious and artistic civilisations, the seafaring traders of ancient Crete, known today as the Minoans. Whether Minoan seamen traded in raw opium, sold medicines which contained it, or unwittingly carried its seeds inside other freight is not known, but they brought opium to new lands.

Minoan civilisation flourished between 2000 and 1400BCE, and is famous for its opulent palaces, voluptuous serpent-wielding priest-esses and strange bull-leaping cult. According to later Greek mythology, Minoan culture was dedicated to the god Minos, who judged the dead and sacrificed people to the Minotaur – a half-man, half-bull creature kept captive in the labyrinth of dark tunnels beneath the royal city. The contentious rebuilding of the palace of Knossos by the British archae-ologist Sir Arthur Evans between 1921 and 1935 epitomises our odd familiarity with these people, inasmuch as there is a feeling of 1930s romanticism about the human figures portrayed here.

The Minoans forged their empire based on securing trade routes across the eastern Mediterranean Sea. From the Aegean islands to the coast of Turkey, from the great ports of the Levant and Egypt to Cyprus, Minoan sailors knew them all. Startling evidence sometimes surfaces to bear witness to their voyages. For example, a Minoan sanctuary has been discovered in the Nile Delta at the ancient city of Avaris (modern Tell El-Daba), an inland port colony where Cretan merchants estab-lished a foothold around 1600BCE. According to Professor Manfred Bietak from Vienna University, who excavated the site, the sanctuary's frescoes of bull-leaping immediately recall the style of those in the 'House of the Frescoes' at the Minoan capital of Knossos. He believes that 'several Minoan artists were at work there [Avaris], some of them artists of the highest standard'.[36]

Zakro, on the island's eastern shore, was a small palace, yet had numerous store rooms as well as a library of clay tablets inscribed with the mysterious script we refer to as Linear A.[37] Still undeciphered, these tablets may record maritime business deals with Crete's trading partners. From the palace's main gate, winding narrow streets led down to a harbour where Minoan ships docked to unload their goods.

Though they were best known as traders, the Minoans also developed a vibrant religious life, and appear to have used opium in many of their rites, according to some compelling evidence found by archaeologists during the twentieth century. In 1903, Arthur Evans uncovered several female figurines, realistically modelled on human bodies and shown handling snakes; their bare-breasted postures and elaborate costumes has since led to them being considered to be portraits of fertility goddesses or priestesses. Then in 1935, at Gazi, located six kilometres from Knossos,[38] local peasants stumbled across two enigmatic terracotta figurines, also bare-chested and wearing distinctive dress. It was an extraordinary discovery. Both of the Gazi figures raised their hands in a ritual gesture, and the larger of the two sported an elaborate hairstyle held in place by three movable pins in the shape of opium-poppy capsules decorated with vertical score lines. Subsequent excavations at Gazi have uncovered a tubular pottery vessel, similar in shape to Cretan ceramics that are sometimes described as 'water pipes' and which could have been used for inhaling opium fumes. Whoever was worshipping these fertility-goddess statuettes seems to have associated opium with their rituals.

This particular opium connection was reinforced in 1974, by the discovery of a treasure trove of ivory objects in a sanctuary at Kition in Cyprus. Among the Late Bronze Age artefacts was an intricately carved, smoke-stained tubular vessel that has been identified as an opium pipe.[39] In a tomb dating to around 1300 BCE at the same site, two polished carnelian poppy-pod beads were found as part of a magnificent necklace.[40] Today, the semi-precious carnelian enjoys a widespread Mediterranean folkloric reputation as a mineral that pacifies people, making them slow to anger.[41]

The late doyen of Minoan studies, Professor Spyridon Marinatos (1901–74), called the large Gazi figure the 'Poppy Goddess' and said that she was a patroness of healing.[42] As the excavator of the battle-fields of Marathon and Thermopylae, and discoverer of the Minoan port of Akrotiri on the island of Thera, Marinatos's opinion was rightly influential. He considered that the deeper colour of the vertical lines on the pins represented the dark hue of dried opium sap, and that the goddess's dreamy expression and closed eyes exhibited the torpor of narcotic intoxication. 'The women of Crete . . .' he believed, 'understood the effects of opium which they tended, as a mystery of the goddess, and dispensed in cases of suffering or despair.'[43] Marinatos's digging at Gazi further revealed that the room where the figurines had been found was dark, windowless and subterranean, an ideal place to host opium-fuelled rituals dedicated to the underworld.

If this reading by Marinatos and others is accurate, then it could be suggested that the priestesses of Minoan Crete may have directed the society's religious use of the opium poppy, communicating its well-known medicinal and soporific qualities and bringing them to material form. Tombs for the dead were dug into the earth, which was seen as the true mother of fertility, connecting mythological beliefs with human mortuary activity – and fostering the very growing conditions favoured by the flower.[44] These associations resonate with later Greek myths, particularly those which tell of King Minos's links with the dead and Hades, and the subterranean lair of his Minotaur at Knossos.

High in the Cretan mountains which rise up from the eastern Plain of Lasíthi is the Diktaean Cave, later identified as the place where Zeus, father of the gods, was said to have been born. Here, a Late Bronze Age carnelian bead was uncovered, beautifully rendered as a poppy capsule. At nearby Ierápetra, three more were found in Minoan-era tombs.[45] These beads, together with a superb necklace of carnelian poppy-capsule pendants from Mari in Syria, and the Kition examples, may have been used as amulets, whose symbolic powers were represented by their poppy-capsule shape. Annie Caubert, a conservator from the Louvre museum in Paris, regards the Syrian pendants as 'mainly of Egyptian origin and can be dated to the New Kingdom'.[46] They may have travelled around the eastern Mediterranean on Cretan ships[47] – as so many other goods did.

AROUND 1400 BCE, the Minoans were conquered by the new superpower of Greece. The Mycenaeans were the first mainland Greeks to flourish, from between 1650 and 1100 BCE, but like the island-based Minoans, they were a seafaring people. They spoke the earliest Greek language, and left traces of it in the script we know as Linear B, which was translated during the 1950s and is clearly derived from the Minoan Linear A. Mycenaean writing shared its predecessor's function as a record of trade and administration. This intimate relationship suggests that the Mycenaeans were familiar with Minoan religion and presumably also with its opium-using rites. No word for opium has yet been found in Linear B inscriptions,[48] but archaeology has revealed tantalising hints of the drug.

Heinrich Schliemann, the discoverer of Troy, first excavated Mycenae in 1874. In deep shaft-tombs, he found extraordinary golden treasures from the Mycenaean age, including a seal ring. In perfect miniature intaglio, it shows a woman sitting beneath a tree offering plants to another woman who stands before her. The plants look identical to poppies, as do others shown on another ring and a bead seal found at Thisbe near the Gulf of Corinth.[49] This Mycenaean jewellery is suggestive but inconclusive evidence for the use of opium in early Greek rituals and beliefs.

Nevertheless, the opium poppy's ethereal connections with the mythological world of the dead appears in Homer's epic history of the Trojan War, episodes of which appear in his *Iliad* and *Odyssey*. If the war was an historical event, it probably occurred during the twelfth century BCE, some two hundred years after the demise of the Minoans and the rise of the Mycenaean power.[50] Whether Homer was a real person or not, and scholarly opinions vary, the two epics were first written down some time later, most likely during the eighth century BCE. According to Homer, Paris, Prince of Troy, eloped with Helen, Queen of Sparta. The Greeks took a terrible revenge when King Agamemnon of Mycenae, the brother of Helen's husband, King Menelaus, marshalled a vast fleet and besieged Troy for ten years. The Greek kings finally destroyed the city by smuggling their warriors into Troy hidden inside the gift of the Trojan Horse. After the sack of Troy, Homer tells how Helen, now reunited with Menelaus, sailed for Greece via Egypt. Trapped by contrary winds, they waited for fair weather, during which time Helen met Polydamna, an Egyptian woman famous for her medical knowledge. Polydamna gave Helen secret remedies to take back with her to Sparta. Years later, at a dinner party arranged by Helen for her royal court, the guests began to reminisce about the Trojan War. Grief engulfed them as they talked about the many heroes who had died, and the disappearance of the great warrior Odysseus. With her friends depressed and tearful, Helen recalled one of Polydamna's remedies. Homer takes up the story:

She lost no time, but put something [nepenthes] into the
wine they were drinking, a drug potent against pain and
quarrels and charged with forgetfulness of all trouble;
whoever drank this mingled in the bowl, not one tear
would he let fall the whole day long, not if mother and
father should die, not if they should slay a brother or
a dear son before his face and he should see it with his
own eyes.[51]

What could the miraculous nepenthes be? Arguments have raged for millennia. Some refuse to believe it existed at all, saying it was a literary device invented by Homer for dramatic effect. Theophrastus, the great herbalist, who lived in the third century BCE, was convinced that no plant had such power, and that nepenthes was a metaphor for Helen's charms – but that does not ring true, since Egypt was known to the Greeks as the home of many 'healing herbs'. Some eight hundred years after Homer's account of the fall of Troy, the Roman historian Diodorus Siculus mentions that Egyptian women had long used opium for its power to 'chase away anger and grief'.[52] The renowned physician Dioscorides (40–90CE) identified nepenthes as a mix of opium and the powerful anaesthetic and psychoactive plant henbane, which can be lethal in large doses.[53] If the queen of Sparta spiked the wine of her banqueting guests, it would be the earliest record of a narcotic drink, a precursor of sorts to the addictive brew of opium and wine known two thousand years later as laudanum.[54]

The Trojan War may be history, or it may be allegory; Helen's narcotic nepenthes might have been opium or it might have been some figment of Homer's imagination – it is impossible to know. But in 1908–9 archaeologists excavated what they identified as the 'shrine of Helen and Menelaus' on the hills outside Sparta, and discovered several lead pins in the shape of poppy heads or maybe pomegranate buds.[55] Twenty years later, a different team investigating the sanctuary of Artemis at Sparta discovered bone pendants and an earring, all of which were shaped like opium-poppy capsules.[56] Plutarch, the Greek historian (46–120CE), recorded that the divinely beautiful Helen had been abducted from this exact shrine by her father Zeus.[57]

THE TROJAN WAR, as told by Homer, was the epitome of the 'beautiful death'. Yet even those heroic endeavours that were told down the ages revived an enduring sorrow, as Helen's guests discovered as they remembered their comrades who had fallen in battle. There was no escaping the grief for the war dead – except, perhaps, by taking the fruit of the poppy.

Long after the destruction of Troy, in the fourth and fifth centuries BCE, poppies appeared in the myths of classical Greece. Poppies, for instance, flowered on the banks of the River Lethe – the stream of forgetfulness, one of the five rivers of Hades – which flowed through the shadowy underworld and circled the cave of Hypnos, the god of sleep. The souls of the dead were obliged to taste the river's waters, so as to lose all memory of what they had said and done in life.[58] For the Greeks, and later the Romans, the opium poppy was the gods' own medicine, infused with 'Lethean sleep' according to the Roman poet Virgil.[59]

The explosion of Greek and Roman literature during the classical age has left a stronger trail of evidence for the poppy in mythology and in history. In his *Argonautica*, an account of Jason's quest for the

Golden Fleece, Apollonius of Rhodes refers to the poppy growing in the sorceress Hecate's magical garden, which lay at the edge of the known world. Nearby, on the shores of the Black Sea, was the ancient city of Colchis, one of several areas regarded by modern biologists to be a place where the opium poppy may have originated.[60]

In the Dark Ages, sometime between 750 and 650BCE, the pastoral Greek poet Hesiod left the first written record of the poppy – *Mekone*. He recalls that near the great city of Corinth there was in ancient times a place called Mekonê, or 'poppy town', inspired by the sea of poppies which surrounded the settlement during springtime and early summer. The word we know today, however, is thought to derive from *opion*, the Greek word for 'poppy juice', which later became opium in the Latin of the Roman Empire.[61]

It was at Mekonê that the earth goddess Demeter – mother of Persephone, the queen of the underworld – was said to have first experienced the wonders of opium.[62] Demeter reigned over fertility, death and rebirth. She taught mortals the skills of agriculture, and as the 'bringer of seasons', she energised the eternal rhythms of nature. As the 'mistress of harvests' she was wedded to the wheat fields and their ever-present poppies. So intimate was the relationship between goddess, grain and flower, that ears of wheat and heads of poppy were the goddess's primary emblems in statues worshipped by her cults. Her agricultural powers and symbols were celebrated in verse, as in the pastoral poetry of Theocritus, who in the second century BCE wrote that Demeter 'smiles on us with sheaves and poppies in either hand'.[63] And her cult was popular beyond Greece, including in the city of Shomron (Samaria) in Judea. There, King Herod issued bronze 'two-prutot' coins between 44 and 40BCE that bear an image of a stem and a round fruit at its head which has been identified as a poppy capsule.[64] In the second century of the Christian era, the Greek-born traveller Pausanias, author of the ten-volume *Description of Greece* which he wrote based on his travels through the classical world, passed through Mekonê, then renamed Sicyon. In the Sanctuary of Aphrodite he saw a seated gold and ivory statue of Aphrodite herself, who held an apple in one hand and a poppy in the other.[65]

Why would a goddess eat opium? The answer is itself a dark allegory, in which the Greeks invent Olympian gods who are immortal translations of their frail selves, and of the fickle cycles of nature upon which humanity's survival depended. In the myths that sprang up from this world, Demeter's unlucky daughter, Persephone, was assaulted by the lust for earthly men and women that the gods so often indulged in. One day, as she was picking wild flowers, Hades, the king of the underworld, ripped open the earth, drove his chariot through the gaping chasm and abducted her. Imprisoned in the realm of the dead, she was ravished by Hades and became his queen. Unable to find her daughter, Demeter desperately wandered the land, searching night and day. The life of the earth came to a standstill as the grief-stricken goddess grew ever more frantic and exhausted. Most of all, Demeter neglected the wheat and corn, and with no grain to harvest, mortal men and women cried to the gods for help before they starved to death. What happened next is told in two different versions.

One version of the myth tells how Zeus, the king of gods, forced Hades to return Persephone to the earth's surface as long as she had eaten nothing during her stay in the underworld. Hades agreed, having already tricked Persephone into eating six pomegranate seeds. A new bargain had then been struck, so that she would return for the six months of spring and summer, but must descend again to Hades' realm for the winter. Demeter was overjoyed when her daughter returned, and the earth too rejoiced and became fruitful again.

The other version saw the gods take pity on Demeter in a startlingly different way – by causing opium poppies to spring up at her feet. Overcome by the swirling fumes, the distraught goddess fell into a deep rejuvenating sleep. When she awoke, refreshed, she returned to earth and energised it, and the wheat and corn grew once again. In this version of the story, poppies are essential to the grain harvest upon which mortals depend. The poppy's rabid fertility – observable in the huge numbers of seeds it produces – seemed, in Persephone's fate, to be for ever associated with the growth of wheat, corn and barley.[66]

Demeter's perpetual loss of and reunion with Persephone, and her grief and joy, stand as a parable for the agricultural year. This imagery has been frequently rendered in art, as on a beautiful terracotta from southern Italy in which Persephone rises from the land of the dead holding a wheatsheaf and a poppy in her hands.[67] It is impossible now to disentangle the myths of springtime rebirth and autumnal harvests from deeper philosophies of life and death. Thus it is no surprise to encounter the poppy in Greek funerary rituals of the dead, or to realise that Persephone wore the poppy bloom as a symbol of her death-like imprisonment in the underworld. The playwright Aristophanes enshrined the memorial uses of the poppy when he recorded that it was woven into garlands worn by the dead. Demeter's loss symbolises a mother's grief for her 'dead' daughter, and speaks to the despair felt by all humans when their loved ones depart. In this ingenious, emotional fable, the poppy rises to ease the suffering of the bereaved.

Demeter's agonies over her daughter represented people's anxieties over the success or failure of the coming harvest, and were marked by the Greeks in several ways. The *Thesmophoria* festival was dedicated to the goddess and celebrated annually to promote earthly fertility. Only married women could participate, and little evidence has survived concerning the various activities of the three-day event – all was to be kept secret. It is known, however, that poppies were used to make cakes for ritual meals and offerings, and while the oil-rich seeds were an obvious ingredient, 'poppy juice' too is mentioned in an inscription at Demeter's shrine at Priene near Ephesus in Asia Minor (modern Turkey).

More is known about another major expression of devotion to Demeter – the annual pilgrimage and ritual of the Eleusinian Mysteries. Held at Eleusis, just outside Athens, this rite in honour of the earth goddess had its origin in an agrarian cult which stretched back to Mycenaean times, around 1500BCE. It morphed into a state-organised event during the Hellenistic era (323–146BCE), when mystery cults became fashionable. In late summer, bustling crowds would gather at the great cemetery of Kerameikos outside the walls of Athens. Thousands of men and women, from slaves to courtesans, politicians, generals and later even Roman emperors, made the pilgrimage. The only require-ment was that participants had not committed murder, and were not 'barbarians' – which meant that they had to speak Greek. Incense swirled, and the sound of flutes and drums filled the air, as the throng surged forward on a twenty-kilometre procession to Eleusis. As they approached the entrance to the town, the initiates were scrutinised by two giant statues of Demeter. She wore on her head a basket decorated with the poppy and symbols of the harvest,[68] and all around the temple were carved stone images of the narcotic flower.[69] The rites were enacted in the subterranean depths of Demeter's eponymous temple, a reference to the underworld kingdom of Hades, many of whose statues were also adorned with poppies. The pilgrimage was popular for some two thousand years.

Secrecy was everything, and no written account was ever made in classical times – the penalty for divulging the rites was death. Only the initiates knew what transpired in the various rituals, though they included the *kiste*, a sacred chest, and the *kalathos*, a lidded basket (the

contents of both remain unknown). The lack of hard facts has excited
the imagination of historians, with Thomas Taylor writing in 1791 that
the *kiste* contained a phallus, seeds sacred to Demeter and a golden
mystical serpent.[70] But, piecing together a jigsaw of clues, scientists
specialising in psychoactive plants, such as the American ethnomycolo-
gist R. Gordon Wasson and the Swiss chemist Albert Hofmann (who
invented LSD), have suggested that participants experienced a magical
vision after drinking a potion called *kykeon* – a concoction of wheat or
barley mixed with water and perhaps spiked with opium.[71] The narcotic
effects of *kykeon* may have been enhanced by the contamination of
the grain by the psychoactive fungus ergot, whose powerful properties
earned it the name St Anthony's Fire in later medieval times.

The Eleusinian Mysteries suggested the pain of death could be
redeemed through rituals which promised resurrection, as surely as
spring follows winter. The experiences of the initiates seem to have
included visions that promised rewards in an afterlife. Around 50BCE,
the Roman philosopher and statesman Cicero wrote in his *Laws* that
the Mysteries brought humans 'out of our barbarous and savage mode
of life and educated and refined to a state of civilisation . . . we have
learned from them the beginnings of life, and have gained the power
not only to live happily, but also to die with a better hope'.[72] Despite
such widespread praise for and participation in the Mysteries, their
power to alleviate peoples' anxieties about the natural rhythms of life
and death faded as Christianity took hold during the fourth and fifth
centuries. The pagan version of life after death through initiation at
Eleusis became a heresy, and resurrection was now reinterpreted as
being tied to the new idea of original sin. The Christian afterlife had
been guaranteed by Jesus' sacrifice, but only those who adhered to
his teachings for their whole lives could expect to enjoy the afterlife.
In the year 392, the anti-pagan Roman emperor Theodosius issued a

decree to shut down Demeter's sacred shrine and end the Eleusinian rites, and in 396 what was left of the pagan sites was desecrated by Christians who accompanied Alaric the King of the Goths during his invasion of Greece.

THE POPPY DID NOT solely take root in the underworld and the earth; it infiltrated the very home of the gods, Mount Olympus. Hermes, the messenger of the gods, was a truly shaman-like figure, responsible for leading the souls of the dead to the underworld. He was overlord of the gods of sleep: Morpheus, the god of dreams; Hypnos, the deity of sleep; his twin brother Thanatos, the lord of death; and Nyx, the goddess of night. All, it seems, invoked the power of opium to cast their spells over mortals dwelling on earth, and were shown in art crowned with poppy wreaths, or carrying them in their hands. Morpheus is commonly depicted holding a bunch of poppies – the tool of his trade – and the enchanting Nyx can often be glimpsed handing out poppies as she brings on the night.[73]

Poppies were used in ceremonies and cults related to other gods as well. They adorned statues of Apollo and Aphrodite, and poppy capsules are found on figurines of these deities, bas-reliefs, vases, tombstones, coins and jewellery. In the wells and waterlogged soils surrounding the sanctuary of Hera, the queen of the gods, on the island of Samos, archaeologists have found evidence of ritual sacrifices and votive offerings including carved ivory poppies and poppy seeds. These appear to have been gifts to the goddess in her role as yet another divine provider of fertility.[74] Asclepius, the god of medicine, induced sleep and dreams to affect his cures. Sleep was oblivion, a temporary respite for the living, an eternal rest for the dead, the greatest healer available to both gods and men. In the statues erected to Asclepius, he is shown wearing the poppy in the fashion of his supernatural siblings.

Opium was well known to mortal healers, too. Hippocrates (460–377BCE), the founder of modern medicine, frequently mentions the poppy in his remedies.[75] He is precise in his descriptions, identifying and distinguishing between the appearance of the white poppy, the fire-red poppy and the black poppy, but does not give any information concerning whether or not they are all varieties of the opium-bearing plant. (The black poppy seemingly derives its name from the fact that its seeds are black rather than the lighter hue of white poppy seeds, though later Roman writers such as Pliny the Elder and Dioscorides identify it as the opium poppy.) Hippocrates also understood the varying therapeutic powers of the unripe poppy, the ripe pod and poppy juice, the last of which he considered as particularly effective due to its narcotic and cathartic qualities. This 'hypnotic poppy', he adds, yields seeds of great nutritional value.[76] Celsus, the first-century CE Roman physician describes *lacrymœ papaveris* (opium juice) as a hypnotic and painkilling drug, while his contemporary Dioscorides writes of the soothing powers of the 'flowing poppy', so called because its juice flows from it.

Despite the feeling of well-being experienced by opium users, the dangers of addiction and overdose were already well known. One ancient commentator, Mnisidemos, regarded the proper use of opium as 'by inhalation for inducing sleep, all other uses being harmful'.[77] Theophrastus warned that a strong dose could summon a painless death for suicides, or serve as an untraceable poison for an assassin.[78] Around 340BCE, Herakleides of Pontus graphically explained one custom of euthanasia: 'Since the island [of Kea] is healthy and the population lives to a ripe old age, especially the women, they do not wait until they are very old for death to take them, but before they grow weak or disabled in any way, take themselves out of life, some by means of the poppy, others with hemlock'.[79] Hannibal, the Carthaginian general, reportedly kept opium in his signet ring, and finally used it to meet his end in 183 BCE.[80] The Romans too appreciated its ambivalent medical properties, teetering as they did between calming and killing. In 55 CE, Agrippina, Emperor Claudius's wife, poisoned her fourteen-year-old stepson Britannicus with opium, clearing the way for her son, Nero, to assume the purple.[81]

During the first century CE, Dioscorides gained his peerless medicinal knowledge by accompanying the Roman armies, and observing first-hand the customs and traditions of the peoples under the empire's rule. He lists several kinds of poppies in his magisterial *De Materia Medica*, which he wrote between 50 and 70 CE. The corn poppy, he said, was a medicine: 'Having boiled five or six little heads of this (with three cups of wine to reduce it to two), give it to drink to those whom you would make sleep.'[82] The opium poppy fascinated him, and he wrote at length about how its sap was harvested from the capsule, and how when its leaves and pods are boiled in water they induce sleep. The juice, he observed, was most potent when thick, 'heavy in odour, and soporific, [and] bitter to the taste'.[83] Taken in small quantities, he observed, 'it is an anodyne and . . . promotes digestion, being useful for coughs and intestinal disorders; but too much being drunk plunges one into a lethargy of sleep, and it kills'.[84] A century later, Claudius Galen, personal physician to the emperor Marcus Aurelius, gave his take on the subject: 'Opium is the strongest of the drugs which numb the senses and induce a deadening sleep; its effects are produced when it is soaked in boiling water, taken up on a flock of wool and used as a suppository.'[85]

AS BEFITTED ROME'S IMPERIAL AMBITIONS, the poppy and war were intertwined from the earliest days of the Latin confederacy. The seventh king of Rome, Lucius Tarquinius Superbus (535–496BCE), was known for his bloodthirsty will to power. Besieging the city of Gabii, he concocted a stratagem to win it by subterfuge, ordering his son Sextus Tarquinius to pretend to defect to the enemy. The inhabitants of Gabii accepted Sextus and made him the commander of their army, whereupon he sent an envoy to his father to find out what his next move should be. Tarquin was in his flower garden, and instead of giving the messenger a spoken response, he walked up and down striking off the heads of the tallest poppies. He told the envoy that there was no message, but that his son should be told exactly what he had done. Sextus interpreted 'Tarquin's poppies' as a secret command to exile or slay the leading men of Gabii, which he did. With no opposition, he subsequently surrendered the city to his father.

The opium poppy was not only a harbinger of death. Pliny the Elder (23–79CE) calls the black poppy hypnotic by virtue of the juice which flows from slitting its bud as it begins to flower. He reports that the juice was allowed to thicken, then kneaded into small loaves, which were dried in the shade – an alluring (but not lethal) snack to serve Roman society. At Pompeii the remains of a poppy-seed cake were found as a votive offering to Isis/Demeter; they were probably deposited there during the first century.[86] When archaeologists excavated a farmhouse at Villa Vesuvio, outside Pompeii, they uncovered a storage vat full of opium-poppy seeds alongside those of other medicinal plants and small animal bones, suggesting that here were the traces of a folk remedy.[87] Both the corn poppy and the opium poppy appear in garden scenes at Pompeii's villas. The opium poppy is on a mosaic in the 'House of the Fawn', and corn poppies appear in wall paintings in the 'House of the Fruit Orchard', placed next to two Egyptian statues.[88]

Opium's use as a sedative, painkiller and narcotic was known to the Ptolemies, the Greek successors to Alexander the Great, who had conquered Egypt in 332BCE and displaced the pharaohs. Andreas of Karystos, the personal physician to King Ptolemy Philopator, who ruled in the third century BCE, warned against using pure opium for eye troubles, because 'if it was not adulterated those who smeared their eyes with it were blinded'.[89]

Yet, the most astonishing aspect of the Ptolemies' relationship with the narcotic flower was an early attempt to grow it as a cash crop. Fields were sown around Alexandria with the seeds to be crushed into oil.[90] Locked away in fragmentary papyri in museums across the world are detailed records of opium-poppy growing by farmers and landowners during the middle of the third century BCE. Some of these poppy fields were impressive. In one papyrus letter dated 252BCE, we read: 'Horos to Zenon, greetings. By [3 February] there will be 130 arouras [36.4 hectares] sown with poppy. If you please, do come and see me so you can feast your eyes on the sight . . . Farewell.'[91] Ultimately, however, the experiment failed, and large-scale poppy growing was abandoned.

Despite the short-lived commercial interest in poppy oil, there is no mention in these documents of the effects of opium on the harvesters or of the many folk healers and quacks who would have been keen to acquire the poppy heads for their own profit. The value of opium resin as a medicine was considerable, and the pods would not have been thrown away once the seeds had been harvested. When the experiment collapsed, the semi-wild opium poppy would find root in wheat fields and rubbish dumps, supplying enough for family medicines and religious use.

By the time Octavian conquered Egypt for Rome in 60BCE, opium was an ingredient in a famous remedy, *diakodion* ('from the poppy capsule'), which, when added to a variety of other ingredients, was considered a potent remedy against arthritis, headaches and stomach pains,[92] and opium remained in everyday use into late Roman times. At the Egyptian city of Oxyrhynchus, which has yielded an unmatched wealth of ancient documents, a papyrus fragment dating to the third century CE captures part of a remedy for a now unknown ailment: it prescribes meconium (poppy tea) mixed with beaver musk on a piece of pottery and then diluted with raisin wine.[93] Three hundred years later, in the sixth century, a Coptic Christian medical papyrus testifies to the continued use of opium as a favoured painkiller, even despite the drug's associations with Egyptian mysticism in a society converted to Christianity and about to be overtaken by Islam.[94]

IT WAS THE GREEK-SPEAKING Coptic world of Byzantine Egypt that the Arabs conquered in 641CE, and when they arrived in Alexandria they found opium cultivated nearby.[95] They soon named the plant *Abou-el-noum* – the 'father of sleep'. Over the next two hundred years, Muslim scholars translated and incorporated the knowledge of the classical world into their own language and culture. Medicine was especially valued, and with some Arab improvements, Dioscorides' five-volume *De Materia Medica* remained in use until the sixteenth century.

Egypt was the centre of early Muslim opium-poppy growing. For six hundred years, between 660 and 1260, during the Umayyad and Abbasid dynasties, processed opium was carried around the caliphate, and traded by land and sea to Europe, India and China. At first, Muslims used opium for painkilling rather than for pleasure. The ninth-century court of Baghdad employed physicians who were ardent champions of the drug's efficacy – as an anaesthetic during surgery, and as a self-administered panacea in the home.[96] The Persian polymath Avicenna (Abu-Ali-Ibn-Sina) described opium as the most powerful stupefying substance. His magisterial fourteen-volume compendium of Islamic medical knowledge, the *Canon of Medicine*, completed in 1025 and translated into Latin in 1175, remained an authoritative source until the seventeenth century. It was perhaps no coincidence that Avicenna lived for many years in the Persian city of Isfahan, an area renowned then, as now, for its opium-poppy fields, and that he died of an opium overdose.[97]

Opium's medicinal qualities were championed in 1527 by the Swiss alchemist-physician Paracelsus, who had returned from travels in Arabia with a famous twin-handled sword in whose pommel he kept his 'Stones of Immortality' – a compound of Theban opium, citrus juice and 'quintessence of gold'. His magical cures were not for the poor. It may well be that Paracelsus himself was an addict, as were so many other physicians at the time. So common was opium across Europe, at least among the well-to-do, that less than a century later Shakespeare wrote in *Othello*:

> *Not poppy, nor mandragora,*
> *Nor all the drowsy syrups of the world,*
> *Shall ever medicine thee to that sweet sleep*
> *Which thou ow'dst yesterday.*

Opium was an established medicine in Europe by this time, not least because of the lucrative Ottoman trade in Egyptian opium. The drug accompanied spices and other substances tinged with the exotic properties of the East. While travelling along an Arab caravan route at this time, the French naturalist Pierre Belon reported seeing fifty camels laden with opium and bound for Europe.[98] By 1650, Monsieur Pomet, chief herbalist for the French 'Sun King', Louis XIV, noted that opium from Cairo and Thebes was the best quality to be had.[99] Thomas Sydenham (1625–89) – the 'English Hippocrates' – regarded opium as the most valuable of God's remedies given to humankind. His zeal for the poppy was such that he wrote, 'Medicine would be a cripple without it'.[100]

Little changed over the next century of 'Enlightenment'. In 1732, Thomas Dover – famous as the rescuer of Alexander Selkirk from his island prison off South America, and whose story inspired Daniel Defoe to write *Robinson Crusoe* – concocted 'Dover's Powder', a mixture of opium, saltpetre, liquorice and the emetic South American plant *ipecacuanha*. Dover had at one time been an apprentice to Sydenham, and had learned much from his master. Dover's Powder had originally been meant to relieve gout, but soon he marketed it for all kinds of ailments, from colds to fevers to dysentery, and for children as well as adults. The dangers of addiction were known in Dover's day, but there was no moral outrage surrounding the drug's use.[101]

For three thousand years, the opium poppy was the most efficacious psychoactive plant known to humans. People were dangerously ambivalent about how to use its powers: whether and whence to use it to soothe pain, induce dreamy encounters with the numinous, or kill. As the nineteenth century dawned, we were finally in a position to reveal opium's secrets through the enlightened science of chemistry. At the same time, an innovative literary movement was embracing the drug as a means to explore man's place in nature – and rebuke such technically minded rationality. Yet neither science nor art could escape the new economic and political order, from which imperialism and complex financial systems were born, and with them new globe-spanning wars. And again, the poppy would find a role to play.

3

OPIUM DREAMS

THE SPLENDOURS OF ANCIENT GREECE AND ROME were a mirror in which Britain and other nineteenth-century European imperial powers saw themselves as masters of the world. Idealised and fanciful as these projections were, Britain in particular regarded herself as the heir to the Roman Empire, and to the earlier intellectual achievements of Hellenism. The nation's wealthy absorbed the attitudes and values of classical civilisation as they journeyed through Italy on their Grand Tours, matriculated at their prestigious schools and universities and built their great cities in the neoclassical style.

The epics of classical literature – the tales of the Trojan War and Homer's escapades – were revered and imitated. Napoleon styled himself as Alexander, and the story of Hannibal's defeat of the Romans at Cannae became the model for how battles should be fought – with a view to total annihilation. The masterworks of Athenian sculptors were transported from Greece to London, where they became the Elgin Marbles and were placed behind the classically inspired columns of the British Museum. Almost more than any other event, this demonstrated how

European powers used the past to justify and ennoble their imperialistic present. The passion for the distant past conjured an equally distorted vision of the medieval world – the Arthurian legends and reawakened notions of knightly chivalry.[1] Yet this confection of reworked 'Golden Age' imagery was an aristocratic veneer uneasily laid on top of profound social and economic changes that were remaking the world.

Industrialisation was the engine of British imperialism – the fuel of an empire on which the sun never set. Fuelled by mercantilism, capitalism, self-confidence and military might, the British (and their rivals, the French and Germans) exported their attitudes and mythologies around the globe. Inevitably, they clashed with others, and with each other, as they did so.

Poppies were transfigured during the nineteenth century, symbolically and commercially, and they played their role in changing the world. The Janus-like death imagery of the opium and corn poppies – the 'long sleep' of opium narcosis twinned with the ubiquitous corn poppy of freshly churned battlefields – appeared as these European powers debuted the first of their great modern wars on the battlefield of Waterloo. There, the ground was quickly smothered by scarlet corn poppies, and the tradition arose that the blood from the fallen had turned into blood-red petals.[2] Empires went to war over the opium poppy, and the vast profits from the trade helped bankroll the Industrial Revolution as its factories churned out machines of mass destruction. A deadly ambivalence is a quality inherent in the narcotic plant. While one aspect of the flower helped finance the mechanisation of battlefield violence, the other alleviated the sufferings of the men involved by disclosing its chemical secrets for the manufacture of painkillers.

The extraction of narcotic derivatives such as morphine, which dulls pain and induces euphoria, opened the way for the 'industrialisation' of opium for medical use. In 1806, Friedrich Sertürner, a German pharmacist's assistant, isolated a crystalline salt from opium. It was an organic compound with alkaline properties – a new chemical substance that would become known as an alkaloid.[3] He called it morphium – the 'secret of opium', after Morpheus, the Greek god of dreams – and it was ten times more powerful than raw opium.

Morphine eased pain, anxiety and insomnia, and by the 1820s, it was widely available in Europe, along with codeine, its less powerful and less addictive cousin. These 'miracle medicines' were revolutionary. With morphine and codeine, harsher wars were made physically bearable for soldiers and survivable for their anxious or bereaved families. In turn, the drugs laid the foundations for increasingly large armies to cope with the ever more frequent and terrible injuries produced by industrialised war. The idea that the harmless red corn poppy would prove equally powerful in helping the casualties of war deal with their emotional and psychological sufferings lay in the future.

The opium poppy took centre-stage in one of the most immoral episodes of history: the so-called Opium Wars, which took place between 1839 and 1860. These conflicts saw the British Empire officially trafficking opium, and using military might to force narcotic addiction on the people of China. During these years, Britain created the largest, most successful and most lucrative drug cartel the world had ever seen. The vast wealth accrued by the Empire would be spent in four years of war, from 1914 to 1918.

THE CHINESE QING DYNASTY EMPEROR Tao-kuang summoned Lin Tse-hsü, a fifty-three-year old scholar and trusted court official, to the Forbidden City in Beijing in October 1838.[4] Lin's reputation for integrity and morality made him the perfect choice to carry out his master's decree – to stamp out the evil of opium addiction. Although the narcotic had been outlawed in 1800, a thriving black market fed the habit of at least four million Chinese addicts. Every year, some thirty thousand chests of processed opium were smuggled into China by European merchants engaged in otherwise legitimate trade in teas and silks.

Imperial commissioner Lin moved swiftly, threatening public execution for Chinese addicts and those officials who did not clamp down on opium. Showing his humane side, Lin offered an amnesty to addicts as long as they undertook treatment to break their habit. And a deadly habit it was, as an article on the drug trade in New York's *Merchants Magazine & Commercial Review* pointed out:

> *There is no slavery so complete as that of the opium taker – once habituated to his dose as a stimulant, everything will be endured rather than the privation; and the unhappy being endures all the mortification of a consciousness of his own degraded state, while ready to sell wife and children, body and soul, for the continuance of his wretched and transient delight.*[5]

Killing the trade meant strangling the supply, and here was tragedy in the making. While China produced small amounts of opium, most of the drug which had hooked the Chinese was not home-grown but illegally smuggled from India on board British ships. Nestling alongside legal cargo, bales of opium were offloaded at Lintin Island in the Bay of Canton, a hotbed of bribery and vice, and sold to Chinese middlemen.[6] Lin confronted the British, demanding they hand over any opium they possessed, and promise never to carry it again on pain of death. The warning was ignored, with the British depending on corrupt Chinese officials to continue the trade, even to the point of using Chinese navy vessels to transport the contraband opium ashore.

Lin made a show of strength on 25 March 1839, barricading the streets surrounding the foreign merchants' dockside neighbourhood, and blockading the river with imperial navy junks. Captain Charles Elliot, the senior British authority in Canton (modern Guangzhou), announced that he would not be bound by Chinese laws, yet despite this the merchants agreed to hand over their illicit stores, and almost 1.3 million kilograms (three million pounds) of opium were surrendered. In what was the largest-ever destruction of a narcotic, the vast stockpile of confiscated opium was emptied into three huge water-filled trenches. The drug was then turned to liquid by mixing in salt and lime, a concoction referred to disparagingly as 'foreign mud'. The resulting slurry was eventually siphoned into the bay. Lin, with a typical flourish, made a ritual address to the spirit of the South China Sea, advising all sea creatures to retreat to deeper water 'to avoid contamination'.[7]

The opium affair might have ended there, but the trade was not freelance and opportunistic – it had mighty backers. As Captain Elliot himself admitted:

> The trade in opium had been encouraged and promoted by the Indian government, under the express sanction and authority of the British government and Parliament, and with the full knowledge also, as appears from the detailed evidence before the House of Commons, on the renewal of the last charter, that the trade was contra-band and illegal.[8]

Soon events spiralled out of control. After several small-scale naval engagements in which the Chinese came off worse, 3 November saw two British warships inflict a humiliating defeat on Lin's war junks, sinking five of the Chinese fleet and seriously damaging many other vessels. In June the next year, British gunboats and marines arrived from Singapore, blockaded Canton's approaches and seized strategic coastal positions. A single British vessel, the steel-hulled paddle-ship *Nemesis*, was able to dominate the Pearl River and its tributaries between Canton and Hong Kong. Elliot informed Emperor Tao-kuang that he demanded 'satisfaction and redress' for Lin's actions at Canton. Within a year, in August 1841, the British had destroyed the ill-equipped Chinese forces on land and sea, captured the city of Chinkiang (modern Zhenjiang), and controlled the sprawling rice fields of southern China.

Lin was dismissed, and his successor Qi-shan decided not to defend Canton, instead ransoming it from the British for six million silver dollars. By the summer of 1842, the British controlled Shanghai at the mouth of the Ch'ang Chiang (Yangtze River), and on 29 August Chinese officials boarded a British warship and signed the Treaty of Nanking.[9] A year later, a second treaty ceded the island of Hong Kong to the British and opened up the ports of Canton and Shanghai to Western trade. Hong Kong, with one of the best natural harbours in the world, was to become the hub for the opium trade with British India.

The terms of the treaty were humiliating and punitive, and showed the British Empire's opium politics in their worst light. China was forced to grant Britain most-favoured-nation status for trade; pay nine million silver dollars as reparations to the merchants whose opium Lin had destroyed; and accept that Westerners were subject to their own national laws, not those of China.

Opium was habit-forming in politics and in war just as it was in private life, and more humiliation lay ahead for China and its people.

The Chinese emperor was understandably reluctant to honour the terms and conditions of the treaties that ended the First Opium War in 1842, but British imperialism itself was hooked on opium's vast profits. These factors combined to trigger the Second Opium War, which lasted from 1856 until 1860. The United States had extracted an advantageous trade treaty from the Chinese, which provoked the envy of the British to the point where they insisted on exercising their right to most-favoured-nation status. First among their demands: China must exempt all British goods from import duty; open all her ports to foreign trade; permit the establishment of Western embassies in Peking (now Beijing); and legalise the importation of opium from British India and Burma.

The Chinese stalled, but the situation exploded on 8 October 1856 when Chinese officials boarded the Hong Kong-based merchantman *Arrow* and arrested its British crew under suspicion of smuggling and piracy. The British invoked the clause of the Nanking treaty, which had agreed that foreign vessels and their crews would not submit to Chinese law. Britain and France joined forces, and in 1857 a combined naval force seized Canton, taking several key Chinese forts near T'ien-ching (now Tianjin) a few months later. Britain and France allied themselves with Russia and the United States to force China to open up more of her ports to Western trade in the Treaty of Tientsin in June 1858. A year later, the Chinese were dragging their feet again on enacting the agreement, but surrendered totally when the Royal Navy showed its might by shelling Chinese forts at the mouth of the Peiho River.[10] Still worse was to come. When the Chinese refused to allow the European powers to establish their embassies in Peking (Beijing), the British and French attacked the city and destroyed several of the Chinese emperor's summer palaces.

Hostilities were ended on 18 October 1860 by the Convention of Peking, an agreement that granted a major role to opium in the economic and political ties that China forged with her imperial rivals. The Chinese agreed to pay millions of dollars in reparations to Britain, France and their merchants; to open up yet more ports to foreign trade; and to cede Chiu-lung (Kowloon) to Britain. In effect, all remaining constraints on opium trafficking were removed.

Shortly thereafter, the Chinese themselves joined in the trade and began cultivating the poppy far and wide across the country. Addiction inevitably rose in the decades that followed, so that by 1880 China was actually importing 6,500 tons of foreign opium annually. By 1906, it was producing more than 35,000 tons of its own opium, consumed by almost fourteen million of its people. The biggest mass addiction to any narcotic in history developed, as twenty-seven per cent of Chinese men became wedded to the poppy flower.[11]

Two further injustices were added to the Peking Convention, and arguably represent the most penetrating and influential consequences of the narcotics trade. China permitted foreign Christian missionaries to proselytise freely, thereby undermining centuries of Confucian self-sufficiency and degrading traditional Chinese culture and belief. It also allowed indentured Chinese labourers to be transported to the United States and Canada. This massive injection of cheap Chinese labour would make possible the construction of America's transcontinental railways, enabling the emergence of the United States as a major economic power.

Astronomical wealth was created on the back of untold misery. During the fifteen years from 1835 to 1850, some 246 million silver dollars drained out of China to pay for opium imports. And the numbers increased exponentially, year after year. The New York Daily News for 15 October 1858 reported that official British sources claimed their export-import trade with just Canton and Shanghai between 1844 and 1856 amounted to the extraordinary sum of 438 million pounds sterling. As the Bombay Gazette wryly noted on 20 November 1849,

'British India now really seems to be supported by the cultivation of a poisonous drug, and selling it or smuggling it into China . . . [where it is] supplied under the British flag, and sanctioned by Parliament itself, for wholesale slaughter'.[12] The wars fought by Britain and other imperial powers for the right to thrust opium on the Chinese were lucrative beyond imagining, and fuelled the rise of the global financial system that underwrote colonialism, industrialisation and further conflicts.

THOMAS ARNOLD, the eminent Victorian and professor of history at Oxford University, branded opium as a sin and the Opium Wars as indefensible. Opium addiction seemed to him 'so wicked as to be a national sin of the greatest possible magnitude, and it distresses me very deeply'. Yet, as Britain prosecuted these heinous acts abroad, an influential literary and artistic set was emerging at home in which the taste for opium was fashionable as a rebuff against the 'evil' and 'destructive' forces of industrialisation and imperialism.

The Romantic Movement reflected a wider trend towards romanticism in literature, art and music. The shift had been put into motion during the final decades of the eighteenth century as a reaction against the cold calculations of science and a rational view of nature that had marked the Age of Enlightenment. Romanticism urged a simpler, folklore-influenced view of the natural world, which was raw but innocent, and untrammelled by the dark forces of an increasingly urban society. Adopting a Romantic worldview would, it was believed, unleash one's emotions and imagination to reveal the power and beauty of nature's infinite variety. Such ideas were heralded by Robert Burns when he drafted his epic *Tam o' Shanter* in 1791. In it, he testified to the poppy's fragile beauty, enticing to the eye but impossible to possess: 'But pleasures are like poppies spread; / You seize the flower, its bloom is shed'.

In Britain, Romantic ideals blossomed in the writing of such luminaries as William Wordsworth, Samuel Taylor Coleridge, Elizabeth Barrett Browning, John Keats, Sir Walter Scott, Percy Bysshe Shelley and Lord Byron. Many of them took opium – usually in the form of laudanum – to heighten their artistic sensitivities or dull the effects of depression and physical pain. The Romantic poets created a truly pastoral poetry: 'Opium, and the liberty of thought it produced, was instrumental in the development of the Romantic ideal'.[13]

One of the founders of the English Romantic Movement, Samuel Taylor Coleridge, identified himself as a philosopher as well as a poet. Although he never finished his studies at Jesus College, Cambridge, Coleridge won the Browne Gold Medal for an ode on the slave trade during his time there. By the early 1800s, he was addicted to opium, drinking as much as two quarts of laudanum a week. He had left his wife and quarrelled with his friend William Wordsworth, allegedly over his drug use. Still, in 1816 he had established his reputation with the publication of two poems, 'The Rime of the Ancient Mariner' and 'Kubla Khan', the latter of which he claimed to have written during the euphoria of an opium-induced dream.

'Kubla Khan' conjures an exotic, opium-fumed Oriental palace:

> *In Xanadu did Kubla Khan*
> *A stately pleasure-dome decree*
> *Where Alph, the sacred river, ran*
> *Through caverns measureless to man*
> *Down to a sunless sea*

And for Coleridge, phantasmagoria and death were never far away:

And sank in tumult to a lifeless ocean:
And 'mid this tumult Kubla heard from far
Ancestral voices prophesying war!

Such originality inspired Wordsworth, who developed his 'conversa-
tion poem' style, in which everyday language expressed poetic feelings. It soon became a standard form for English poetry. If Coleridge's
laudanum habit aroused much of his most inventive and memorable
verse, then the opium poppy is at the root of the pastoral poetry that
grew to dominate English letters over the next century.[14]

Opium also ensnared Thomas De Quincey, author, intellectual
and literary friend of Coleridge and Wordsworth. Physically weak as
a child, De Quincey was by all accounts precociously intelligent, as
well as wilful, and as an adult he was known for being an opinion-
ated polymath. He spent several months tramping the countryside as
a wayfarer before in 1802 entering Worcester College Oxford, where
he had his first taste of opium.

De Quincey believed in Britain's imperial right to conduct the
Opium Wars to protect her trade and commerce. Colonel Henry Watson,
a family friend, had owned the ship which had sailed with the first
official consignment of opium to Macao in 1782, and had then begun
smuggling the drug on his own account.[15] In 'The Opium Question
with China in 1840', an article written at the time and republished in a
volume of his collected works in 1897,[16] De Quincey wrote that it was
inevitable that a mighty British Empire would triumph over a decadent
'oriental' kingdom. He was repulsed by all things Asiatic, and especially
Chinese, and creatures of the East found their way into one of his opium
nightmares: 'I was kissed, with cancerous kisses, by crocodiles, and lay
confounded with all unutterable slimy things, amongst reeds of Nilotic
mud . . . I escaped sometimes, and found myself in Chinese houses.'

Like many people at the time, De Quincey's habit of taking opium for pleasure developed out of purely medicinal needs – in his case, relieving neuralgia. By 1813, he was consuming opium every day, partly due to this illness, but also to alleviate the grief he felt over the untimely death of Wordsworth's three-year-old daughter Catherine, whose wildness and innocence had attracted his poetic imagination.[17] He increased his daily doses in the years that followed, during which he suffered greatly, with depression driving dependence and leading to ever greater expenditure on the drug. Always short of money, he made a virtue of necessity in 1821 when he was persuaded to publish his fantastical and nightmarish experiences in a series of articles for the *London Magazine*. The memoir proved so popular that it was soon republished in book form under the title *Confessions of an English Opium-Eater* and making him England's most notorious user of the drug.

Confessions was socially influential as well as commercially successful. It gives us a glimpse of De Quincey's opium habit, its pleasures and terrors, and reveals the easy availability of the narcotic in the early nineteenth century. His first encounter with the drug, he says, was on a rainy Sunday afternoon in London, when he bought a tincture of opium in a druggist's shop, describing the shop-owner as the 'unconscious minister of celestial pleasures!'.[18] De Quincey was captivated by opium at once:

> *Here was a panacea . . . for all human woes; here was the secret of happiness, about which philosophers had disputed for so many ages, at once discovered; happiness might now be bought for a penny, and carried in the waistcoat pocket; portable ecstasies might be had corked up in a pint bottle.*

His enthusiasm knew no bounds:

> *O just, subtle, and mighty opium! that to the hearts*
> *of poor and rich alike, for the wounds that will never*
> *heal, and for 'the pangs that tempt the spirit to rebel,'*
> *bringest an assuaging balm; – eloquent opium! that*
> *with thy potent rhetoric stealest away the purposes of*
> *wrath, and, to the guilty man, for one night givest back*
> *the hopes of his youth, . . . and, to the proud man, a*
> *brief oblivion . . . Thou only givest these gifts to man;*
> *and thou hast the keys of Paradise, oh just, subtle, and*
> *mighty opium!*[19]

He took opium in wildly fluctuating amounts for the rest of his life, his most productive periods of writing coinciding with his maximum intake of laudanum. His *Confessions* inspired many literary giants of the age, from Edgar Allan Poe to Nikolai Gogol, and was even mentioned by Sir Arthur Conan Doyle in his Sherlock Holmes adventure 'The Man with the Twisted Lip'.[20]

While Coleridge and De Quincy were notorious for their opium dreams, they were not the only devotees of the drug. Prime Minister William Gladstone reputedly drank laudanum in his coffee before debates in Parliament. Laudanum's potent mix of opium, wine and spices was equally prized by American founding father George Washington, Florence Nightingale, abolitionist William Wilberforce, novelist Louisa May Alcott and innumerable less celebrated men and women who benefitted from its painkilling properties. Many began to use the drug to treat the lingering pain of debilitating medical conditions, such as dental problems (Washington), back pain (Nightingale) and ulcerative colitis (Wilberforce). Elizabeth Barrett Browning, who starting taking opiates at fifteen to treat 'nervous hysteria' from a spinal injury, was inspired by its effects: 'I am in a fit of writing – could write all day & night – ... in an hourly succession of poetical paragraphs & morphine draughts', she wrote in 1843.[21]

While poets praised opium's liberating effects in verse, this was artistic cover on a grim reality. At a time when doctors had few powerful remedies, opium-based medicines treated every ailment from insomnia, diarrhoea and rheumatism to dysentery, cholera, malaria and bronchitis.[22] The opium poppy, in its many guises, underwrote the health of nineteenth-century Europe and America. Thomas Jefferson, one of America's founding fathers, grew his own opium poppies in the garden of his country estate at Monticello, Virginia to produce the laudanum that alleviated the headaches and rheumatism he suffered in later life.

THE UNITED STATES would become obsessed with the legal status of opiates during the following two centuries, yet depended on them to a considerable extent in key events which defined its own nationhood: the War of Independence; Chinese immigration to build the transcontinental railroad; and the cataclysmic Civil War of 1861–5. During the War of Independence, which ended in 1783, American and British armies had been struck by battlefield shortages of opium, and both sides had grown their own narcotic poppies to provide painkilling relief for their soldiers.[23] By 1840, two decades before the Civil War began, opium and morphine were widely used as medicines. However, from the 1840s to the 1890s, American opium consumption increased fourfold, with the number of addicts estimated to be as high as 300,000 in 1896.[24]

Since the 1700s, quack patent medicines laced with opium had been sold in almost every general store across America. The hucksters who peddled such concoctions were masters of eloquent hyperbole, and often spent vast sums on advertising and promotion. Those who bought the products were easily swayed by the claims made for elixirs that were little more than fancy bottles of uncut opium blended with innocuous liquids.

Comforting cordials with names such as Ayer's Cherry Pectoral and Mrs Winslow's Soothing Syrup were said to cure every real and imagined illness, bad nerves, fractiousness in children and even marital complaints.[25] The potions became especially popular among women, as it was socially unacceptable in many places for them to drink alcohol. One advertisement, shocking today, shows a loving mother dangling a vial of flavoured opium liquid over a baby, presumably her own, whose hands reach towards it just a little too eagerly. Some brands targeted women, claiming that their mixtures would relieve 'female troubles' associated with menstruation and the menopause. By the late nineteenth and early twentieth centuries, between sixty and seventy per cent of opiate addicts would be middle- and upper-class white women.[26]

Patent medicines tightened the grip of the opium poppy on these addicts to a remarkable degree. In 1858, one newspaper listed 1,500 different patent medicines; by 1905 a patient could choose from 28,000 of them.[27] Long before the American Civil War began, opiates were commonly available across the continent, a talismanic feature of what has been called the 'Great Binge' – a nineteenth century characterised by various narcotics that were legal, widely available, widely consumed and deeply embedded in everyday culture.

For instance, cocaine was patented in 1862, and initially prescribed to combat morphine addiction; it would later be added to such efferves-cent treats as Coca-Cola, which was originally sold in Atlanta, Georgia in 1888 as a temperance alternative to alcohol.[28] In the final decades of the century, the Bayer pharmaceutical company attempted to produce codeine – also a derivative of the opium poppy – and created heroin instead. Heroin was at first marketed as a non-addictive substitute for morphine, and as a medication especially suitable for children.[29]

These developments, as revealing as they are of the potency of the opium poppy, paled against the repercussions of the Civil War. For the first time, the poppy and its derivatives would be called to serve as combatants on the field of battle. Their enemy was the pain inflicted by the technologically advanced weapons available to the Union and the Confederacy – including the highly reliable Springfield Model 1861 and Enfield 1853 rifles; Ketchum grenades; the Vandenburgh volley gun; and the multi-barrelled, rapid-fire Gatling gun. The wounds and maimings inflicted by these weapons could be relieved by powerful opiates, widely regarded as the best medicines available. The narcotics could also help soothe the mental trauma of infantrymen, as well as the pain of infections and disease. The American Civil War would offer many lessons for the First World War, but above all the conflict served as a massive medical trial of the efficacy of opium. Could men endure the agonising horrors of industrialised death and maiming with its help?

Opium, said the Union army's surgeon-general, 'was used almost universally in all cases of severe wounds, and was particularly useful in [dealing with] penetrating wounds of the chest, in quieting the nervous system and, indirectly, in moderating hemorrhage'.[30] This view was widespread, and Civil War army doctors mixed opium with other medicines to control the greatest battlefield killers of all – dysentery and diarrhoea. While opiates did not cure, they did alleviate pain, and military physicians returned to them again and again.

Terrifying wounds caused by artillery shrapnel fired at point-blank range were treated by daily doses of morphine, sometimes administered with the newly invented hypodermic needle rather than as pills or mixed in drink as laudanum. The wounds of some soldiers were so dreadful, and their pain so unbearable, that they had to be dosed every four hours.[31] Amputations too were common, and to avoid the spread of gangrene, arms and legs were removed 'full-quarter' – where they joined the body, rather than simply at the wounded extremity. Only opium and morphine could help the wounded survive the shock of such brutal surgery.

The scale of suffering created an insatiable hunger for painkillers. As a result, the opium poppy cast its double-edged spell over the Union and Confederate armies, both of whom cultivated their own fields of narcotic poppies across Virginia, Tennessee, Georgia and South Carolina to satisfy the demand from their battlefield surgeries.[32] The Union army alone produced ten million opium pills, three million ounces of opiate preparations such as laudanum, and some thirty thousand ounces of morphine during the war.[33] Such was the urgent need for opiates that normal medical procedures were often bypassed. Nathan Mayer, surgeon-major for the Union army, didn't have time to dismount his horse, so poured what he called 'exact doses' of opium into his hand, and let wounded men lick it from his glove as he rode by.[34]

Shortages of battlefield medicines hit the Confederate army hard, whether it was opiates or the chloroform and ether that were widely used as anaesthetics. One response was the compilation of huge books, often exceeding five hundred or six hundred pages, in which were listed large numbers of home-grown substitutes. These included Indian tobacco, bush honeysuckle, *Cannabis sativa* and wild lettuce. The properties of the locally available southern white or red poppy featured in these catalogues are somewhat ambiguous. Some among the Confederates regarded it as yielding poor-quality opium, while others praised its anaesthetic qualities, and believed it to be as potent as the rare, expensive commercial opiates that arrived on the European ships that managed to evade Union blockades.[35]

It was no surprise that many disabled veterans paid the price of addiction for the gift of life. One 1865 estimate calculated that no fewer than 400,000 Civil War veterans were addicted to morphine.[36] Still, arguments rage over the extent of addictions caused by the war. The numbers of patients all but speak for themselves. The Union army recorded 1.6 million men suffering from diarrhoea and dysentery, 300,000 from afflictions such as typhoid, scurvy and venereal disease, and 250,000 from wounds.[37] To these can be added 30,000 who endured the trauma of amputation, and thousands of Confederate prisoners who suffered in Union prisoner-of-war camps. The vast majority of these men were treated with opium, morphine or local substitutes. It is unlikely that doses of opium given to such numbers of men would not have produced a single addict, yet between 1861 and 1865, there appears to have been not one reported case.[38] Medical reports submitted to the Union army's surgeon-general between 1862 and 1865 are equally silent on opium or morphine addiction, though they record soldiers' cravings for tobacco and alcohol.[39]

Sceptics who disbelieve in widespread opiate addiction argue that in many cases morphine was rubbed into the raw flesh of wounds, a practice that may account for the large quantity of the drugs consumed during the conflict. The absence of evidence is possibly due more to cultural factors than anything else, however. Opiates were legal and ubiquitous and generally viewed as all-purpose miracle drugs. Many physicians, especially in the military, were concerned with the immediate sufferings of their men, and did not always recognise the addictive qualities of either opium pills or morphine. Some accounts from the Civil War even suggested that the power of opiates to help relieve pain was not recognised fully enough, and that they should have been used more frequently. The agonies of some men were so severe, it was argued, that the choice must lie between administering morphine and amputating a limb.[40] Given what we know today about the addictive characteristics of opiates, many soldiers must have become addicted.[41]

After the war, more than 100,000 men continued to suffer from the diseases, wounds and traumas of their battlefield experiences – for which opium and morphine had originally been prescribed. Thousands more were admitted to hospital, where they were again prescribed opium for their physical or mental conditions. Large numbers of veterans were sent to prison, and found ways to have tea, coffee, whiskey and other contraband smuggled into their cells.[42] Wouldn't opium have been among the things they craved to end their suffering?

If few doctors appreciated the addictive power of the narcotic, then it is hardly shocking that few references to dependency appear either in medical reports or newspapers of the time.[43] Apothecaries – experts in drugs, and legally permitted to sell opiates – seem not to have recognised the extent of addiction.[44] Church ministers had difficulty recognising opium addicts,[45] and the general public did not notice them. Many veterans, however, were easily identified by the leather bag hung around their neck, in which they kept morphine tablets and sometimes a syringe.[46]

Yet opium's hold over these damaged veterans was only one dimension of the nation's drug addiction: opiates also played a vital role in prosecuting the Civil War by relieving the pain of civilian grief and loss. In 1868, Horace Day revealed this tragic legacy in his book *The Opium Habit*:

> *Maimed and shattered survivors from a hundred bat-*
> *tlefields, diseased and disabled soldiers . . .* anguished

and hopeless wives and mothers, made so by the slaughter of those who were dearest to them, *have found . . . temporary relief from their suffering in opium.*[47]

DURING AND AFTER THE CIVIL WAR, especially in the southern states, homespun recipes for preparing opium for medicinal purposes were widespread. In one local newspaper, South Carolina's *Edgefield Advertiser* for 10 June 1863, there is a startling description of a practice that recalls the poppy fields of the ancient Mediterranean world:

> *When the poppy heads are ripe, with a very keen knife make vertical incisions in them . . . A cream-colored juice will exude from each incision. Scrape off the juice . . . put into a saucer, plate or teacup, place in the shade, and shape while drying.*[48]

Indeed, opium growing, preparation and use was so much a part of everyday American rural life that cheap substitutes had been hunted down and were considered part of good housekeeping. In an issue of the *Mobile Advertiser* dated June 1864, a recipe for 'Lactugarium' instructed one to cut off a 'lettuce-top', scrape off the 'milk' up to six times, and allow it to dry into a brown mass which can then be shaped into a lump and wrapped tightly in paper.[49]

Intimate traces of this habit are sometimes found in unexpected places, and seem to be connected with fallout from the Opium Wars across the Pacific Ocean. During the 1870s, as one of the terms of the 1860 Convention of Peking, thousands of Chinese immigrants had arrived in the United States to work as labourers on the railways. Some found work as merchants and doctors. These new Americans brought with them ancestral beliefs, and more earthly habits. One of these Chinese families started a general store in Virginia City, Nevada, which burned down in the Great Fire of 1875, preserving a snapshot of expatriate Chinese life. In 2004, archaeologists discovered the site, and excavated the remains of sacrificed cats and birds, children's toys and crockery, and an 'opium stash' which included a small glass vial, a slate plate and a pipe.[50] It was in reaction to this imported opium use that cities such as San Francisco and Portland, Oregon began to outlaw opium dens, specifically targeting their Chinese immigrant communities. American citizens remained free to import the drug.[51]

As the nation grew into its emerging role as a world power, its laws turned against the folk practices of the pioneer days. New anti-narcotics legislation would have far-reaching political consequences. Setting the stage was the passing of the 1906 Pure Food and Drug Act, which, by requiring the labelling of foods and drugs, led to a dramatic decline in the production of patent medicines. A more powerful law waited in the wings – and it was a child of war and opium.[52]

After the Spanish-American War of 1898, the terms of victory granted control of the Philippines to the US government. The territory came with an extra gift: a suite of laws inherited from the Spanish that provided for an annual supply of 130 tons of opium to almost two hundred licensed drug dens. A commission of inquiry was convened by the US Congress to explore alternatives to this state of affairs, and a number of American missionaries recently in the Philippines or China made sure to have their voices heard. Based on their testimony, the committee members conveniently 'forgot'

America's involvement in the opium trade during the previous century and argued that Britain's opium trafficking was ruining the Chinese people. It was also worth noting, they said, that the silver bullion China paid to the British for the drug might be better spent on American products. President Theodore Roosevelt named Dr Hamilton Wright opium commissioner of the United States in 1908 – America's first so-called drug czar.

Several international conferences subsequently took up the addiction issue, and Wright and Episcopal Bishop Charles Henry Brent, a veteran of missionary work in Manila after the Spanish-American War, headed to Shanghai to draft an accord. On 23 January 1912 the first international agreement designed to attack the opium problem was signed in The Hague. It required that each signatory nation pass laws to control narcotics within her borders.[53] Five of the twenty-five articles in the treaty specifically targeted opium in China.[54]

In 1914, as war approached, New York representative Francis Burton Harrison sponsored a bill that would be adopted by the House and Senate after incendiary, racist debate. The case for passage invoked 'drug-crazed, sex-mad negroes' and 'the large number of women who ha[d] become involved and were living as common-law wives or cohabiting with Chinese' because they had become opium addicts. But the mighty Harrison Narcotics Act was primarily crafted to bring much-needed regulation and control to the licensing and dispensing of opium, morphine and heroin prescribed by doctors and pharmacists – the main source of opium for chronic users. These professionals now had to register, pay special taxes and keep records of their drug transactions. In an odd twist, those who peddled patent medicines laced with opiates were exempted from paying the tax or being licensed, as long as their spurious remedies did not contain more than two grains of opium, one quarter of a grain of morphine, or one eighth of a grain of heroin.

The true devil was in the detail. After the act was passed, it mutated from a law of regulation to one of prohibition. The words aimed at medical professionals – that they dispense opium 'in the course of [their] professional practice only' – was creatively interpreted by law-enforcement agencies as meaning that because addiction wasn't a disease, addicts were not patients, and so physicians and pharmacists could not prescribe it. The effects were immediate and dramatic, and are considered by some as the origins of the twentieth century's disastrous policies to control the use of 'hard drugs'.

It seemed an odd turning of the tide for the country that had pioneered the dispensing of morphine during its great Civil War.

IN THE VARIOUS WARS that erupted in the second half of the nineteenth century, other nations adopted the use of opiates on the battlefield. Many of these wars were fought on land covered with scarlet corn poppies, helping further to meld the two flowers into one icon. Between 1870 and 1871, soldiers recruited to the Franco-Prussian War fought while surrounded by fields of poppies, then retired with their injuries to field hospitals to be treated by the bloom's opium-yielding cousin.[55] These killing fields were the landscapes known so well to Napoleon, and would later see the battles of the First World War; today vast fields of opium poppies are legally grown on this same ground for the multinational pharmaceutical companies. The cover of *Harper's Weekly* dated 1 October 1870 is graced by an illustration of a make-shift hospital in a church after the previous month's Battle of Sedan, which marked a shift in France's fortunes in the conflict. Though the war would stretch on for several more months, the German forces had won. The cover illustration shows wounded soldiers being treated with morphine watched over by curiously oriental-looking Catholic priests.[56] Was the artist trying to make a political point?

The poppy's symbolism was growing more potent, entwining the conduct of war and the creation of art ever more tightly. In September 1870, Claude Monet fled France for Britain to avoid conscription into the French army. Safely out of reach in London, he spent much of his time with fellow artist and 'father of Impressionism' Camille Pissarro. These encounters greatly influenced Monet's painting style, but so did the events in his homeland. As the Franco-Prussian War reached its climax and France was brought to a humiliating defeat, his moods became darker and he suffered bouts of depression, which were not helped by the battlefield death of Frédéric Bazille, a fellow Impressionist, and godfather to Monet's son Jean.

When the war ended, Monet returned to France, his prosperity enabling him to move to the small village of Argenteuil on the River Seine near Paris. Inspired by the scenery, he stayed there for eight years and created the paintings that made him famous. Not least of these was *Wild Poppies, Near Argenteuil*, painted in 1873 in the shadow of the recently ended war. Monet's masterpiece endows the poppies with a strange luminosity that makes them seem to shimmer as they catch the light. There is no suggestion that Monet intended to commemorate his friend Bazille, or the casualties of the war, yet it is fitting that he produced this most famous image of the corn poppy in what was to be its last appearance as a simple flower rather than as the symbol of a lost generation.

Monet seems to capture, in brushstrokes, the praise heaped on the corn poppy by the poet, artist and thinker John Ruskin. In 1875, Ruskin published one of his handbooks, in this case on botany, with a typically fey Victorian title: *Proserpina, Studies of Wayside Flowers*. Alongside scientific descriptions, he made room to say the poppy was 'All silk and flame: a scarlet cup, perfect-edged all around, seen among the wild grass far away, like a burning coal fallen from Heaven's altars'.[57] It was 'painted glass; it never glows so brightly as when the sun shines through it. Wherever it is seen – against the light or with the light – always, it is a flame, and warms the wind like a blown ruby'.[58]

The Romantic poets' descriptions of the corn poppy, together with their everyday use of opiates, fuelled a confusion of ideas about the two related flowers. Opium poppies bloom in several colours, not just white, and grow all over Western Europe, not just around the Mediterranean and further east. They bloom alongside the always red corn poppy, and both species scatter themselves among rolling wheat fields. Art imitated nature, however, and Romantic images of corn poppies were infused with the mind-altering qualities of opium. Writers described one species and then ascribed to it the power of the other. John Keats, one of the Romantic Movement's major figures, became famous for odes that overflowed with sensual imagery. In his poem 'To Autumn', he wedded the corn poppy's exuberant red petals, which open in summer, to the opium poppy's timeless tranquillity – 'Or on a half-reaped furrow sound asleep / Drowsed with the fumes of poppies'. Keats travelled to Rome in late 1820, hoping that its warmer climate would alleviate his tuberculosis. It didn't, and his health rapidly deteriorated. In his final days he entreated his friends and doctor for laudanum to ease his pain. They refused, worried that he might use it to commit suicide. He died on 23 February 1821, aged twenty-six.

The corn poppy became a literary fantasy flower, alongside the grander blooms of roses and daffodils. Unlike these scented flowers, the odourless poppy had a darker side, standing on the border between the natural and supernatural worlds.

With uncanny prescience, the opium-addicted poet Francis

Thompson dwelt on narcotic oblivion in his poem 'The Poppy', written in 1891. He sees 'this withering flower of dreams', 'the sleep flower', 'the sun-hazed sleeper'. Ominously he observes the poppy 'With burnt mouth, red like a lion's it drank / The blood of the sun as he slaughtered sank'. A little more than two decades later Thompson's anxious, violent floral imagery had been transplanted from a euphoric pastoral stanza dedicated to a beloved daughter to a terrifying reality of sighting poppies and bodies on the killing fields of the First World War.

4

BARBED-WIRE BATTLEFIELDS

WAR, PAIN, GRIEF AND FORGETFULNESS DREW THE opium and corn poppies ever closer throughout the nineteenth century. But they had not yet merged into the Remembrance Poppy that we know today. One tragic ingredient was missing. And in its grotesque and unparalleled slaughter, the First World War provided what all the previous century's conflicts could not – a final toll of tens of millions of dead, maimed, bereaved and vanished from across continents.

A tenacious and defining myth of the Great War is the freezing, muddy, icy trench, endlessly barraged by the flames of artillery shearing through leaden skies. This was a true image, but not always, and not everywhere. This was a modern war fought on ancient divisions, with massed ranks of men charging across summer fields of wheat speckled with countless poppies under a burning sun.

Flying high above the Somme in the summer of 1916, the young English fighter pilot Cecil Lewis became well acquainted with the terrifying landscapes of war. He also could not help but notice the delicate crimson flower sprouting in the devastation. He exclaimed, 'among the devastated cottages, the tumbled, twisted trees, the desecrated cemeteries . . . the poppies were growing!'[1] He saw 'Clumps of crimson poppies, thrusting out from the lips of craters, straggling in drifts between the hummocks, undaunted by the desolation, heedless of human fury and stupidity, Flanders poppies, basking in the sun'.[2]

Similarly, Captain Rowland Feilding arrived at the front-line trenches near the village of Cuinchy, France in June 1915 in time to witness soldiers rushing wildly across a No Man's Land that was ablaze with scarlet poppies.[3] In his countless letters to his wife he described the flowers just as vividly as the assault of rifle and machine-gun fire.[4]

In the early years of the conflict, those nursing the wounded and the dying could still find comfort in the blooms. Katherine McMahon, a volunteer nurse arrived in France in July 1915. Fresh from America, she had not yet absorbed the terrors of the war, and wrote almost wistfully of how her hospital camp lay in a valley facing the English Channel whose nestling hills were cloaked in poppies.

The men in the trenches were also drawn to the corn poppy's flaming petals. Fred Hodges, a veteran who served to the last day of the war, remembered: 'One day I picked a bunch of red field poppies from the old grassy trench and put them in the metal cup attached to my rifle . . . I was acutely conscious of them growing there in the midst of all that man-made destruction'. Into a filthy dugout in Flanders, infested with flies and lice, Sapper Jack Martin brought a little homely comfort. On a makeshift table 'we have a vase of small marguerites and flaming poppies . . . The vase is an old 18-pdr shell case that we have polished up and made to look very smart'.[5]

Private Len Smith would become an accredited war artist, but throughout the war he illustrated his recently discovered diary with cartoons, landscapes, portraits and postcards. Alongside miniatures he painted of poppies, he wrote of the battlefield scenes that he glimpsed from the trench: 'With much caution one could even peep over the top and it was lovely to see groups of red poppies . . . Considering the numerous shell holes they were very numerous and made a very brave display – I know they thrilled me intensely'.[6] Pressed between the pages of the diary are traces of a corn poppy. The scribbled caption records: 'Actual Flanders Poppy from "No Man's Land" 1916'.[7]

Olaf Stapledon, serving in France with the Friends' Ambulance Unit, wrote a letter to his cousin in 1916 describing 'a mound of ruin overgrown with bright poppies, cornflower, & mustard'.[8] It was an apparition which would become familiar to the American troops freshly arrived the next year – from Belleau Wood to Cantigny to Chateau Thierry, the battlefields appeared as an endless sea of poppies and wheat. It was not so much that the scarlet flower grew up from the graves of the dead but that countless thousands of men fell on land that was little more than an ocean of poppies and their own blood.

For the soldiers of the Great War, the proliferation of the wild flowers came to symbolise the conflict's goals of freedom and regeneration. The flowers were also seen to provide a literally tactile connection between the living and the dead – the roots reaching into graves below and the petals reaching into hands above.[9] Writing about nature helped many infantrymen to cope with the horror of their experience. Here was a means for measuring their sufferings, but also for protecting themselves against utter oblivion; their words might survive if nothing else. The spirit of this idea was captured by an anonymous photographer in 1918, who took a picture of two Australian soldiers sitting in a field and gazing intensely at the wild flowers that surrounded them. Were they reflecting, perhaps, on the deaths of comrades and their own escape from disaster?[10] That same year, an American, William Stidger, who was working for the YMCA on the French battlefields, wrote how he turned away

> *from all the suffering to find a blood-red poppy bloom-*
> *ing in the field behind him; or a million of them cover-*
> *ing a green field like a great blanket . . . I thought to*
> *myself: They look as if they had once been our golden*
> *California poppies, but that in these years of war every*
> *last one of them had been dipped in the blood of those*
> *brave lads who have died for us, and forever after shall*
> *they be crimson in memory of these who have given so*
> *much for humanity.*[11]

It was a disturbing clash: the romanticism of the bloom and the modernity of the blood and viscera spilled by industrialised war on a mass scale. For some, it was much easier, much more comforting, to deny this reality, to see only the poppies growing on the fields where the battle no longer raged.

Flowers possessed an uplifting connection with youth and beauty, but, through their own rapid fading, with death and decay as well. The simple and fragile corn poppy had latent qualities resurrected by the effects of war. Its abundant black seeds became metaphors for the vast numbers of dead, its shimmering petals a crimson metaphor for 'the missing' – a heart-rending euphemism for the countless men blasted into nothingness by the combatants' high explosives. Yet they also embodied the ancient meaning of fertility and renewal – a floral display of hope for the future. And though the cynic saw countless thousands die to fertilise the fields of France and Belgium, others embraced that hope for the future of civilisation. As the war thundered on, its voracious appetite for men's lives exceeded the hopelessly naive underestimates of the opposing nations. The poor little poppy, so recently eulogised by Monet's painting, shouldered an increasingly heavy load along the battlefields of the Western Front. Endless columns of young, virile men in battalions and regiments replenished the ranks – continually cut down but always replaced, fading away yet constantly flowering again.

The corn-poppy fields seemed as endless as their own suffering and the death toll. Here were the seeds of something new: a mixing together of poppy and death on an industrial scale. Images of the crimson bloom fused with scenes of carnage, fields of mutilated and rotting bodies. Yet somehow, amid this savagery, the corn-poppy petals were reimagined as the fragile spirits of the dead, rising from the blood-drenched earth.

A botanical truth underpinned this gruesome reality. Before the war, the soil of Belgian Flanders was not rich enough in lime to allow poppies to flourish in great numbers. The shattered rubble of village walls and of men's bones blasted lime and calcium into the landscape, creating the conditions necessary for carpets of corn poppies to bloom. So rapidly did the poppies appear on the devastated battlefields, that they seemed almost as supernatural heralds – announcing the presence of the otherwise silent and uncountable dead. In an echo of Waterloo, it was as if the blood-red poppy nourished those who lay beneath the ground.

It was no wonder that the war poets would immortalise it as the beacon of resurrection.

TALL, IMPOSING, with boundless energy, John McCrae was a consummate man of action. A sharpshooter with medals from the Boer War, he would not be remembered for his bravery under fire, his inspirational leadership on the South African veldt, or the rapid pro-motion these qualities brought. He would, instead, be immortalised by his poem.

McCrae's physical presence and military bearing were matched by an enquiring mind and a romantic and sensitive character. He was a doctor with a talent for writing medical essays, and also deeply religious. As a devout Presbyterian, he had memorised his Puritan prayers even before he could read. Typical of his time, this energetic and educated man wrote poetry, though more as a pastime than a passion.[12] In this he was part of the pastoralist Georgian tradition which saw the world in almost whimsical Romantic terms.

Born in 1872 in Guelph, near Ontario in Canada, McCrae's Scottish ancestors had a venerable military heritage, and it is tempting to trace his later literary fame to his mother's influence, as, unusually for a woman of the mid-nineteenth century, she was well read and fluent in Greek and Latin.

Having left the army after the Boer War to pursue a medical career, McCrae rejoined immediately shortly after he heard the news that Britain had declared war on 4 August 1914, and he was in the first wave of patriotic Canadians who sailed to Europe. On arriving in England, he spent several months training on Salisbury Plain, then journeyed to France in February 1915. He was quickly moved on to Belgium and appointed lieutenant-colonel of the Canadian Army Medical Corps. Fatefully, he retained his previous rank as a doctor-major in the First Brigade of Canadian Field Artillery.[13]

April 1915 saw him stationed near Ypres, the city in Belgian Flanders whose medieval splendour had been smashed in early bom-bardments. When he arrived, it was being levelled in the Second Battle of Ypres. Working from a casualty dressing station dug into the bank of the nearby Yperlee Canal, he tended the injuries of countless men wounded by the relentless enemy attacks on the city. On 22 April, the Germans unleashed a choking fog of chlorine gas over the Allied lines and announced the advent of a new form of warfare, in contravention of the gentleman's code of war that had been forged at the Hague Convention of 1899. Many men did not survive. It was at this time that the British army opened Essex Farm Cemetery adjacent to McCrae's bunker. Every day he watched young men being carried to their premature rest there. He later recalled how 'we are weary in body and wearier in mind. The general impression in my mind is of a nightmare'.[14]

Among the men who soon found a home in the cemetery was McCrae's friend Lieutenant Alexis Helmer. Fair-haired and blue-eyed, Helmer had graduated from McGill University just before the war and quickly proved himself to be a born leader of men. Only twenty-two, he had risen to be an officer of First Brigade Canadian Field Artillery. At 8 a.m. on 2 May he was standing next to his own field gun in the midst of a heavy German bombardment. Moments later, he was blown to pieces by shellfire. His shattered remains had to be gathered up in sandbags. They were arranged in human form inside an army blanket, and then buried at sunset at Essex Farm Cemetery.[15]

At the ad hoc funeral, McCrae stood in for the chaplain, who was absent that evening. With no training in burying the dead, let alone a friend lost in such a horrible way, he recited from memory extracts from the Order for the Burial of the Dead. 'O God of spirits, and of all flesh, who hast trampled down Death, and overthrown the Devil, and given life unto thy world: Do thou, the same Lord, give rest to the soul of thy departed servant, Alexis Helmer, in a place of brightness, a place of verdure, a place of repose, whence all sickness, sorrow and sighing have fled away.'[16] Staring at the freshly dug earth, and with the din of battle still ringing in his ears, he continued: 'We brought nothing into this world, and it is certain we can carry nothing out. The Lord gave, and the Lord hath taken away; blessed be the name of the Lord.'[17] A wooden grave marker was then pushed into the freshly dug earth.

Crouching in the entrance to his first-aid dugout at dawn the next day, McCrae looked out on the bright wild poppies and simple wooden crosses marking the makeshift graves. As soon as he came off duty he walked over to an ambulance, sat on its tailgate and tore a page out of his dispatch book. As the poppies shimmered in the morning light, he began scribbling, pausing occasionally to glance up again at Helmer's grave. He composed the fifteen immortal lines of 'In Flanders Fields' in the next twenty minutes.

> *In Flanders fields the poppies blow*
> *Between the crosses, row on row,*
> *That mark our place; and in the sky*
> *The larks, still bravely singing, fly*
> *Scarce heard amid the guns below.*
>
> *We are the Dead. Short days ago*
> *We lived, felt dawn, saw sunset glow,*
> *Loved, and were loved, and now we lie*
> *In Flanders fields.*
>
> *Take up our quarrel with the foe:*
> *To you from failing hands we throw*
> *The torch; be yours to hold it high.*
> *If ye break faith with us who die*
> *We shall not sleep, though poppies grow*
> *In Flanders fields.*

His poem was 'born of fire and blood during the hottest phase of the Second Battle of Ypres', according to McCrae's friend Lieutenant-Colonel Edward Morrison.[18]

AS THE OLD CENTURY PASSED, the Victorian era had given way to a golden age of naive innocence and self-satisfaction – the Indian summer of Edwardian Britain. It began with the accession of King Edward VII in 1901, and was swiftly followed by the coronation of King George V in 1911. In literary circles, the mood gave birth to pastoralist Georgian poetry, an often pale and whimsical imitation of the earlier Romantic tradition. Georgian poetry was less of a vibrant celebration of the countryside than its predecessor had been, but rather a 'weekend ruralism', and a 'pastime for the governing class'.[19]

Romantic verse found physical form in the designs of art nouveau, which flourished from 1890 to 1910.[20] Rhythmic motifs of curving flowers, tree branches and robes spoke to nostalgia for the innocent, pre-industrial age and the 'whiplash' inherent in modern life.[21] This philosophy of art and language had been developed as an escape from grinding, dehumanising industrialisation, and many of the artists' worst nightmares of the industrial age would be fulfilled in the horrors of the war.

The new Romantic poetry of an upper-class, make-believe rural idyll was carried to the battlefields of France, Belgium and beyond by young educated British officers. Among them was the charismatic Rupert Brooke, whose talents were admired by Virginia Woolf and who was called 'the handsomest man in England' by W.B. Yeats. Before the war, in a café in Berlin, Brooke had penned a typically Georgian eulogy to Nature (with a capital N), entitled 'The Old Vicarage, Grantchester':

Smile the carnation and the pink;
And down the borders, well I know,
The poppy and the pansy blow.

In similar vein, Brooke described to a friend in 1914 a brief stay in a country cottage in Gloucestershire which had 'a porch where one drinks great mugs of cider, & looks at fields of poppies in the corn'.[22]

Brooke captured the jingoistic British enthusiasm for a war that was widely expected to be over by Christmas. Such feelings were not born of direct experience, as Brooke never went into combat. His idealism was most famously voiced in his sonnet 'The Soldier', in which he conjured imperial imagery more appropriate to the Victorian era:

If I should die think only this of me:
That there's some corner of a foreign field
That is forever England

Catching the public spirit of the early war years, his poems were perfect fodder for the nation's politicians, who, like the poet, had not grasped the true nature of modern warfare. 'They used Brooke's poems as war propaganda, immortalising him as the young warrior keen to lay down his life for his country', according to one guide to the poets of the war.[23] Mythical, secluded, unspoiled Arcadia – *Et in Arcadio ego* ('Even in Arcadia there am I', death) – would be turned into a battlefield, and nature itself was soon to conspire with industrialised weapons to produce a world which would leave comforting verse far behind.

Not long after the start of hostilities in August 1914, flowers – which, just a generation before had been catalogued to serve as a secret language of love – were bestowed with a wholly modern and disturbing symbolism. It was said that 'a standard way of writing the Georgian poem was to get as many flowers into it as possible'.[24] However, the poppy's bright scarlet hue, so redolent of freshly spilled blood, made it an obvious signifier for young soldiers raised on pastoral poetry and its pre-war obsession with red flowers of all kinds, and its presence in the killing fields would eventually help it to replace its competitors as a memorial flower.[25] Until 1918, though, it was the rose, not the poppy which symbolised the English army at war. The national flower of England evoked strong romantic connections.[26]

Typical of such early flower-filled poems was 'A Song' by Charles Alexander Richmond, an American clergyman and academic who did not fight in the war. Though the poem begins with the rose, it also manages to draw on the poppy's narcotic imagery, which was already making its presence known on Europe's battlefields:

> *O, red is the English rose,*
> *And the lilies of France are pale,*
> *And the poppies grow in the golden wheat,*
> *For the men whose eyes are heavy with sleep*

Herbert Asquith spoke in similar vein in his 1915 poem 'The Fallen Subaltern':

> *As goes the Sun-god in his chariot glorious,*
> *When all his golden banners are unfurled,*
> *So goes the soldier, fallen but victorious,*
> *And leaves behind a twilight in the world.*

Such appeals to romantic nature were perhaps a cloaking device to mask the horrors of war.[27]

Yet while nature was an integral part of the 'myth of the war experience'[28] and the stubborn belief in soldierly immortality that was rife among recruits (and those who recruited them), it could also be that the destruction of the French and Belgian countryside heralded the disappearance of the whole pre-war world. The comforting certainties of the past were no more. Nature was being crushed, landscapes annihilated; men were being sacrificed on the altar of nineteenth-century ambitions pursued with twentieth-century technology.[29]

The war poets capture a sense of this rapidly changing world in a medium tailored to convey what plain prose cannot. It was thus with Lawrence Binyon, whose prescient elegy, 'For the Fallen', was written a few weeks after the war had begun. Binyon wrote of young soldiers and their 'straight limbs, and true, steady and glowing eyes', as if they were fighting some barbarous tribe on a far-flung shore of empire. Despite his pre-war language, Binyon sensed something more was at stake, and envisioned the tragedy that was to come. Magnificent, painful and universal, his prophetic words are recited annually at the Festival of Remembrance at London's Royal Albert Hall. As the audience is showered with red poppy petals, the poem recalls the dead:

> *They shall not grow old, as we that are left grow old:*
> *Age shall not weary them, nor the years condemn.*
> *At the going down of the sun and in the morning*
> *We will remember them.*

The terrible experience of the First World War, and the struggle to record it, forged a new poetic sensibility. The Arcadian flowers, birds and fields of Georgian England were deformed – twisted into poppies tortured by barbed wire in fields strewn with shattered bones.[30] Bombs obliterated the rural peace; nightingales sang during battle. The endless heavens that had inspired so many pre-war eulogies became the narrow slits of sky seen from the depths of a rat-infested trench.

The Battle of the Somme changed the war for the military, the public and poets alike. Pastoral illusions could not withstand the 19,240 deaths and 35,493 wounded that were tallied on the first day alone. The once Romantic countryside was soon bedecked with poppies, which at times seemed to mock the living with a satanic hue. Soldiers' experiences of the destruction gave rise to the idea that the poppies, nourished by blood, had captured the souls of the fallen. The work of Wilfred Owen, Siegfried Sassoon and Isaac Rosenberg epitomised the bitter disillusionment, the sense of futility and waste of life during the war, and stood in contrast to the patriotic warrior ideals of Georgian poetry.

Some soldier-poets began angrily to expose the suffering and agonies of their fellow men on the battlefields, giving voice for the first time to the gut-wrenching realities of the conflict. Owen, for one, repudiated the hypocrisy that had brought such renown to Rupert Brooke. In his most famous poem, 'Dulce et Decorum Est', Owen twisted the knife:

> *If you could hear, at every jolt, the blood*
> *Come gargling from the froth-corrupted lungs,*
> *Bitter as the cud*
> *Of vile, incurable sores on innocent tongues,*
> *My friend, you would not tell with such high zest*
> *To children ardent for some desperate glory,*
> *The old Lie: Dulce et decorum est*
> *Pro patria mori.*

Here there was no glory in dying for one's country.

With a more accessible touch, Sassoon satirised those at home who remained ignorant of the sufferings of soldiers. He was notably bitter towards politicians, likening Parliament to a drunken, raucous music hall in his poem 'Blighters':

> The House is crammed: tier beyond tier they grin
> And cackle at the show . . .
> I'd like to see a tank come down the stalls . . .
> And there'd be no more jokes in Music Halls
> To mock the riddled corpses around Bapaume

The bitterness among the soldier-poets did not fade after the war. In his 1919 poem 'Aftermath', Sassoon asks his readers: 'Have you forgotten yet?', and reminds them, 'Do you remember the rats; and the stench / Of corpses rotting in front of the front-line trench'.[31]

Rosenberg, a soldier-poet who did not survive the war, came from a working-class Jewish family in east London. He was torn between sympathy for the dying and his feelings of helplessness to save them. No details were spared. In 'Dead Man's Dump', he wrote: 'A man's brains splattered on / A stretcher-bearer's face'.[32]

Rosenberg saw the change in the weather of the war, and the tragedy of nature turned against men. Not surprisingly, his poppy is a different flower from the Romantics' immortal bloom. Just weeks after the beginning of the Battle of the Somme on 1 July 1916, he penned 'In the Trenches' on a spare scrap of paper. As with John McCrae, he focuses his attention on the poppy, but Rosenberg uses harsher, raw language – words that would have seemed impossible a few months earlier. Poppies and men are inseparable, broken and bloody, smashed by shellfire in the trench at dawn:

I snatched two poppies
From the parapet's edge,
Two bright red poppies
That winked on the ledge.

Behind my ear
I stuck one through,
One blood red poppy
I gave to you.

The sandbags narrowed
And screwed out our jest,
And tore the poppy
You had on your breast . . .
Dawn – a shell – O! Christ
I am choked . . . safe . . . dust blind, I
See trench floor poppies
Strewn. Smashed, you lie.

Yet he was dissatisfied with this effort, and a few weeks later he returned to the poem and rewrote it as 'Break of Day in the Trenches', now widely regarded as one of the finest of all Great War poems.[33] The poppy remained centre-stage, but it had grown more insidious:

The darkness crumbles away –
It is the same old druid Time as ever.
Only a live thing leaps my hand –
A queer sardonic rat –
As I pull the parapet's poppy
To stick behind my ear

. . .

What do you see in our eyes
At the shrieking iron and flame
Hurled through still heavens?

. . .

Poppies whose roots are in man's veins
Drop, and are ever dropping;
But mine in my ear is safe,
Just a little white with the dust.[34]

The poppy had come to symbolise 'the shell-shredded dead and their crimson blood',[35] appearing as a single bloom announced by a rat – the hated pests who feasted on the bodies of the dead. These previously innocent flowers were truly vampires, biting into the veins of dead men and sucking up their blood as nourishment from the earth to sustain its brief life.[36]

Rosenberg died at dawn on 1 April 1918, almost exactly three years after the death of Rupert Brooke and the writing of 'In Flanders Fields' by John McCrae.

THE IMAGINED EUPHORIA of the poppy became real for the injured once morphine was administered. Just as in the American Civil War, opium took on a hero's role in the medical tents. But the hero could also morph into an enemy. Addiction remained a menace, particularly because of the easy availability of the now mass-produced drug. The danger was greater after a soldier had served time in the trenches. Why wouldn't the dreamy lassitude produced by the opiates be infinitely preferable to the horrors of full consciousness?

The US army's surgeon-general warned that 'All habitual drug takers are liars',[37] and that every step should be taken to make secure the large quantities of painkillers in the battle zone.[38] As 'soldiers of the Medical Department have been recently arrested for selling morphine and cocaine stolen from the Medical Department . . . [such drugs] . . . should be kept at all times under lock and key'.[39] On a few days' leave away from the trenches, British army captain J.C. Dunn journeyed through the countryside behind Le Tréport, in northern France, and commented on driving past fields where the poppy was being cultivated – to produce morphine, within earshot of the guns.[40] More curious, perhaps, were the morphine gift boxes available from Harrods department store in London as late as 1916. Complete with syringe and spare needles, the boxes patriotically announced that they were 'A Welcome Present for Friends at the Front'.

Opium was not only used to treat the wounded. For several months in advance of the British attack on the Ottoman-Turkish lines in Gaza in November 1917, aeroplanes dropped packets of cigarettes along with propaganda on the Turkish trenches. Soon the Turkish soldiers welcomed these airborne gifts. On 5 November, the day before the attack, the British again dropped thousands of packets, but this time each cigarette had been saturated with opium. Within hours, the British had taken Gaza from the stupefied Turks, many of whom were unable to speak, let alone fight; some soldiers were discovered fast asleep.[41]

While the Gaza campaign was almost comical, other examples of the repercussions of the use of opium during the war were not. After four years of battle and ten years of opium addiction, the Hungarian poet and soldier-doctor Géza Csath poisoned himself at the Hungarian-Serbian demarcation line in 1919. Johannes Becher, a German poet and novelist, banished his war experiences through an intense addiction to morphine,[42] a dependence which displaced the physical reality of the war with a mental turmoil provoked by the drug. Opium gave Becher a heightened sense of his own morality. He could no longer see a difference between the rightness of the enemy and his own country's politicians, who he now considered his foes too.[43]

By coincidence, in May 1915, as McCrae was writing his poem and as the war began yielding huge numbers of wounded men in desperate need of morphine, American doctors were being arrested and imprisoned for supplying opiates to addicts. The *New York Medical Journal* announced

> *As was expected . . . the immediate effects of the Harrison anti-narcotic law were seen in the flocking of drug habitues to hospitals and sanatoriums. Sporadic crimes of violence were reported too, due usually to desperate efforts by addicts to obtain drugs, but occasionally to a delirious state induced by sudden withdrawal.*[44]

Later the same year, the 'drug crisis triggered by the passage of the Harrison Act was reportedly in full swing. The journal *American Medicine* declared, 'Narcotic drug addiction is one of the gravest and most important questions confronting the medical profession today'. The august editors wrote 'A particular sinister sequence . . . is the character of the places to which [addicts] are forced to go to get their drugs and the type of people with whom they are obliged to mix. The most depraved criminals are often the dispensers of these habit-forming drugs'.[45]

The Harrison Act had made a crisis out of a problem, and its effect dovetailed in a curious way with the catastrophe of the First World War. The sudden outlawing of opiate use in America in 1915 produced what some believe to be the first use of the term 'Soldier's Disease' among ageing Civil War veterans – a disease that would be feared over the next decade. But the Harrison Act was also a rallying call against American involvement in the global conflict. Alarmed by the prospect of the United States being drawn into the Great War, the Yale professor Jeanette Marks wrote *The Curse of Narcotism in America: A Reveille*, in which the opium addiction of Civil War soldiers was put forward as a warning against going to war:

> *Did you know that there is practically no old American family of Civil War reputation which has not had its addicts? . . . [I]t was the 'army disease' because of its prevalence . . . [W]ith the war that hangs over us, the drug evil will spread into a giantism of even more terrible growth than the present . . . [T]here are something like 4,000,000 victims of opium and cocaine in this country today.*[46]

Astonishing as these numbers are, they were actually greatly exaggerated, as were Marks's fears of an explosion of new American addicts after the war. According to the records, few US soldiers returned home in 1918 and 1919 addicted to morphine, though the reason for this is not entirely understood. The answer may simply be one of maths: only 204,002 American casualties were reported during the First World War, compared to 281,881 wounded and another 224,097 who were hurt or fell ill during the American Civil War.[47] Sadly, eighty-year-old veterans of the Civil War were still living in old soldiers' homes stricken with chronic opium addiction into the late 1920s.[48]

The issues of opiate addiction exemplified the changing nature of war. Pre-war ideals would buckle and fail in the face of the weighty losses at the Somme in 1916 and at Passchendaele the next year. Across

Europe, the war was shaking the old order into chaos. Farm workers and office clerks put on uniforms and marched to the front. Lists of the dead were published daily. Young men were absent from city streets. Women were put to work in munitions factories. Trains clattered across the doleful English countryside carrying wounded soldiers, refugees, prisoners of war and civilians unfortunate enough to bear a German or Turkish name. In France and Britain, Zeppelin airships loomed in the sky, and together with the fearsomely named Gotha bombers, dropped death from on high. There were also rare but spectacular 'sound and light' shows when armaments exploded at factories, bringing front-line destruction to the hearts of these nations.

The overall effect was to bring death and wounding, grief and loss, to almost every family in Britain. Many felt a profound but unfocused desire for some form of elegy, of remembrance.

LIKE HIS FELLOW POETS, McCrae was a product of his time, and so was his poetry. He drew on the popular fashion of Georgian pastoral verse, yet juxtaposed it with the stark reality of his wartime experience. Edward Morrison later recalled that the two of them 'often heard in the mornings the larks singing high in the air, between the crash of the shell and the reports of the guns in the battery just beside us'[49] – a new pastoral experience, to say the least. McCrae's poem built a bridge between the past and the present.

The wind-blown poppies of 'In Flanders Fields' grew between the sad rows of temporary wooden crosses in a battlefield cemetery, a sight that many soldiers knew too well. The poem homed in on their everyday life as soldiers, their sense of brotherly duty as well as sacrifice.

And it seemed to issue an anxious plea – laying responsibility on the living to continue the fight. Yet in May 1915, more than a year before the cataclysm of the Somme, McCrae's poetry had not entirely lost its pastoral innocence. That would be gone soon enough, with the angry and agonising imagery of death that would appear in the 'protest poetry' of Wilfred Owen and others, and destroy the neo-Romantic Georgian style.[50] Whether or not McCrae's poem foretold the idea of 'a corner of a foreign field that is forever England',[51] there is a sense when reading the poem that it was written just in time.

'In Flanders Fields' is two poems in one. The first two stanzas are a peerless elegy to the pastoral mood, where the innocent dead are set in counterpoint to sunrise and sunset, lark song against artillery barrages, grave-marker crosses and a rolling endless sky. These verses touch all the pressure points of English society's sensitivities, and were almost predestined to strike a chord in the wider English-speaking world. But then a dramatic change occurs. The third and final stanza wrenches the reader out of this romanticised and idealised world, imposing an obligation on the living to keep the memory of the dead alive, to make their sacrifices worth more than a sombre but fleeting remembrance. But the poem also implores – almost shames – the living to 'keep the faith'. Its sudden change of pace and tone challenges the reader not to mourn the dead so much as take up the fight. This new message is a 'call to arms' and a passing on of the torch of freedom. It sits uneasily alongside the poem's opening verses in a way that could not have been achieved after the summer of 1916, and the hitherto unimaginable casualties of the Battle of the Somme.[52]

The dual nature of McCrae's poem is reflected too in its ambiguous use of poppy imagery. McCrae shifts between the two species. The pastoral imagery of the first two stanzas conjure the corn poppy, while the final verses play on the opium poppy's sleep-like narcosis. The poem's final lines are the first conception of a hybrid Remembrance Poppy. There McCrae says that if faith is broken *the dead will not sleep*, although they are covered with poppies in the battlefields of Flanders.

Within a month of writing the poem that would be his legacy, Lieutenant-Colonel McCrae left the front lines to take up a new posting just outside the French channel port of Boulogne. He took with him the lines scrawled on paper, polished them a bit for public consumption and sent the finished poem to the London *Spectator*. In a decision that may have haunted the paper's editor for the rest of his life, the poem was rejected. A few months later McCrae had better luck, and 'In Flanders Fields' was printed in *Punch* magazine on 8 December 1915. The poem was run without a byline. McCrae could never have imagined that his words would strike such a chord. They were a touchstone for the transformation by which the common corn poppy became the symbol for all who died in war – the lost and the found, the loved and the lonely.

The poem was an immediate sensation in the trenches and at home. The corn poppy was rechristened the Flanders Poppy, and the image of its fragile blood-red petals rooted itself in the psyche of the English-speaking Allies. Yet while death in Ypres had been the catalyst for the poem, the subject was universal. McCrae's subject was the fear that soldiers would be forgotten once dead, and that their sufferings would be in vain, a mounting concern as the casualty lists grew. But here was a flower, an emblem of remembrance that in its simplicity represented the eternal hope which banished such fears.

In the spirit of the times, the poem became a peerless propaganda tool, raising men, money and morale, and, according to the cynical, luring more patriotic young warriors to an early death. McCrae was constantly asked for permission to use the poem to support the ongoing war effort.

Poppy propaganda worked, alongside appeals to patriotism and duty. In Britain, men flocked to enlist in Lord Kitchener's volunteer army in time for the Battle of the Somme in July 1916, and many came from Canada, similarly, for the Armageddon that was Passchendaele a year later. These battles played their part in the Allies' victory, but not without great cost. McCrae's poem, much like its forebears from epic Greek mythology, invited brave and true men to lay down their lives in endless sleep for the generations not yet born. And as more men died, the more the poppy took root in the shattered fields of the Western Front and in the imagery of the fallen.

McCrae did not live to see his immortal verse give birth to the Remembrance Poppy. In January 1918, while stationed at Wimereux, just north of Boulogne, he was appointed consulting physician to the British armies in France. However, the news came as the flu virus arrived at the camp. He was struck down. Soon, his illness was aggravated, by asthma and the lingering effects of the gas he had inhaled on the battlefields. His lungs became infected, and he was transferred to a nearby officers' hospital, where he lapsed into a coma on 27 January 1918 and died in the early hours of the following day.

But the poppy had not finished with John McCrae. Immediately after his death, his fellow officers searched the surrounding fields in the hope of finding winter poppies to lay on his grave, believing that they would have reminded him of Flanders.[53] Fate stepped in, but not in the shape of the fragile corn poppy, but rather in the shape of things to come. Unsuccessful in their search, McCrae's comrades ordered instead a wreath of artificial poppies from Paris.[54] Quite by chance, John McCrae's wreath was the first appearance of the millions of Remembrance Poppies to come.

The opium poppy may have brought pain-easing sleep and dreams to the wounded, but the harmless corn poppy was becoming almost narcotic in its own way: it helped to give expression to the grief of millions who knew soldiers who had died or suffered in the war. In time, the Remembrance Poppy would become a symbol whose palliative role on the spiritual plane equalled anything the opium poppy had achieved on the physical one.

'In Flanders Fields' was adopted as a collective expression of emotion among the war generation across the Allied countries, and would form part of the Remembrance Day commemorations that would soon be held on 11 November each year. While McCrae's poem immortalised the poppy and helped to make it a visible sign of remembrance, McCrae and the place of the Remembrance Poppy's conception have been immortalised too. In 1985, seventy years after the poem was written, the provincial government of West Flanders unveiled a commemorative stone to John McCrae at Essex Farm cemetery, a stone's throw from his first-aid bunker. Breaking with Belgian tradition, which dictates that monuments carry the royal cipher of the wartime King Albert, this sculpted white stone bears an engraved poppy beneath McCrae's name and the date of the poem's composition, 3 May 1915.[55] Eight years later, in 1993, the dugout medical station, still nestled beneath the banks of the Yperlee canal, was refurbished and opened to the public as a war heritage site. In McCrae's homeland, his poem has achieved near-mythical status, its manuscript becoming one of Canada's most enduring war artefacts.[56] Canadian schoolchildren memorise the verse. Given the nation's bilingual status, an official French version – 'Au champ d'horreur' – has been written.

In April 1915, a month before John McCrae wrote his poem, Rupert Brooke died. Brooke was buried on the Aegean island of Skyros, almost in sight of Troy, and mourned as a patriotic hero. The young poet had given voice to the aspirations of British politicians and public alike,[57] but those optimistic aspirations would be vanquished within the year.

Although 'In Flanders Fields' was composed in the same Georgian style used by Brooke, there were no heroes or bright-eyed young warriors on show in McCrae's verses. The poppy was no longer a Romantic symbol. It was a symbol of the shell-torn bodies, an emotional calling card for remembrance and respect.

The last breath of pure Georgian poetry was its most famous. It fixed together the potent symbolic might of the corn poppy and the healing power of the opium poppy. It combined appearance with substance – fragile crimson petals and the relief of mental anguish. It united two poppies in one, and would go on to create a commemorative emblem that would capture people's imagination long before it had any manifestation in the physical world.

POETS DIE, but their works survive, and the poppy's evolving symbolism still conveys the truth of the trenches to us, a century later. It is impossible not to see the corn poppy as a mirror of the unnaturally short lives of the men whose fighting churned up the soil. The poppy grows, fades and grows again, in an endless cycle of rejuvenation, an ongoing commemoration of the dead bound to the rhythms of nature.[58]

Those soldiers who survived would have their physical and emotional wounds tended by the poppy – treated with morphine and bestowed with tributes alike. But reality could not be escaped, not even in the sleep and dreams that were the currency of the narcotics trade. Ivor Gurney, a war poet who fought and survived, was for ever haunted by his experiences. Gurney concludes his poem, 'To His Love':

Cover him, cover him soon!
And with thick-set
Masses of memoried flowers –
Hide that red wet
Thing I must somehow forget.

For a while, soldiers and the bereaved alike endeavoured to forget the pain of wounds and personal loss in order to continue living. But they strove 'never to forget' the generation that had died too young.

On the deserted battlefields, Chinese peasants, who had been transported half way round the world by the British for the job, began clearing the debris of war.[59] They were paid to search for and bury the Allied dead in cemeteries set among rolling fields of corn poppies. In such places, corn poppies did not speak of the hidden dead, but rather advertised the memory of those fortunate enough to be rescued from oblivion and given at least a semblance of dignity with a formal military burial.

The fact that poppies naturally grow on disturbed ground simultaneously signified new life as well as death, and for many this helped temper the human propensity to view such places as spiritually and morally troubling. The endless fields of scarlet petals were an organic counterpart to the endless rows of wooden crosses dotting innumerable landscapes. Later, when those flimsy crosses were replaced with durable Portland stone in the Imperial (now Commonwealth) War Grave Commission cemeteries, the flower's brief life made it all the more poignant. Poppies perfectly and painfully represented the short lives of so many Great War soldiers. The poppy fields were ephemeral; the fields of gravestones would endure, seemingly, for ever.

The idea of the poppy as a flower of remembrance was not fully formed on the battlefields of the First World War. Broken soldiers' experiences were not enough to make the poppy a symbol of renewal and commemoration for the wider public. For every soldier who died, a larger number of family and friends were struck down by grief. A 'Remembrance Poppy' had to be about the civilian experience, too.

The rejuvenation of poppies was almost complete. The historical stage was set, the poetic imagery in place and the numbers of dead sufficiently legion. The inspiration for the Remembrance Poppy was missing, however. It would appear from nowhere, and in a most unlikely place.

5

THE POPPY LADY

It was a day of omens. On 9 November 1918, dawn broke over the Château Neubois near Spa in Belgium with an air of foreboding. Within hours, its occupant, Kaiser Wilhelm II, had abdicated, and would soon be staring out of the window as his silver train jolted him into exile in the Netherlands. In less than forty-eight hours, the First World War would end in armistice, an agreement signed in another railway carriage at Compiègne outside Paris. One of the most powerful men on earth was now little more than a refugee.

When he heard the news, a twenty-nine-year-old German soldier recovering from a mustard-gas attack suffered a relapse of his temporary blindness. That night he brokered a deal with God: in return for his sight, he vowed to dedicate his life to politics. Adolf Hitler kept his vow,[1] and exactly twenty years later, on 9 November 1938, the sound of breaking glass announced the Nazi terror of Kristallnacht.

In one of the more disturbing coincidences of history, that same night in 1918 saw a meeting of the occult and Aryan 'Thule society' in Munich. Wilhelm's abdication prompted a messianic speech by

Grandmaster Rudolf von Sebottendorf, who warned of the chaos that would engulf Germany – 'In the place of our princes of Germanic blood rules our deadly enemy: Judah'.[2] The Thule society would later sponsor the Deutsche Arbeiter Partei, only to see it hijacked by the Führer and be reborn as the Nazi Party. In his chilling and prophetic rant, Sebottendorf exhorted the brotherhood to fight 'until the swastika rises victoriously out of the icy darkness'.[3]

But the young Hitler and the old grandmaster were not the only ones to experience visions of a new world on that fateful day.

In New York City, a middle-aged spinster hurried to her gloomy basement office at Columbia University. Grey clouds scudded overhead and rain threatened. A spectacular future beckoned to the forty-nine-year-old schoolteacher. She would dedicate the rest of her life to healing the wounds opened by the Kaiser's global war. Within the hour she would invent one of history's most startling and evocative symbols.

MOINA BELLE MICHAEL was born near Good Hope, Georgia, USA, on 15 August 1869, into a family whose ancestral roots were in Belgian Flanders and among the French Huguenots of Brittany. She had begun teaching at the age of fifteen, and had spent her life educating young minds in the church schools of her home state. Unworldly in many respects, she had embarked on a fateful trip to Europe in the spring of 1914, visiting Britain, France, Belgium and Switzerland. Bad timing caught her in the German city of Cologne during the last week of July, where she saw German soldiers primed for the imminent invasion of Belgium.

She later recalled her impressions. 'They were like brutes to me – from the tips of their haughty helmets to the polished hob-nails under their heavy boots, clanking with showy spurs. Instinctively I feared and disliked them', she wrote.[4] Everywhere, it seemed, she saw posters of the Teutonic 'super soldier' sitting astride his warhorse, holding aloft a flaming torch. Schooled in the Bible, and intensely moral, to her these steel-clad warriors were messengers of the Apocalypse.

The countdown to war quickened, and Michael fled to Rome just in time. She worked briefly for the US authorities in aiding the return of stranded tourists to America. At last it was her turn to leave, and she travelled to Naples to await a ship. Even her escape was dramatic. Two years before, the ocean liner *Carpathia* had rescued the survivors of the *Titanic* from the Atlantic's icy waters. Now it hove into view to rescue those stranded by the rising tide of war. Slipping through the minefields outside Gibraltar, then zigzagging for weeks to avoid patrolling German submarines, the *Carpathia* finally reached New York, and Moina Michael made her way back to her Georgia school.

It was only in September 1918 that Michael left her classroom in the belated hope of joining the war effort. With patriotic fervour, she took leave of absence to enrol on a training course at the YMCA's Overseas War Secretaries (OWS) headquarters at Columbia. Enthusiastic as she was, age was against her, and after completing the course she was denied the opportunity to return to Europe. However, recognising her verve and dedication, Dr J.W. Gaines, president of the OWS, kept Michael on in the office until January 1919, when all the staff were to set sail for France. It was in these difficult times and unpromising surroundings that Michael had the epiphany which would change her life and the lives of millions she would never meet.

The OWS were celebrating their twenty-fifth anniversary on the morning of 9 November 1918, and the delegates were meeting in the room above Michael's cramped and dingy office. She sat down, waiting to speak to one of them, and glanced at the table strewn with magazines. By chance, she picked up the latest issue of the *Ladies' Home Journal*. She was immediately drawn to a striking colour picture of ghostly soldiers rising from a field of grave-marker crosses and blood-red poppies. The illustration accompanied John McCrae's 'In Flanders Fields', also known at the time as 'We Shall Not Sleep'.

Michael had read the poignant verses before, but this time they stopped her in her tracks. She imagined the silent voices of the dead whispering in her ears. They called out from the French and Belgian battlefields half a world away, imploring her to keep the faith. She later recalled, 'This was for me a full spiritual experience'.[5] As she contemplated that most frail of flowers, she grasped its emblematic promise, 'that [the] blood of heroes never dies'.[6]

The shades of the dead seemed to clamour around her, beseeching her to convert the simple flower into a sacred emblem of their sacrifice. This, she decided, was the purpose of her life. She had never married, and now never would. She had no children of her own; instead, the poppy would become her 'spirit child'.[7] Transfixed, she pledged her soul to 'that crimson cup flower of Flanders, the red Poppy which caught the sacrificial blood of ten million men dying for the Peace of the World'.[8]

The tide of emotion compelled her to respond to McCrae's final imploring stanza:

> *Take up our quarrel with the foe:*
> *To you from failing hands we throw*
> *The torch; be yours to hold it high.*
> *If ye break faith with us who die*
> *We shall not sleep, though poppies grow*
> *In Flanders fields.*

Leaning over her desk, she grabbed an envelope and penned a poem of her own, hastily entitled 'We Shall Keep the Faith':

> *Oh! You who sleep in Flanders' fields,*
> *Sleep sweet – to rise anew,*
> *We caught the torch you threw,*
> *And holding high we kept*
> *The faith with those who died.*
> *We cherish too, the poppy red*
> *That grows on fields where valor led.*
> *It seems to signal to the skies*
> *That blood of heroes never dies,*
> *But lends a lustre to the red*
> *Of the flower that blooms above the dead*
> *In Flanders' fields.*
> *And now the torch and poppy red*
> *Wear in honour of our dead.*
> *Fear not that ye have died for naught*
> *We've learned the lesson that ye taught*
> *In Flanders' fields.*

She knew that her effort would not be remembered for its literary qualities, nor renowned for the power of its imagery, but rather for what it voiced. Her words captured the spirit of the time, and, she hoped, would ease the conscience of so many who were wondering why the war had been fought, why so many young men had died. And it endeavoured to address the burning question, *What could ordinary men and women do to show their respect and gratitude?* Poetic skill was not among Michael's talents; determination and single-mindedness were.

Given the age-old associations of the corn and opium poppies, it seems appropriate that Michael's reunion with McCrae's famous words drew her towards an ethereal encounter with the dead. And although nothing more than another coincidence, the chain of events was curiously underlined by the fact that Michael's father, John Michael, was a veteran of the American Civil War. A native of rural Georgia, John Michael had fought on the Confederate side in some of that conflict's most famous battles, and the county that the family called home had been a centre of poppy growing for morphine to treat the war wounded. As a child growing up in the South, Michael had heard first-hand about the ravages of the war on soldiers' families. Though there is no evidence that her father had been wounded, his health had been poor after the war, and as a young girl she had helped to support her family. At the very least, her father must have heard of the 'Soldier's Disease' which afflicted so many veterans. Yet we do not know if any of this came to her mind as she penned her poem.

Just as she finished writing, several OWS delegates appeared at her desk, and she shared her verses with them. They too were inspired. On the spot, they offered her ten dollars to buy some flowers and brighten up the dull office. She announced, as she later remembered in her memoir, 'I shall buy red poppies – twenty-five red poppies. I shall always wear red poppies – poppies of Flanders Fields'.[9] She pointed to McCrae's poem in the magazine to explain herself, and the delegates returned to their meeting, magazine in hand. So impressed were they that almost all of them asked Michael for poppies to wear.

Try as she might, not a single poppy was to be found on the university campus. Her quest had begun.

She rushed from the office to scour the city's novelty shops for artificial poppies, but with no success. On the point of giving up, and as if by divine providence, she made her way finally to Wanamaker's store, and was served by a young female shop assistant. Michael's mission had a tragic resonance for the assistant, who revealed that her own brother had been killed on the Western Front, and was 'sleeping among poppies behind the battle lines of France' in a grave only a few months old.[10] And Wanamaker's had silk poppies available to buy.

Michael reached for her purse and secured one large red poppy for her own desk and twenty-four smaller silk-petalled ones for the delegates. When she returned to the university she was immediately swarmed by the delegates, who were eager to have a poppy for their lapels. After pinning one of the small flowers to her cloak collar, she handed out the rest to the crowd. She had bought the poppies with money freely given, and had handed them out to all who asked. This was the first Poppy Day, albeit unofficial and unrecognised, with poppies exchanged for a donation, not sold. A tradition was born.

It was a momentous day for the commonplace corn poppy. In the wake of Michael's poetic vision and scribblings, a run of random events had been woven together into the birth of an international ritual.

Two days later, the guns fell silent on the Western Front, as the Armistice of 11 November 1918 took effect.

DRIVEN BY AN IRREPRESSIBLE ZEAL, Michael began campaigning for the poppy's adoption as the memorial emblem for all those young Americans who slept in Flanders Fields, and as a fundraiser for the wounded survivors and their families. Her campaign soon led her to Lee Keedick, the formidable head of the Lee Keedick Lecture Bureau, a leading speakers' agency in New York.[11] Keedick would later sign up famous figures such as H. G. Wells and Howard Carter, the discoverer of Tutankhamun's tomb, for North American lecture tours.[12] He had a reputation for driving a hard bargain and considerable connections in the New York social and business worlds. There was no one better placed to help make Michael's dream a reality.

Keedick was about to set out on a European tour to gauge public sentiment in the wake of the Armistice. Indeed, he was already putting together a roster of star speakers for the following year. But Keedick instantly recognised the public-relations value of the poppy emblem.[13] On 13 December 1918 – the day Michael's YMCA colleagues left for Europe – he drew up a contract to launch her poppy campaign.

Yet in their headlong rush to capitalise on the popularity of McCrae's poem, the kindred spirits made an error of judgement. Although a simple, single poppy bloom had tugged at Michael's heartstrings on that morning at Columbia University, they abandoned the symbol. In its place, Keedick fashioned a montage of images and colours he thought would better command the public's attention. In the centre he placed a 'Torch of Liberty' around which a poppy was entwined; the logo, now referred to as the 'Flanders Victory Memorial Flag', was embellished with the colours of all the flags of the Allied nations. It was a wondrous mix of jingoistic associations, but the language of symbols is elemental, not intellectual.

In February 1919 the memorial flag was launched to a flurry of press coverage, and initially looked likely to prove popular. Michael was encouraged when New York's Calvary Baptist Church adopted it.[14] Keedick was so confident that he patented the design and produced flags and decorative pins for sale. On 14 February, Canadian fighter pilot Colonel William 'Billy' Bishop was scheduled to address New York's Carnegie Hall. Bishop had shot down seventy-two enemy aircraft during the war, a feat for which he was awarded the Victoria Cross. He was hailed as the top ace of the British Empire, and feted as a hero during a series of public-speaking engagements across North America. Keedick seized an opportunity when he saw one, and when Bishop addressed his enthralled audience at Carnegie Hall he did so on a stage decorated with poppies and draped with a huge Flanders Victory Memorial Flag. But even Bishop could not muster support for the patriotic emblem. The memorial flag failed to spark the American imagination.

The problem was pinpointed by one reporter who wrote that when confronted with the huge flag, 'the audience stared wonderingly at this "banner with a strange device," speculating at its significance'.[15] The purity of the poppy's message had been lost, and in its place was a confusion of competing signals. Was this an American symbol, or an Allied one? Was it a badge of victory or an emblem of remembrance? It was everything and nothing.

Michael returned to Georgia. She gave endless speeches to whip up support for her beloved poppy, but it didn't work. Everyone seemed to support her ideals, but no individual or organisation stepped forward to champion the memorial flag design. A few months later, with the public indifferent and more lucrative business to attend to, Keedick himself lost interest and abandoned his creation. At this time, Michael wrote of her deep despair. 'Discouragement all but defeated me,' she said.[16]

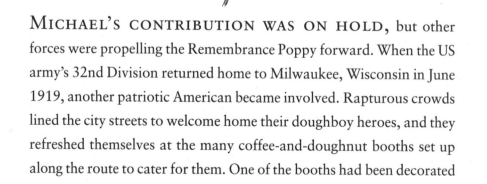

MICHAEL'S CONTRIBUTION WAS ON HOLD, but other forces were propelling the Remembrance Poppy forward. When the US army's 32nd Division returned home to Milwaukee, Wisconsin in June 1919, another patriotic American became involved. Rapturous crowds lined the city streets to welcome home their doughboy heroes, and they refreshed themselves at the many coffee-and-doughnut booths set up along the route to cater for them. One of the booths had been decorated with red paper poppies, and was twice stripped bare by enthusiastic customers who wanted to wear the flowers as a sign of their support for the troops. By the end of the day, the crowd had left donations on the counter totalling several hundred dollars in exchange for the poppies.

Mary Henecy, one of the unsung heroines of the poppy emblem, was working in the refreshment booth that day. She had witnessed the spontaneous donations, and proposed to her local branch of the American Legion that poppies be distributed on the streets in the days leading up to Memorial Day,[17] with any money raised used by the Legion to help rehabilitate returning veterans. The idea won support, and poppies were given out a year later, on the Saturday before Memorial Day 1920.[18]

In Georgia, Michael was contemplating a return to her teaching career, or perhaps a belated attempt to gain a university degree. In the midst of her indecision and discouragement, she felt the wind change. She discovered that the Georgia branch of the American Legion was meeting in Atlanta in August, and decided to attend the convention. She lobbied vigorously to have the poppy adopted as their official memorial flower – and she succeeded. Every 11 November, members of the Georgia branch would wear a poppy as an emblem of remembrance.

Fired up by their own enthusiasm, the Georgia delegates promised to champion the poppy's cause at the Legion's national convention in Cleveland, Ohio in September 1920, in the hopes of having it embraced by all chapters. Michael's confidence returned. The poppy, she believed, was back on track. On 29 September, the American Legion passed the Georgia delegates' resolution. Michael was overjoyed.[19]

Among the visitors to the Ohio convention was an elegant, energetic and well-connected French widow named Anna E. Guérin who would help to export the poppy emblem around the world. Guérin shared Michael's passion for the poppy as a symbol of remembrance – a flower that combined battlefield memories with personal poignancy – but

Guérin's ambitions were greater: to reach millions of buttonholes across all the Allied nations. To do this, she realised that she must transmute the transient, fragile poppy bloom into a durable, marketable form. One could not count on nature's delicate petals, especially on Remembrance Day, nor could one depend on finding a cache of artificial flowers at a Wanamaker's or a refreshment booth. Instead, Guérin would mass-produce simple poppies in silk.

Inspired by John McCrae's call and Moina Michael's response, Guérin had begun making artificial poppies in Paris soon after the war. She campaigned tirelessly, championing her 'flower of remembrance' across France, speaking at every convention and servicemen's organisation that would give her a platform. She spoke with fervour, beseeching veterans and their families to wear a red silk poppy in honour of the French war dead. In 1919, she visited the United States to support the 'Victory Loan', a package of financial assistance to get France back on its feet. While there, she had asked the American Legion to support a Poppy Appeal too. Returning home, and with the backing of Madame Jeanne Millerand, the wife of French president Alexandre Millerand, she founded the Paris-based Ligue Américaine Française des Enfants.[20]

Guérin's efforts to enlist American allies were rewarded on her visit to the Cleveland convention. Michael's Georgia delegates may have convinced the Legion to adopt the poppy, but it was Guérin who was acclaimed onstage as 'the Poppy Lady of France'. It was an emotional moment, and she later recalled how 'my joy was so deep that tears filled my eyes and I could hardly contain my emotion'.[21] With the Legion's stamp of approval, there was a huge market for Guérin's silken petals. Her intention was to sell French handmade poppies to the American Legion, which would then distribute them across America.

Guérin finessed her plan with a brilliant entrepreneurial idea. Her silken poppies would be made by war widows who lived in the devastated battle zones of northern France. The flowers would be sold wholesale not only to the American Legion, but to veterans' associations around the world. These organisations in turn would sell the flowers to the public and use the funds to benefit their own maimed soldiers and bereaved families. Part of Guérin's share would be donated to French children orphaned and made destitute by the war. Two months later, on Armistice Day, Guérin's organisation, La Ligue Américaine Française des Enfants, covered the graves of American soldiers in France with poppies in an act meant to grab at the emotions and solidify the flower's emblematic significance.[22]

GUÉRIN WAS TIRELESS. In August 1921, she made a trip to London to show a sample of her poppies to Colonel E.C. Heath, the general secretary of the newly founded British Legion.[23] On 10 June of that year, the Legion had coalesced from four postwar groups dedicated to members of the armed forces – the Comrades of the Great War, the National Association of Discharged Sailors and Soldiers, the National Federation of Discharged and Demobilised Sailors and Soldiers and the Officers' Association. Guérin enquired whether the Legion might want to use the poppy in order to raise funds for its services, with a percentage set aside for her own work in France.[24]

Her timing was perfect. One of the Legion's founders, Douglas Haig, 1st Earl Haig, had been Britain's senior commander during the war, and had led the forces at the horrific Battle of the Somme, where 600,000 Allied servicemen lost their lives. The red poppy touched him greatly, and the Legion adopted it as part of its Appeal Fund, with which he would be personally associated until his death in 1928. Nine million poppies were ordered for the first Poppy Day to be held in Britain on 11 November 1921.[25] Following Michael's precedent, the poppies were not to be sold at a fixed price, but given in exchange for a voluntary donation. Britain's first Poppy Appeal raised £106,000 – the equivalent of £3.1 million today.

Remembering and honouring the war dead, and supporting the maimed and bereaved, were aims that touched almost every family in the nation. If there were any doubts about how best to commemorate the lost and help the wounded, they would be quickly dispelled by the tag attached to each poppy which announced 'British Legion Remembrance Day'. On the reverse, the poppy appealed to the fellow feeling of the Allies: 'Made by the women and children in the devastated areas of France'.

These French poppies were of crimson silk, with a metal pin for attachment to clothing. To accompany the fluttering petals, the British Legion prepared a leaflet. An illustration of a soldier and a battlefield cross standing amid a sea of poppies accompanied reprints of McCrae's and Michael's poems. The leaflet's anonymous author announced:

> *The Sale of Flanders Poppies on Remembrance Day gives an opportunity to every man, woman and child to subscribe to Earl Haig's Appeal . . . If we are to hand to coming generations an untarnished record of the Great War, we must see to it that so long as our surviving warriors live, every effort must be made to keep them and their dependants from want attributable to war service.*[26]

The leaflet offered a very British mythology around the poppy and its wartime appearance too in a piece entitled '"THE THIN RED LINE" on the Western Front'.[27] The poppy's nearly instantaneous blooming across the battlefields after an artillery barrage was invoked: 'in a few days the crocus and poppy were making beautiful the far-flung graveyard'.[28] It took time for human beings to erect their memorials, memorials which time itself would quickly sweep away, but 'Nature required no time to set up her great memorial, for her poppies grew on the newly made graves; an ever-recurring and never-dying memorial'.[29]

The poppy, the leaflet said, was no longer the flower of dreamy Persephone. Watered with the blood of soldiers, it had grown into a symbol of faith. Neither poppies nor fallen soldiers would ever truly die, 'and the red petals shower down everlasting pictures of the blood so freely shed'.[30] The final flourish in the essay was a striking and evocative turn of phrase which joined imperial British history with the memory of more recent conflict-memory: 'Here is our greatest thin red line – the poppy path from Nieuport to Bapaume – the line that none can ever break'.[31]

LOOKING BACK WITH THE HINDSIGHT of a century, and with the help of testaments such as these, the poppy now seems an obvious choice to symbolise the war dead. Yet, as Earl Haig and the British Legion were championing the poppy in the autumn of 1921, a shrill, discordant voice was heard. In November, Lieutenant-General G. M. Macdonogh unveiled a war memorial at Beaumont College, Old Windsor, and uttered a remark which ran counter to the prevailing mood. The poppy, he thundered, is 'a pagan flower, it was the emblem of the dead and the last thing they wanted to do was to forget them'.[32] Macdonogh fell back too hastily on his upper-class education in the classics, in which the opium poppy, not the corn poppy, carried the burden of symbolism.

As Macdonogh's outburst made clear, there was genuine confusion among the British public about whether the emblem was the corn poppy or the opium poppy (as there still is today). Both the corn poppy and the opium poppy grew in England, the former mainly scarlet but sometimes orange or pink, the latter ranging from white to purple to red.[33] For a century or more, English poetry and literature had blended the appearance and symbolism of the innocent and the narcotic. And more so, the English poppy hid a darker secret – it was not quite as innocent and romantic as it seemed.

Since before the eighteenth century, home-grown opium poppies had become a staple of English folk medicine, and in some counties it was cultivated in almost every back garden.[34] Opium solutions were commonplace in the nineteenth century, when, as in the United States, various concoctions, such as Infant's Quietness and Soothing Syrup, could be bought to calm unruly children. Godfrey's Cordial, a mixture of opium and treacle, was so popular that the amount of narcotic it contained was investigated by an 1843 parliamentary report.

Among the impoverished and hard-working farm labourers of East Anglia's fenland, poppy tea was a common cure for rheumatism and malaria.[35] Brewed as an infusion of boiled poppy heads and stems, it was on sale in many rural shops and on market stalls, and according to legend was added to locally brewed beers into the twentieth century.[36] Captain J.C. Dunn observed on the eve of the Battle of the Somme that his native Norfolk fields were far richer in poppies than were the battlefields of France. He probably meant the comment innocuously, but it might just have concealed an interesting truth.[37]

The amount of opium use in the fenlands was astonishing. At Whittlesea, a town of 3,700 souls, there were five chemists who dealt

primarily in opium, and even during the 1920s, years after drug legislation was enacted, opiates prescribed for veterinary purposes were being
taken by local people – an accepted practice there.[38] In some rural communities at least, there was no confusion between the two kinds of poppy.

The members of the British Legion knew their history too, and
were aware of the poppy's status as the flower of oblivion – among
both mortals and the gods. Unlike the lieutenant-general, the Legion
confronted the issue head-on, vowing to resurrect the poppy as the
flower of remembrance. Both the Legion and Macdonogh had, each
in their own way, failed to grasp that the poppy had two faces, one of
remembering but the other of forgetting.

Macdonogh remained in a minority with his attitude to the
Remembrance Poppy, however. Greatly impressed by the success of
the 1921 Poppy Day, Major George Howson MC approached the
British Legion and suggested that, in future, British poppies be made
by wounded British soldiers. Howson had inaugurated the Disabled
Society after the war to improve the quality and availability to the war
maimed of artificial limbs, and now saw an opportunity to combine
both good works. Howson's proposal was accepted, and the Disabled
Society's poppy factory opened for business in June 1922. At a stroke,
Anna Guérin's French poppies were doomed. The poppy factory, now
in the London suburb of Richmond, has become a living war memorial,
and in a turn of phrase as modern as it is evocative, has been called
'the Factory of Remembrance'.[39]

THE SUCCESS OF THE FIRST POPPY APPEAL delighted
the British Legion, and for 1922 an incredible thirty million poppies

were ordered and an ambitious publicity campaign was organised.[40] Poppy posters appeared all over the country, and in London the latest technology was pressed into service. Giant electric signs flashed out from Piccadilly Circus, rousing the passers-by with 'Earl Haig's Special Message – Buy Poppies for Remembrance Sake'.[41] The second Poppy Day was an even greater success than the first, with the proceeds totalling £204,000, double those of the previous year. The Remembrance Poppy had stormed public sentiment, and was established in the landscape of commemoration.

Guérin's tireless efforts to spread the poppy message did not end in Britain, and she continued to forge an international spirit of remembrance. Her reputation was such that in the farthest corners of the English-speaking world, the poppy was adopted even among those whom she herself had never visited. As one example, in September 1921, a month after Guérin's visit to London, one of her representatives, Colonel Alfred Moffatt, championed the poppy to the New Zealand Returned Soldiers' Association (NZRSA). He was so persuasive that an order for 350,000 small and 16,000 large silk poppies was sent to Guérin's Ligue Américaine Française des Enfants. While New Zealand's aim was to launch an inaugural Poppy Appeal to mark Armistice Day on 11 November 1921, the ship bearing this precious cargo was delayed and arrived too late. By accident, the nation's first Poppy Day did not commemorate Armistice Day, but instead ANZAC Day – for the Australia and New Zealand Army Corps, who fought together during the Gallipoli campaign in 1915 – the nation's other major commemorative event, held annually on 25 April 1922. The first ANZAC Day had been held in 1915, when news of the troops' successful landing reached New Zealand on 30 April and the government announced a half-day holiday. The day was christened ANZAC Day the next year, and announced as a public holiday in 1920.[42]

The soldiers and families of the ANZAC may have had a particular, unique association with the geography of their countries' service in the Great War. Australia's and New Zealand's soldiers had suffered appalling losses at Gallipoli. When ANZAC forces stormed ashore on 30 April, they were greeted by a Homeric landscape carpeted with springtime poppies as well as an intractable Turkish foe. Just south of the landing beach was Poppy Valley, which got its name from a field of brilliant red poppies near its mouth. Reflecting the unfolding events, Poppy Valley at its southern end would soon be renamed the 'Valley of Despair'.

The deadly struggle unfolded in the shadow of Troy, just a few miles across the Dardanelles, which separated the Gallipoli peninsula from the Turkish mainland. In the ancient past as well as in 1915, corn poppies and opium poppies grew side by side across the landscapes of battle. The heroic efforts of ANZAC forces and their terrible losses defined their role in the war, and became a political touchstone of identity and independence after 1918.

Distance from the war seemed to amplify the poppy's commemorative power. Despite the five-month delay in getting the poppies 'Down Under', New Zealand's first Poppy Day was a resounding success. Many outlets exhausted their supply of poppies before midday. In total, 245,059 small poppies were sold for one shilling (5p), and 15,157 of the larger variety sold for two shillings each. Altogether, and after expenses, the NZRSA collected £13,166, of which £3,695 went to Guérin's French league. The remainder was kept by the NZRSA to help New Zealand's own unemployed veterans and their families during the winter of 1922.[43]

In 1921, the Returned Sailors and Soldiers Imperial League of Australia – the forerunner of today's Returned and Services League of Australia (RSL) – recognised the poppy as its own memorial flower. A million poppies were ordered from the widows and orphans of France and were sold for one shilling each, with the money divided between their French makers and the Australian League. As the prelude to its first Poppy Day, the League announced:

> *In adopting the Poppy of Flanders' Fields as the Memorial Flower to be worn by all Returned Soldiers on the above mentioned day, we recognise that no emblem so well typifies the Fields whereon was fought the greatest war in the history of the world nor sanctifies so truly the last resting place of our brave dead who remain in France.*

Such statements reflected a postwar atmosphere of heightened respect for the dead. Raw from the terrible losses of the war, the Australian conscience displayed an overwhelming desire to preserve the sanctity of Armistice Day. No commercial activity should contaminate the purity of commemoration. Poppy Day was decreed always to be the day before 11 November. Australia's Remembrance Poppies were designed to be exact replicas in size and colour of the real blooms found in Flanders Fields. The intention was not just to remember and honour the dead, but to symbolise the shared commemorative imagery among all Allied nations, and express respect for the common battleground of France.

For Australians and New Zealanders, wearing the poppy was a political and moral declaration.

ELSEWHERE IN THE COMMONWEALTH, Guérin was finding converts in 1921. On a visit to Canada, she met with the Great War

Veterans Association, the precursor to the Canadian Legion. Fiercely patriotic, the Canadians embraced the poppy like no other nation, not least because they saw their own John McCrae as the catalyst for the poppy phenomenon. It was a meeting of minds, as McCrae's 'In Flanders Fields' had not only inspired Michael and Guérin, but was clutched tightly to the collective heart of all Canadians after the war.

Canada officially adopted the poppy as a remembrance emblem on 5 July 1921, with the first Poppy Day Appeal held in November of that year, alongside the similar efforts in Britain and Australia. Guérin recalled her impressions of the event in Montreal, where the windows of shops and houses were emblazoned with poppies, and 'every citizen, big and little, wore a red poppy in his button-hole in memory of the men who lie asleep in "Flanders Fields"'.[44]

But in Canada, as in Britain, Guérin's artificial poppies carried the seeds of their own demise. There was a rapid and inevitable impulse to replace French poppies with ones made by the nation's own needy veterans. Remembering the dead was only part of the poppy's attraction; it also came to express Canadians' pride in the emerging nation's conduct during the war, and to become a symbol of Canadian nationhood. For instance, before the war, most Canadians had never heard of Vimy, a small hamlet nestled against an imposing ridge in northern France, just a few miles from the Belgian border. The town had been quickly occupied by the Germans, and thousands of Frenchmen had lost their lives in attempts to dislodge the glowering enemy from its strategic stronghold on the ridge's commanding heights. Then in April 1917, against all odds, Canadian soldiers stormed Vimy Ridge, and after bitter fighting, overcame the Germans.

More than a military victory, it was a sign that Canada's army had come of age. The sacrifices and courage of the Canadians at Vimy became legendary, and were seen as a bloody scar of the birth of the nation. In Canada, wearing a poppy became a peerless statement of identity – a proclamation in scarlet of the power of warrior ancestors to be reborn in the modern world.

ANNA GUÉRIN'S EARLY SUCCESS left an enduring mark. But while her French outfit would sell millions of silk poppies, the lessons learned in Britain and Canada were quickly taken up, and in America a backlash was gathering. Michael felt that something was not right about French-made poppies being sold in the United States for the financial benefit of the French.[45] She had worked hard to see the poppy adopted in her own country, then watched as Guérin hijacked her efforts. She sounded personally hurt that the poppy campaign's charity was flowing back to France: 'We've done our bit for France. Why not let us make the Poppies? Why not use Poppy money to rehabilitate our own needy veterans and their needy families? Our children and wives need food, shelter and clothes. Why not help us here at home?'[46]

Michael was not alone in her feelings. Many disabled and un-employed American ex-servicemen shared her frustration. But there seemed no way out of the arrangements that were in place.

She needn't have worried. Guérin's world had started to implode. Five months earlier, on 12 May 1921, the *New York Times* had breath-lessly reported: 'Rival Societies in War of Poppies'. The article shared news of a dispute between two American groups claiming to represent the French league, and thus the right to sell poppies on Memorial Day in the United States.

The controversy had begun a few weeks earlier when Guérin had arrived in the United States armed with letters from Madame Millerand, the president of the French league. With typical panache, she rapidly organised the American French Children's League to sell poppies on behalf of the French parent organisation. But another group, calling itself the American-Franco Children's League had also appeared on the scene. It had been founded by Bishop Herbert Shipman, a heroic US army chaplain who had been invalided home from the Western Front and ran his poppy campaign from an office on Madison Avenue in Manhattan. Guérin and Shipman saw the dangers and the opportunities of this public-relations boon, and in a truce negotiated at the Waldorf Hotel they decided that their two groups should merge in time for Memorial Day, on 30 May.

One Mrs Mercedes McAllister Smith disagreed. A vociferous and strident character, McAllister Smith had personally ejected a female heckler from a meeting because the woman had a German accent.[47] She was also the go-getting New York State chairman of Guérin's now officially defunct American and French Children's League. McAllister Smith rejected the proposed merger and continued selling poppies as before.

The imbroglio soon became a political embarrassment. Guérin maintained her alliance with Shipman, while McAllister Smith recruited the newly elected American president Warren G. Harding as honorary president of her breakaway organisation. This unwittingly but effectively pitted the president against a representative of the wife of the president of France. It was particularly awkward, since Harding had been impressed with a remembrance ceremony in New York City which Guérin had helped to arrange: she had suggested that a statue of Joan of Arc be smothered in poppies, and dressed one of the young girls from head to toe as a scarlet bloom.[48] Harding had found it to be a charming and effective tribute. He did not want to take sides in the fight, but he found himself in a diplomatic knot. Numerous government officials got entangled in the French league affair.[49]

With Guérin's ambitions descending into farce, events were clearly moving in Michael's favour. She breathed a sigh of relief in September when, at the annual convention of the American Legion, held that year in Kansas City, Missouri, the auxiliary division voted to engage disabled American war veterans, many of whom were languishing in hospitals, to manufacture Remembrance Poppies for US Memorial Day.[50] She was satisfied. 'These poppies which you buy on Poppy Days in the United States are the ones thus fashioned by the maimed, gassed and wounded men of the World War', she said.[51] It had been a tortuous affair, but Michael's perseverance had gained the upper hand over Guérin – it had all been worth it. Appearances, however, can be deceptive.

In the glow of her victory, Michael settled into the Pullman coach that would take her home to New York. She picked up a local newspaper, ready to catch up on the news of the day. In it, she found a report on the convention's final resolutions. In disbelief, she read how the delegates had adopted the daisy as their official emblem. The poppy had been repudiated – downgraded, in Michael's eyes, and passed on to the American Legion's auxiliary division to be used only for memorial purposes.[52] Who chose the daisy and why, remains a mystery. Although its romantic associations with love and springtime were well known,[53] such qualities were not key to honouring the dead and wounded, or to caring for their families.

Her trademark energy rekindled by this new challenge, she fired off countless appeals to anyone of influence to get her beloved Flanders Fields Memorial Poppy reinstated. Her letter to the American Legion prompted an official reply that remains a masterpiece of bureaucratic double-speak. The Legion, it said, was delighted to receive her letter, but the decision could not be reversed.

Distraught and depressed, Michael's faith wavered once again. Her thoughts were invaded by other powerful symbols, such as the rainbow and Christ's sacred chalice from the Last Supper. But these came to her in vain. Try as she might, she couldn't abandon the poppy and everything it meant to her. With religious zeal, she argued that there was 'no meaning, no symbolism, no appeal, no appropriateness in the DAISY as a Memorial symbol for my Buddies sleeping in Flanders Fields'.[54] Her emotions reached fever pitch as she implored the American Legion to reinstate her flower. 'There could be no symbol of the World War Sacrifices but the Poppy'.[55]

With this betrayal upsetting Michael's plans, further scandal rocked Anna Guérin's organisation. In December, McAllister Smith launched a $200,000 lawsuit for slander, claiming that Guérin, Herbert Shipman and others had conspired to blacken her name and affect her ability to sell poppies for Memorial Day. She alleged that the defendants had called her an adventuress and a jailbird, and demanded legal redress.[56]

The year 1922 would be a testing time for the Remembrance Poppy. From the start, Michael's passionate obstinacy failed to change the Legion's policy. Then, Guérin's French league was dissolved, taking its annual supply of French silk poppies with it. Both women were frustrated at every turn.

Never short on ideas, Guérin approached another organisation, the Veterans of Foreign Wars of the United States (VFW). She explained her goals, impressed them with her dynamism and then persuaded them to take over the Poppy Appeal from the American Legion as well as the ruins of her own group. In May, the VFW organised the first nationwide sale of poppies for Memorial Day. Although relying on the last shipment of Guérin's French poppies, the event was a great success, raising large sums for American veterans.[57] Encouraged by the results, the VFW national convention, held in Seattle, moved to adopt the poppy as its official memorial flower that August. In a few months, the Remembrance Poppy was triumphantly resurrected.

It was all too much for the American Legion, which had wrong-footed itself by abandoning the poppy the previous year. As memorial poppies bloomed all around, the Legion was stuck with the daisy. A rancorous exchange of letters between Legion and VFW members ignited opposing passions. One Legion member accused the VFW of stealing the American Legion's poppy, and that the VFW did not 'represent, in any appreciable degree, the veterans of Flanders Fields'.[58] Barely able to control his rage, Norman Hall, editor of the VFW's *Foreign Service* magazine, fired back that 'members of the VFW are vastly more representative of the veterans of Flanders Fields than the Legion is'. Hall concluded with a bitter salvo, accusing the Legion of 'attempts to gather undeserved praise and unearned funds by besmirching an organization that has added more glorious pages to American history than the American Legion ever will'.[59]

Political winds unwittingly fanned the flames, but ultimately the VFW's reputation was enhanced. President Harding wrote from the White House, 'I find myself heartily in sympathy with the purpose of the Veterans of Foreign Wars and American War Mothers in their request that the people, at large, shall wear on Memorial Day a poppy, the Inter-Allied Memorial Flower.'[60]

As October arrived, a disgruntled American Legion changed its mind again at its national convention in New Orleans. It passed a new resolution 'that the poppy is hereby declared to be the official American Legion flower, instead of the daisy'. This was a high-level climb down, and disguised a world of internal politicking and arguments that had been thrown into stark relief by the unexpected success of the VFW. The fundraising potential of the poppy had belatedly been realised, and the Legion decided to launch its own Poppy Appeal for Memorial Day 1923.

The battle was on for the hearts and minds of the American public, with the humble memorial poppy as the weapon. It claimed its first victim in December 1922, when Mercedes McAllister Smith's suit in the French-American 'war of poppies' was dismissed in the New York Supreme Court.[61]

American-made, red crêpe-paper poppies appeared in 1922, but there would not be enough to satisfy the demand in the following year. Faced with an inevitable shortage for the 1923 Memorial Day observances, the VFW acquired the remaining surplus of Guérin's silk poppies and negotiated with a New York City firm of artificial flower manufacturers to make up the rest of the shortfall. This short-term solution worked, but the VFW's embarrassment, and the need to ensure a reliable future supply led to it following the British Legion's example in London, but with a very American twist.

In February 1924, the VFW stole another march on the American Legion by registering the name 'Buddy Poppy' with the US Patent Office. It was coined by the poppy-makers themselves to honour their comrades who had died or were maimed, and its motto was 'to honour the dead by helping the living'. Already in the previous year, Babe Ruth, the New York Yankees' legendary baseball player, had presented the first official Buddy Poppy to President Harding.

Finally, after so many attempts, the Buddy Poppy fired the public's imagination. Its new name resonated with American informality, and spoke to the friendships between the nation's veterans and their fallen friends. Inevitably, such powerful imagery evoked pride as well as patriotism across America's armed forces. By April 1931, Buddy Poppy production had reached four million flowers for that year's Memorial Day commemorations. It was a decade after the Great War and the Great Depression had taken hold, leaving many American families broke. At a White House ceremony that spring, President Herbert Hoover was presented with a Buddy Poppy by Hazel Markinson, a seven-year-old girl whose father, a veteran of the war, had died. To accompany the press release, the president wrote a letter to the commander-in-chief of the VFW:

My dear Commander:

I warmly commend the annual 'Buddy Poppy' Campaign which is conducted under the auspices of the Veterans of Foreign Wars of the United States as a means of general civilian contribution in the relief work for disabled and needy veterans and their dependants. It not only gives employment to disabled veterans, but also it aids in the maintenance of a National Home for Widows and Orphans of deceased veterans in Eaton Rapids, Michigan.

Yours faithfully,
HERBERT HOOVER[62]

THE PRODIGIOUS ENERGY and obsessive dedication of Moina Michael and Anna Guérin propelled the poppy on the path to global domination as the symbolic flower of remembrance. Both women became known as the 'Poppy Lady', though to avoid confusion, Michael was often called the 'Poppy Princess' while Guérin was the 'Poppy Lady of France'. Inevitably there was friction between the two women, whose relationship, as far as we know, was fraught and competitive. Michael emerges as the major figure because, unlike Guérin, she wrote her own history in *The Miracle Flower*, published in 1941. This idiosyncratic little book, self-aggrandising and humble by turns, is shot through with religious imagery yet remains a compelling account of the troubled birth of this evocative symbol.

Tensions between the two women can be traced between the lines of *The Miracle Flower* – particularly in the account of Guérin's first appearance on the American scene. The women were kindred spirits, yet Michael could not bring herself to mention Anna Guérin by name. She refers to her several times simply as the 'French visitor',[63] and once even as 'Madame _____', as if she had either forgotten Guérin's name or decided that for some reason it should not be published.[64] By contrast, even the smallest bit-part player in her story – a Mr J.G.C. Bloodworth, an American Legion delegate too busy to talk to her – is named in full. When she was obliged to acknowledge Guérin's efforts, Michael adopted a grudging tone, as when she wrote, 'Her utilization of our sacred Memorial Poppy' or 'She sent her French women (widows) across to London to sell poppies'.[65] Michael wrote her book twenty years after the events she describes, yet even from that distance she had difficulty conceding the major role that Guérin played in creating the Remembrance Poppy we know today.

Interviewed in February 1939 by the Federal Writers' Project, a US government New Deal initiative that funded the recording of oral histories during the Great Depression, Michael was astonishingly candid about her life, if somewhat free with her version of history. By this time, she was living in a single room in the Georgian Hotel in Athens, Georgia. Sporting a gold pin with full-blown poppy buds bordered with pearls, she greeted her visitor with more than a hint of irony – 'welcome into my living room, library, office, dining room, kitchen and bedroom', she said.[66]

After skipping through memories of her youth, Michael recalled how Guérin had caused her difficulties when she had brought her poppies to the United States. These French blooms competed with poppies made by disabled American veterans, Michael said, but, she made clear, she eventually won the day. Madame Guérin had given up and returned to Europe, where she introduced the poppy to Britain.[67]

Michael glossed over the truth when it came to Guérin, and reserved her bitterness for unnamed others. In an extraordinary outburst, she said, 'Just think what I have caused the world to realize from the sale of poppies each year! Just seventy million dollars. Yet the world don't donate one penny toward my support and I have barely enough to buy actual necessities'.[68] Self-pitying perhaps, and not strictly accurate, yet there was an awkward and undeniable truth in her words. Her 'spirit child' had consumed her life.

Moina Michael and Anna Guérin invested years of their lives to establish the poppy as the international flower of commemoration. By the mid-1920s their task was done. But while Guérin all but disappeared, Michael's life became so closely entwined with the poppy that it was nearly impossible to separate the woman from the flower.

Recognition, honours and awards showered down on the Poppy Princess during the inter-war years. When Columbia University celebrated its 175th anniversary in 1929, Michael was the only woman who rated a feature in the special commemorative edition of the *Alumni News*. A year later, she received a Distinguished Service Medal from the women's auxiliary of the American Legion, and in 1931 she was honoured as a 'Distinguished Citizen of Georgia'. In 1937 a commemorative bust was unveiled at the Georgia State Capitol, and in 1940 the American Legion voted her a citation for distinguished service along with a stipend of one hundred dollars a month for the rest of her life.

Even after her death on 10 May 1944 – the same year in which Guérin died – the honours kept coming to this remarkable woman. Just months after her death, the US government christened a 'liberty ship' the *Moina Michael*, and on 9 November 1948, thirty years to the day after her first vision of the Remembrance Poppy, a three-cent postage stamp was issued in honour of her efforts.[69] It was somehow ironic that the woman who complained that she had to pay for every stamp on her countless letters was now commemorated with one. In 1969, Michael was once again remembered, when the Georgia assembly designated part of Highway 78 the 'Moina Michael Highway'.

Though an American spinster and a French widow invented and disseminated the Remembrance Poppy, the flower's future would lay beyond their nation's shores. Michael's poppy remains the official remembrance flower in the United States, but it is not a well-known symbol for most American citizens today. And in France, Anna Guérin would have been heartbroken to discover that, despite all her efforts, her beloved homeland never adopted the scarlet bloom. The nations of the two women who did the most to create the Remembrance Poppy have little interest in their legacy.

But poppies are extraordinary flowers. They bloom in their millions every year, not only in the soil, but also on lapels, hats and car bumpers. They flower too in the countless wreaths placed on the cold, stony memorials built to the dead. In the years following the Great War, they were made by crippled hands and tugged relentlessly at the heartstrings every Remembrance Day. Between the wars, the annual harvest of red cloth poppies on their thin metal strips recalled for many a generation of youth sacrificed on the barbed wire of the Western Front and beyond.

The humble flower

Papaver rhoeas, the corn poppy, an engraving from an illustration by James Soweby published in *Medical Botany*, 1832 (© Florilegius / SSPL). A corn poppy in cross section (*inset*), showing the capsule, or pod, and stamens (© Joe Petersburger / Getty Images).

The bringer of sleep

Papaver somniferum, the opium poppy, an engraving by G. Havell in *British Phaenogamous Botany*, 1834 (© Florilegius / SSPL). An opium poppy head (*inset*) being drawn for sap, from which opium and heroin can be made (© Anthony Bradshaw / Getty Images).

Ancient myths

An Egyptian amulet (*left*), *c.* 4000 BCE, made from carnelian, with a head similar to a poppy pod, was believed to grant protection for the dead as they moved through the afterlife (© Science Museum / SSPL). A stele (*right*), or stone slab sculpture, dated *c.* 880–860 BCE, from Nimrud (the ancient city of Kalhu), Mesopotamia, in which a winged Assyrian diety carries a bouquet of poppy heads. Stone relief in the collection of the Metropolitan Museum of Art, New York.

A terracotta figurine of a Minoan goddess (*left*), *c.* 1400–1200 BCE, with a crown of opium poppies. Jugs (*right*), dating to the Bronze Age, used to transport Cypriot opium to Egypt; the vessel's shape is believed intentionally to evoke a poppy capsule (© Science Museum / SSPL).

Romantic addictions

Laudanum bottles from the nineteenth century, when Romantic figures such as Shelley, Byron and Coleridge became habitual users of opiates (© Science Museum / SSPL).

An 1876 advertisement (*left*) from America promises 'a certain and sure cure without inconvenience' for Civil War veterans and others addicted to opium (© Stock Montage / Getty Images). An art nouveau pattern for wallpapers and fabrics (*right*), from Eugene Grasset's *Plants and Their Application to Ornament*, 1897, features the opium poppy (© Florilegius / Getty Images).

In the trenches

In a rare colour image from spring 1916, a French army patrol poses with poppies sprouting from the earthen walls (photo by the Photography and Cinematography Organisation of the French Army; courtesy of Heritage of the Great War website).

A memorial card (*left*) with Lt Col John McCrae's poem 'In Flanders Fields', printed after his death during active service in France. Vase hammered with poppy motifs made as battlefield souvenirs during the 1920s from spent artillery shell cases (*middle*; © James Brazier), and .303 bullet cartridges crafted into the shape of poppies by artist Stephen Mulqueen (*right*; © Stephen Mulqueen). Soldiers and civilians created so-called trench art throughout the war, as did returning refugees in the decades afterwards.

A scrap of 'therapeutic' embroidery of poppies made by Sgt D. Smith while in hospital in France during the First World War (© Imperial War Museum).

The birth of an icon

One of the British Legion's first silk poppies (*top*; © James Brazier), and an early 'Haig's Fund' poppy seller's badge (*bottom left*). The 'Poppy Lady' Moina Michael's memoir (*bottom right*).

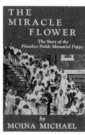

An ex-serviceman (*top*) builds poppy wreaths, 1929 (© Mary Evans Picture Library). It took three hundred men the full year to produce the millions of poppies required for Remembrance Day, including this veteran (*bottom*) putting the finishing touches on poppies during the Second World War (© Mary Evans Picture Library).

A narcotic grasp

Patrolling the opium fields of south-west Afghanistan in 2009, at the height of the fight against the opium-funded Taliban resistance. This cultivar displays a fringed petal (© Getty Images).

Men harvest poppy sap in Nangarhar province, 2012, when opium production was increasing in Afghanistan (© Getty Images).

Commemorative coins issued by the Royal Canadian Mint (*above*) that American defence contractors initially suspected of being radio transmitters planted on them to collect information. An Afghan 'war rug' (*right*) depicting planes approaching the Twin Towers on 9/11; an opium pod appears on the bottom right (© Tony Wheeler / Getty Images).

Remembrances across a century

A poster encouraging support for Victory Bonds during the Second World War, through use of the poppy's potent symbolism (© Imperial War Museum).

"If ye break faith — we shall not sleep"

BUY VICTORY BONDS

A postcard (*above*) commemorating aviator Charles Lindbergh's 1927 'flyover' at Waregham, during which he dropped poppies in memory of the Great War's dead. Remembrance poppies (*right*) at the Roll of Honour, Australian War Memorial (© Richard I'Anson / Getty Images).

Political cartoonist Nicholas Garland's haunting commentary on opium production in Afghanistan, published in the *Daily Telegraph*, February 2008 (© The Daily Telegraph).

RECORD POPPY CROP EXPECTED IN AFGHANISTAN

The 'Victoria Cross' cultivar (*left*) of *Papaver somniferum* (© Chris Burrows / Getty Images). There are cream, apricot, pink, rose, lavender and grey poppy cultivars, as well as the ubiquitous red and white. The Victoria Cross variety seems to have been developed some time between 1856, when the eponymous medal was first cast, and 1890, when it was officially named. A field of opium poppies (*right*) in Salisbury, England, being grown for production of morphine (© Scott Barbour / Getty Images).

Wooden crosses bearing the pictures of fallen soldiers and carrying Remembrance poppies at a memorial field in north-east England, 2012 (© AFP / Getty Images).

The many faces of the poppy will for ever remain with us

6

SOUVENIR
OF WAR

THE BONES OF THE DEAD BLEACHED THE KILLING
fields where war had raged, and from London to Sydney, New York to
Vancouver, grief chafed raw in the souls of the bereaved. Throughout
the 1920s and 1930s, crimson cloth poppies for the living and poppy
wreaths for the dead bloomed, as thousands of pilgrims journeyed to
the battlefields seeking a trace of the sons, fathers, brothers, husbands
and lovers who had not returned. These modern pilgrims fell silent only
to ponder or to weep, setting down their poppies, fixing their memories
to a place, and imagining their loved ones somehow close by.

As postwar reconstruction quickened, visitors were drawn in their
tens of thousands to the impressive new memorials built to commemorate
'the missing' at Thiepval, on the Somme in France, and the Menin Gate
at Ypres in Belgium. At the inauguration of the Menin Gate on 24 July
1927, the Australian war artist Captain William Longstaff was in the
crowd. He was so moved by the sombre event that he said that during a

midnight walk along the Menin Road he had a vision of steel-helmeted men standing in the moonlit cornfields. On his return to London, he painted *Menin Gate at Midnight*, his iconic portrait of ghostly ranks of tombless dead rising up from the field of poppies fronting the new memorial to confront their own missing selves, then turning away to march back to the battlefields where they had died.[1] The painting was an instant sensation, and Longstaff donated it to the Australian War Memorial in Canberra soon afterwards. During a 1928–9 tour of the artwork around Australia, one million people are said to have turned out to see it. A thousand signed reproductions were sold, the image becoming a miniature memorial in many homes.

On the old battlefields, more visceral memorabilia were being sold. In cafés and at roadside stalls, many of the war pilgrims alleviated their pain and sanctified their visit by purchasing unusual mementos, objects known today as 'trench art': embroidered silk handkerchiefs, small carved wooden boxes, brass shell cases.

Many of the souvenirs were empty artillery shell cases decorated with art nouveau floral forms, including some incorporating the poppy, made during and after the war by both soldiers and civilians. They served as 'flower vases' for the mantelpiece or the hall, harking back to the pre-war Georgian fashion for pastoral designs and an ageless fascination with flowers and their meanings. As we have seen, for young men at or near the front, flowers represented the free spirits of the dead whose bodies lay under the earth, and on the soil of graves where they expressed transcendence and rebirth. Sometimes, it wasn't enough to incise a flower onto an old artillery shell. Some men created flowers from smaller scraps from their wartime experience. This can be seen in a record kept by Stanley Keith Pearl of the 5th Field Company Engineers, Australia, of his time spent making a hat-pin stand adorned with metal daisies:

This stand, in the form of a field daisy, was constructed on the Somme in May 1918. Its base is from a 77-mm shell-case and an 18-pounder nose-cap embellished with the Rising Sun worn by a sapper who was awarded the Military Medal. An Army issue purple-diamond colour patch acts as a cushion, while the stalk is a piece of copper conductor from a portable electric light plant for a searchlight at Aubigny. The 'flower' was made from a German water-bottle found near Villers-Bretonneux and a German overcoat button bartered from a 'Fritz' prisoner for a packet of cigarettes. The hat pins are from New Zealand and Canadian Engineers' cap badges, bartered for cigarettes, while the pin shafts are spokes purloined from army bicycles.[2]

These metallic flowers carried no natural scent, yet they evoked a strange new perfume of grief. Made of brass, the shell cases tarnished quickly, and gave rise to a comforting, perhaps therapeutic, rite of frequent polishing. Bereaved women were assaulted by the pungent smell of brass cleaners, and rubbing the metal flower vases until they gleamed often became less a household chore than a sacred act, a methodical way to bridge the gap between the living and the dead. But as the years rolled by and memories faded, the markings of these mementos of bright lives cut short were worn down to a dull lustre.

The material world of the postwar years was disturbed by the presence of these ornaments, leaving a mark on a generation of fatherless children. Unfortunately, only a few documents exist to provide a glimpse into this, such as an item bought by Mabel Jeffries as a souvenir of her wartime service as a nurse in France. Sixty years later, long after Mabel had died, her niece revealed its secret:

Yes, that thing by the fireplace with the flowers on it is really a shell case . . . She brought that back from France for her parents; I thought it was an awfully morbid thing . . . It got to Granny's house and then it came here . . . I often look at it and wonder how many men its shell killed.[3]

The postwar battlefields of the Western Front were black-magic gardens fertilised by the blood and bones of countless young men.

Apart from trench-art blooms created from war debris, there now sprouted real flora also unknown before the war. In Flanders Fields, where once among the intricacies of medieval drainage channels indigenous plants had thrived, an international crop of hearty weeds took root in the fallen trenches. Our Lady's-thistle (*Silybum Marianum*) travelled there from Britain in horses' oats, and huge turnips brought as seeds from Germany now broke the Belgian soil.[4] As at the Colosseum of Rome, where exotic flora bloom from seeds dropped by the spectators who trekked across the empire to watch the gladiators nearly two thousand years ago, the Ypres Salient – the compact, pinched battle zone in Belgian Flanders from which the Allies defended the city of Ypres – commemorated its role as a global theatre of death with its floral displays each spring. Postwar newcomers appeared too, such as alien heather brought from Brittany to commemorate the French who died near Boezinge during the German gas attack of April 1915, and maples and cedars from Canada planted at the Brooding Soldier memorial at Vancouver Corner, St Juliaan, to commemorate two thousand Canadian dead.

This was the surreal landscape of war memory in which the Remembrance Poppy flourished, renewing itself each year, and bringing hope to families decimated by the war. Wearing the poppy was an act of solidarity with the dead and the living, and seemed to promise that such terrible sufferings would never be repeated.

THE AMERICAN AVIATOR Charles Lindbergh flew into history in the summer of 1927 when he steered his monoplane the *Spirit of St Louis* solo across the Atlantic. He made the journey from New York to Paris in less than thirty-four hours, circling the Eiffel Tower before landing at Le Bourget aerodrome on the evening of 21 May. For his achievement, he won the $25,000 Orteig Prize and the pleasure of a hectic round of dinners, receptions and celebrity encounters, including meetings with the French wartime leader Marshal Ferdinand Foch and France's own pioneer aviator Louis Blériot.

While in Paris, Lindbergh was invited by the American Club of Brussels to fly on to Belgium. He eagerly accepted, and twenty-five thousand well-wishers gave him a hero's welcome when he landed there on the afternoon of 28 May. After an audience with King Albert and Queen Elisabeth of the Belgians, Lindbergh was feted at a banquet in the evening. Within thirty-six hours he took off again in *Spirit*, this time bound for London. But fate intervened.

It was 30 May – Memorial Day in the United States – and Lindbergh decided to commemorate the day by amending his flight plan to fly over the Flanders Field American War Cemetery at Waregem, where 368 American soldiers lay beneath serried ranks of wooden crosses. With perfect timing, he banked his monoplane above an assembly of notables and the curious, and threw a bouquet of poppies out of the cockpit. As they floated to the earth, the crowd broke into spontaneous applause.[5] In Lindbergh's mind, it was the Buddy

Poppy that he cast from his plane over these American patriots' graves. For this act, as well as for his historic transatlantic flight, he was awarded honorary membership of the Veterans of Foreign Wars (VFW) later that year.

Lindbergh's 1927 flypast was not forgotten. On its fortieth anniversary, the US air force began a tradition of executing the 'Missing Man' formation over American war cemeteries in Belgium. This famous aerial salute to comrades fallen in war sees four combat jets fly in horizontal formation with one breaking away vertically and flying heavenwards – the eponymous missing man. While the tradition was limited initially to Second World War sites, the First World War cemetery at Waregem was added to the roster of flypasts during the early 1980s. It was an appropriate tribute to the conflict that had invented the idea of 'the missing'.

The most enduring consequence of Lindbergh's aerial commemoration was that it seeded Remembrance Poppies across the battlefields, much as the wind seeds the wheat fields when the pod of the natural poppy expels its fertile riches. This eloquent and poignant act struck an emotional chord in the once fiercely fought over and now devastated area of the Ypres Salient, just eighteen miles from Waregem.

On Sunday, 12 July 1987, Lindbergh's poppy offering was resurrected when paper poppies rained down on those who had gathered at Tyne Cot cemetery near Passchendaele, just north of Ypres. Tyne Cot shelters the graves of almost twelve thousand men, and inscribes the names of some 35,000 missing soldiers. It is built on the once German-occupied slopes of the Passchendaele ridge, which was the objective of months of bloody struggle in 1917. The attack cost hundreds of thousands of casualties on both sides, and the sense of wasteful sacrifice is perhaps stronger here than anywhere else along the Western Front. Today, the tombstones cluster around two concrete pillboxes from whence German machine-gunners wrought havoc on the advancing Canadian troops. In 1987, eyes misted over and a handful of First World War veterans in their late nineties stood shoulder to shoulder with thousands of others and looked up as the sky turned red and ten thousand poppies fluttered down.[6] Patriotic and respectful, Lindbergh's aerial commemoration also opened the door to a world of coincidences and connections that resonated with the ancient roots and modern meanings of the memorial poppy.

The poignancy of such events cannot be denied, but the effect is constantly being reinvented for new generations of audiences. During the annual Festival of Remembrance at London's Royal Albert Hall, thousands of poppy petals are scattered over the audience. At Buckingham Palace in 2005, during the sixtieth commemoration of the end of the Second World War, a Lancaster bomber showered a million red poppy petals over the crowds lining the Mall. Smaller in scale, but equally evocative, was a display of respect and remembrance by Samantha Roberts, whose husband, a British tank commander, was killed just three days into the 2003 invasion of Iraq. On 28 October 2004, this brave widow floated to the earth from fifteen thousand feet suspended from a giant red poppy parachute to raise money for the Royal British Legion's Poppy Appeal.[7]

A final turn in Lindbergh's legacy reveals how the poppy's symbolism meshed with the aviator's own frame of mind. During his Atlantic crossing, Lindbergh said he had an epiphany about the new world he was conquering by air. As he throttled through the clouds and banked above the River Seine, he saw the earth from a God-like perspective. He was convinced that aviation, by shrinking the distances between nations, had the ability to reshape the world for good. Flying over French and Belgian war cemeteries, and especially perhaps by dropping his poppy wreath at Waregem, Lindbergh expressed his belief in the power of universal remembrance to allow the dead to live for ever in our memories, in the hope of bringing an end to all war.

This was a very personal obsession. Over the next decade, Lindbergh would champion a parallel quest: to make the body as well as the spirit immortal. Teaming up with the gifted French surgeon Alexis Carrel, he helped to build the so-called Perfusion Pump, which allowed an animal's organs to survive outside the body and which, with much modification, became the heart–lung machine.[8] With technology enlisted in this life-affirming way, Lindbergh may have hoped to provide yet one more way in which war would be seen as futile.

STARTING IN 1921, the war-wounded of Britain were employed in the British Legion's newly established poppy factory, located in a small room above a shop off the Old Kent Road in south-east London. The beginnings were modest, with just five disabled servicemen assembling poppies from crimson cloth and wire, and painting the centre of the flowers black with enamel paint. By August 1922, forty-one disabled veterans were working in the cramped conditions, many arriving in wheelchairs pushed by their wives,[9] and each man expected to make a thousand poppies a day. Although many of the men had previously been unemployed, some for a long time, and all had single or double amputations, the British Legion's journal described it as 'the cheeriest workshop in London', with the men singing along to records on a gramophone as they went through their day's work.[10]

The operation soon moved to Richmond in Surrey, and then in 1933 moved again, this time to a purpose-built factory nearby, where it remains to this day. These new premises allowed for more war-shattered men to be taken on, with space for machines to be adapted so that, for example, a one-armed man could operate a press to cut the poppies into shape with the stump of his missing limb.[11] Today, wounded ex-servicemen and women from the conflicts in Iraq and Afghanistan are helped back into civilian life on Royal British Legion programmes funded by the Poppy Day Appeal,[12] an arrangement whose social value and symbolism remain both proper and moving.

The factory captured the overriding spirit of bearing visible witness to the dead that typified the inter-war years. The sentiment was caught in a letter to *The Times* in November 1925: 'every penny spent in tributes to the dead, will through the British Legion find its way to the relief of those broken and destitute men, who in giving their health and their jobs, have made a sacrifice as great in spirit as those who gave their lives'.[13] As First World War veteran Alexander Anthony, who had fought on the Somme and at Ypres, said decades later, in 1967, 'I'm a believer, you see. And to me that poppy means everything'. For some forty years he had clung resolutely to the poppy:

> *I have been connected with these poppies for the last fifty years . . . When you know where your donation goes and the amount of money spent on destitute ex-servicemen who have given their all for their country, and you see these badly disabled servicemen making the poppies, then the light in their eyes when you bring them part of this donation is all the justification needed.*[14]

The fact that wearing the scarlet directly supported the broken men of Flanders Fields, who were now making Remembrance Poppies for their nations' commemorations, lent the emblem a special redolence.

The Canadians, too, soon enlisted disabled veterans to make their memorial poppies. Although Anna Guérin had sold her poppies in Canada in 1921, by the next year the Department of Soldiers Civil Re-establishment had set up 'Vetcraft' workshops in Montreal and Toronto. Here, disabled veterans made poppies in honour of their fallen and injured comrades, receiving a small but vital income in return. Three years later, in 1925, the Canadian Legion was formed and began to organise the country's annual Poppy Day Appeal.[15]

One of the first issues of the Legion's magazine, the *Legionary*, highlighted the crucial differences between veteran-made poppies and those made by anyone in any factory. In a single sentence of perfectly turned copy, the author pitched sentiment (the presumed victor) against profit (the obvious enemy): 'The disabled veterans in Vetcraft and Red Cross workshops are creating true memorials, while a poppy replica produced under ordinary commercial competitive conditions is nothing more nor less than an artificial flower'.[16] Such ideals are surely well intended, but even the Legion could not hold out against the power of the market: Vetcraft operations ceased in 1996, and poppy production has since been contracted out to a for-profit company.

For some, the change compromised the poppy's potency as a symbol, but it did not appear to decrease its popularity among the general public. Today, a dazzling variety of poppy images are available to purchase in support of the cause, not merely poppy pins and badges but bumper stickers, jewellery, cutlery and even a range of clothing emblazoned with a poppy logo.[17] For all who wear the poppy in its myriad forms, it is a pledge never to forget those countrymen and countrywomen who have died and suffered in war.

The British and Canadian lead was observed by the Americans, and promptly copied. The VFW opened its first poppy factory in Pittsburgh in 1924, employing disabled soldiers to assemble its Buddy Poppies.

The trademark rights obtained by the VFW decreed that Buddy Poppies with the organisation's label had to be the handiwork of suitably needy veterans employed in VFW-supervised workshops. A National Buddy Poppy Committee enforced this rule and regulated the poppy's specifications – a role it has never relinquished.

Designed as a national initiative, the Buddy Poppy would raise enough money to compensate veterans for their work, support rehabilitation programmes and look after orphans and widows in the VFW's national home. Today, the little red flowers are assembled at eleven locations across the United States – from Biloxi, Mississippi to Grand Rapids, Michigan. The VFW produces eighteen million poppies annually, and in the true spirit of Michael's memorial, it is never sold, but only given in exchange for a donation.[18]

Not all nations were as quick to learn the lesson that people are inspired to give in order to have something made by someone worthy who will directly benefit from any donation. New Zealand's old soldiers had to wait a decade longer than their comrades in Britain, Canada and the United States to reap the full benefits of Remembrance Poppies, as it was only in 1931 that the New Zealand Returned Soldiers Association (NZRSA) organised the war-wounded to manufacture them. Commemorating their sacrifices, disabled Great War veterans from the Auckland and Christchurch Returned Soldiers Associations began making poppies for the New Zealand Poppy Day Appeal. Today, the Christchurch association produces all of New Zealand's Remembrance Poppies.

Whatever ancient symbolism and literary dimensions were attached to the corn poppy or its opium-bearing cousin, it was the veteran-made Remembrance Poppy that helped the heroes of the war to cope with their physical and emotional wounds. Buying a poppy put money in an old soldier's pocket. For many it was as simple as that.

And poppies were not only bought to be worn by the living. They adorned the tombs, stone sculptures and memorial resting places of the dead as well. Moina Michael created the first Remembrance Poppy wreaths in 1919, when she assembled huge, anchor-shaped garlands to be taken aboard a US navy vessel and cast onto the waters in remembrance of all those who had perished at sea.[19] A few years later, in November 1922, the mayoress of Truro, Cornwall saw that an empty wreath frame had been placed on the town's newly erected war memorial, and announced that passers-by could fill the wreath with poppies that they had bought, so making a collective commemoration from their individual acts of remembrance.[20] The royal family gave their seal of approval to the tradition when in 1924 they began to lay wreaths each year at London's Cenotaph.[21] By 1929, almost half a million poppy wreaths were being made by London's poppy factory for a public ritual that had become all but universal.[22]

ON CITY STREETS AROUND THE GLOBE, the poppy was bought by millions, but in Britain the poppy was a singular phenomenon across society. As such it collided with the old and new social attitudes that were reshaping the postwar world, and inevitably the British class system was involved. At first, cloth poppies sold for three (old) pennies (1.25 pence in modern currency) and silken versions for one shilling (5 pence). Soon, five different varieties of poppy were available: the cheap one-penny for the schoolchildren; the three-penny, bought mostly by the working class; the six-penny for the lower-middle class; the one-shilling for the middle class; and the half-a-crown (i.e. two shillings and six pennies) for the wealthy.[23] The relative generosity of each of society's classes can be made out in each poppy's sales figures. In 1929, £518,489 was raised on Poppy Day, of which the working class contributed £200,000 and the lower-middle class £215,000. The vast majority of funds raised came from the nation's poorest, with the wealthiest contributing comparatively little.[24]

This awkward truth did not prevent the higher social classes from hijacking the preparations for the annual Remembrance Sunday event. Local branches of the British Legion ideally included the mayor, a bank manager and a newspaper editor. Female poppy sellers were recruited on behalf of the lady mayoress, and the young ladies themselves had to be of the 'right type' – friends of the committee, members of local social clubs or members of the Girl Guides.[25] While everyone in Britain was expected to repay their debt to those maimed in the war by buying a poppy, Poppy Day activities were organised along lines that ignored the urban realities of the industrialised cities of the north, where so many of the soldiers had joined up. Instead they reflected the politically conservative society of the rural and suburban south of England.[26]

By the late 1920s, poppy wearing on Armistice Day had become a moral duty – so much part of popular culture that the novelist Dorothy L. Sayers could use it as a significant clue in her 1928 murder mystery *The Unpleasantness at the Bellona Club*: the absence of a poppy from a general's personal effects clearly disproved the assumption that he had died on 11 November, as it would have been inconceivable that such a man would have been alive on that day without a poppy in his possession.[27] The newspapers of the time were full of reports of almost everyone wearing a poppy, where 'Rich and poor, young and old, wore the dainty blooms made by women and children in the devastated areas across the seas'.[28]

As elsewhere around the world, where poppies were initially imported from Anna Guérin's French workshops, there was often a shortage of supply: 'If only the organisers of the Poppy Day in Norwich had had an adequate supply of flowers, they might have made a very much bigger success of their Sunday collection'.[29] Similar problems afflicted Canada, Australia and the United States. Greater quantities of poppies would appear shortly, however.

In Britain, it was important to garner publicity for the 'new tradition', and amazing spectacles were staged. A poppy-decked elephant paraded the streets of Leeds in 1924, and in the same year a poppy-covered goat hauled a miniature replica of Wimbledon's war memorial around south London.[30] The poppy-strewn battlefields of the Somme and Flanders were depicted at a more manageable size within the grounds adjacent to Westminster Abbey. A single wooden cross brought from the battlefield grave of an unknown British soldier stood alone for several years at the abbey until, in 1928, passers-by began planting their own poppies alongside it. And thus the Field of Remembrance was born.[31]

Large donations captured the imagination, though did not add greatly to the overall amounts received. Such initiatives included a single petal from a real poppy sold at London's Smithfield Market for five pounds, or a basket of poppies auctioned at Sotheby's for which the first winning bidder would pay ninety pounds, take a single poppy, then re-auction the remainder, until five hundred pounds was raised. Royalty too adopted the fad, with the king, the queen and the Prince of Wales each paying one hundred pounds for a single poppy.[32]

Public enthusiasm for the Remembrance Poppy sometimes took an arguably unintentional sexual turn, as a result of the fact that poppy selling was often deemed to be women's work (and would remain such until after the Second World War). One curious event took place in Leeds, where patriotism was spiced up with carnivalesque eroticism and questionable taste. The *Yorkshire Post* of 11 November 1921 announced: 'The hotels, clubs and other public places will be visited by Ladies clad in red poppy costumes, with red cloaks and hoods and black masks, and pistols that are innocent of anything but a little flash of red light'.[33]

Around the globe, young women were recruited to hawk the Remembrance Poppy blooms. During the 1930s poppies were sold by 100,000 members of the British Legion's Women's Section, who were assisted by 250,000 volunteers (also women).[34] In the United States, VFW volunteers were often pretty young women, who stood in front of giant Stars and Stripes flags surrounded by poppy wreaths and patriotic posters (also featuring attractive young ladies), and handed out poppies to the public for a donation.[35] As Moina Michael struggled to make ends meet in her cramped hotel room, the impoverished Poppy Princess was being upstaged by young beauties collecting money for the flower she had invented.

Hollywood was soon engaged as part of the machine of poppy patriotism. The glamour of the silver screen was attached to the Buddy Poppy, and, in a tradition which stretched from the 1930s into the 1950s, actresses such as Ginger Rogers, Jane Wyman, Doris Day, Virginia Mayo and Natalie Wood were recruited to be Buddy Poppy Girls.[36] As Joan Leslie, the Buddy Poppy Girl for 1941, later recalled, 'When Warner Bros cast me in patriotic films, I represented an All-American girl. I believe in the ideals VFW members stand for and fought for'.[37] This was a two-way street, for the Hollywood studios benefited from having its most alluring and bankable stars posing for publicity pictures with an emblem of America's finest, especially after the United States entered the fray of the Second World War.

Of course, movieland's most famous poppies had little to do with the war. In 1939, overcome by their drowsy vapours, Judy Garland fell asleep in a magical field of poppies in the Technicolor fantasy *The Wizard of Oz*. L. Frank Baum's book, on which the film was based, had been published in 1900, long before the First World War. Yet here we see the two species conjoined, the innocent red corn poppy letting loose the intoxicating fumes of their opium-bearing cousins.

WHAT DID PEOPLE of Depression-era Kansas or London – a generation removed from the Great War – believe it meant to wear a Remembrance Poppy? While everyone wanted to participate, to be seen to respect the memory of the dead and to help the veteran survivors, the meaning of the poppy was individual to each country in which it was embraced. It was clear to many that there were several paradoxes in play. Even in these early days, the poppy's association with opium was one of the oblivion to which the war dead had been conveyed, but it was also the source of the morphine which brought blissful relief to the maimed and wounded. At the same time, it alleviated the pain of loss for the bereaved.

Buying poppies helped the wounded, but for many it meant not having to think about the damaged men in their hospitals and rest homes. This tragic existence was entangled with poppy-making and poppy-wearing and was pushed centre-stage by Herbert Read's 'A Short Poem for Armistice Day'.[38] A paean to the memorial flower and those who made it, Read portrays the suffering of those on the margins of society who make artificial poppies from paper, tin and metal (the grim 'One eye one leg one lung one arm a syncopated sick heart beat'). He describes the Remembrance Poppy as having neither sweet scent nor seed, and how their wire grips the buttonhole. He then adds the poem's most famous and startling image: 'and men like flowers are cut and withered on the stem'. With pinpoint and disturbing accuracy, the poem moves back and forth between real poppies, their artificial counterpart and the men who make them.

In all this worthy activity, it is easy to overlook the astonishing amount of money that was raised by the Remembrance Poppy in the inter-war period of 1921 to 1940. Within a few years of the war's end, the British Legion was raising vast sums in Britain and across the empire. By 1928 Poppy Day receipts had grown to £503,000 in Britain alone.[39] Over the inter-war years, the money raised totalled £10,447,027.[40] In 1939, in the midst of writing her memoir, Moina Michael calculated that every year around the world some $7 million was raised through the sale of her beloved poppies.[41]

There is a subversive link between the sheer numbers involved, of everything from poppies to pennies to armaments to human beings. In the massed ranks of such imagery we perhaps lose sight of individual men, their past lives, their battlefield exploits and the futures they never had – and the inestimable debt owed to them by the living, something that cannot be calculated in pounds and pence. Read's hard-hitting poem pinched the raw nerves of the war generation, but times were changing.

THE NAZI JUGGERNAUT rolled into Poland in 1939, as Moina Michael put the finishing touches to *The Miracle Flower*. Everything the poppy epitomised for Michael and millions around the world lay in ruins. Her dream of world peace was dying, and her idealism and flowery prose seem trapped in a time warp. The 'new chivalry of humanity', with which she had imbued her scarlet emblem, had been brushed aside. Yet the poppy's power to conjure remembrance and inspire the human spirit was more potent than she could have imagined.

Britain steeled herself for a new conflict, and the poppy refused to wilt. While the commercialisation of the 1920s and 1930s had not changed its character, the prism of the imminent war cast a new light on the crimson bloom. The failure of the Great War to secure everlasting peace was seen as a betrayal of the war generation and their sacrifices. For many, wearing a poppy became an uncomfortable act.

Young men changed their opinions, throwing off their poise as the thankful sons who received the benefit of the war generation's sacrifices and growing anxious with fear that it was now their turn to be dragged into conflagration. Already in the early 1930s, students at Cambridge University had used Armistice Day not only to wear poppies as a sign of respect but also as an emblem of pacifism.[42] But a new tragedy seemed to be approaching.

In Britain, the feelings of patriotism, endurance and strength that had been trotted out with the Remembrance Poppy each 11 November since 1921 were vital to a nation about to be put under siege. Politicians asked the public to ready themselves for the struggle ahead, pointing to the past as reason enough to hold fast against the enemy. But these feelings were temporarily converted to doubt when it was announced that the Armistice Day commemorations of 1939 were to be cancelled.[43] After all, Armistice Day was inappropriate when the nation was at war.

However, Poppy Day was not inappropriate, and in the autumn of 1939, the country needed the British Legion more than ever. The public were encouraged to buy two poppies, or pay double for a single one. The appeal was a triumph, and poppies were bought and worn in record numbers. An astonishing £595,887 was collected that year, with one observer recording that out of a hundred people he counted, no fewer than eighty-two were wearing the scarlet flower.[44]

So in many ways, the Second World War revitalised the Remembrance Poppy in Britain. Following the success of 1939, Winston Churchill heartily endorsed the Poppy Day appeal of 1940. It was a sign of the dangerous times that poppy collection boxes sent by train around the country arrived in towns and villages blasted through with bullet holes.[45] But flying-bomb attacks could not stop the poppies of 1944 raising more than £1 million for the first time.

By war's end in 1945, the vast quantity of poppies sold could not be considered without remembering the equally vast bloodshed and suffering that had been added to humanity's conscience in those six years. After 1945, Britain's 1914–18 war memorials were painstakingly re-inscribed with a new crop of names, and the poppy effortlessly made the transition to embody memory and respect for the war dead of both conflicts. Now the poppy was a symbol of the souls lost in all Britain's conflicts, not just in the First World War.

Similarly, in New Zealand the poppy helped to rally people to support the Allies in the new world war. The government granted a special wartime permit to allow the importation of the British cloth from which poppies were made. What had begun as Great War remembrance became a commemoration of all of New Zealand's war dead, and a way of supporting every serviceman and his family. By the end of the war, no fewer than 750,000 poppies had been sold in a country with a postwar population of just 1.7 million – an extraordinary level of support. This widespread wearing of the scarlet bloom throughout the war helped to give the Remembrance Poppy a life beyond the annual Poppy Day Appeal and official commemorations. Poppies began to appear at the funerals of returned servicemen and women, and were taken as patriotic offerings on pilgrimages to battlefields, memorials and cemeteries by this next generation of veterans.

Likewise, Canada immediately decided to commemorate Second World War veterans alongside those of the Great War with its Remembrance Poppy. Returned soldiers were recruited to become enthusiastic new champions for Poppy Appeals through work in the Canadian Legion's Vetcraft workshops. However, not all Canadian soldiers were equal. Extraordinary as it sounds today, it was only in 1966 that Canada's Native Americans who served in either world war were allowed to join the Royal Canadian Legion, despite the fact that they had responded wholeheartedly to the call to arms from as far back as 1914.[46] Indeed, more than 3,500 had served in the First World War, and more than 300 had died. Yet, on their return home, these warriors were often ignored.[47]

Consider the distressing accounts of some First Nation soldiers who returned from the wars. Okanagan Private George McLean was awarded the Distinguished Conduct Medal for 'conspicuous gallantry and devotion', and Ojibwa Corporal Francis Pegahmagabow earned more medals than any other First Nation soldier of the First World War for his excellence in the field as a scout and sniper,[48] but neither could join the Canadian Legion. Both said this made them feel excluded from the annual Poppy Day Appeal and its mission to remember the living as well as the dead. A clergyman from the Cree Nation, Edward Ahenakew, could not believe that this could remain the policy: 'Not in vain did our young men die in a strange land, not in vain are our Indian bones mingled with the soil of a foreign land'. He hoped these brave veterans could take their place by the side of the white people, 'after the unseen tears of Indian mothers in many isolated Indian reserves have watered the seeds' from which their aspirations arose. For years these hopes fell mainly on deaf ears.

Then in 1936 the Canadian Legion took up the veterans' cause with a resolution which stated the Legion would do everything in its power to ensure that Native American war veterans would be treated the same as their other Canadian comrades, particularly in regard to pensions and allowances.[49] Ruth Quesnelle, a Blood Indian woman from Alberta, was married to a now deceased First World War Native American veteran who was long denied membership of the Legion. Husband and wife eventually became members in 1981, and since that time she has sold Remembrance Poppies every year. In her own words, Ruth admits, 'It's an honor for me to sell for the Indian war vets'.

Despite half a century of shameful discrimination, Canada's First Nations wear the poppy (along with an eagle feather) on 11 November, and regard it as a symbol of an experience they share with all Canadians.[50]

In the aftermath of the Second World War there was an outpouring of memorialisation. Some memorials were new, but others simply added names or architectural elements to monuments that commemorated the Great War. These newly inscribed names honoured the fallen, but also testified to the failure of the First World War to achieve its much-vaunted aim of banishing all conflict from the world. In the Canadian capital, Ottawa, the National War Memorial was a cenotaph which had been inaugurated in 1939 to respect the nation's dead from the 1914–18 war, and was rededicated in 1982 to include the Second World War and the Korean War. In 2000, the Canadian Tomb of the Unknown Soldier was added in front of the memorial, symbolising the sacrifices made by all Canadians who had died, or would yet die, in the service of their country. The First World War echoed through this event, as the unknown soldier had been exhumed from the war cemetery of Cabaret-Rouge, in sight of Vimy Ridge; and, on the first Remembrance Day after the reinterment, a new tradition was established: those who had gathered to pay their respects spontaneously cast their Remembrance Poppies on the tomb.

THE POPPY'S TRIUMPH was not universal. Poppy Girls from Hollywood notwithstanding, a curious fate awaited the flower emblem in the land of its birth. After 1945, and especially after the Vietnam War polarised society, the poppy faded from view in America. Still, in the midst of this growing amnesia, a gruff voice from the US counterculture music scene swam against the tide: Captain Beefheart, whose surreal lyrics and seemingly chaotic improvisations entertained many young people at the time, released his song 'Veteran's Day Poppy' in 1969. In the first verse, Beefheart captured the ambiguous essence of the poppy:

> *I cry but I can't buy*
> *Your Veteran's Day poppy*
> *It don't get me high*
> *It can only make me cry*[51]

The poppy has remained the nation's official remembrance flower, but by the late twentieth century it was not much seen among Americans – it lingers still, but below the level of mass consciousness. Since its beginnings, the VFW has produced more than a billion Buddy Poppies, but in 1989 only 18 million were produced, exchanged for an average donation of fifty-five cents.[52] With a population of 307 million, 18 million poppies represents six per cent of the US population. In Britain, 30 million poppies are bought each year by a population of 65 million; in Canada, 15 million are bought from a population of 33 million.

While the Buddy Poppy's fortunes have ebbed and flowed, some individuals keep Moina Michael's campaigning spirit alive. In 1995, the Second World War army veteran Andy Bandalos distributed four thousand poppies from his wheelchair, which was strategically sited in his town of Suffern on the New York–New Jersey state border. Revealing his passion for and dedication to the poppy, Bandalos said, 'I had a lot of buddies killed in the war. Even though I can't walk, I want to do every-thing I can to preserve their memories'.[53] And two years later, an anonym-ous donor gave $13,640 to the Buddy Poppy Appeal in New Jersey.[54]

TODAY, ALONG THE OLD WESTERN FRONT of the Great War, the scars of battle are hidden beneath a blanket of billowing wheat and corn. The battlefields are cut through by new motorways, sectioned by rebuilt towns and new industrial parks and overlaid by the manicured lawns of innumerable war cemeteries. Just centimetres beneath these competing scenes of rural idyll and harsh modernity lie the trenches, dugouts and nameless bodies of the so-called Great War for Civilisation, and in some places covered by or lying adjacent to the far fewer remains of the Second World War which passed more rapidly across this terrain, but which added to the toll of death and destruction. Every summer this grim underworld is carpeted with corn poppies, and every winter coloured by the crimson paper of the Remembrance Poppy.

Single blooms with green plastic stems, miniature wooden crosses with poppy attached and wreaths with handwritten notes are scattered by veterans, relatives and schoolchildren. Some are pressed between the name plaques to the missing at the Menin Gate in Ypres, and at other times a flood of single petals flutters down from the memorial's skylights onto the crowd below. In the alchemical world of the memo-rial poppy, emotion can be so intense that a petal can become a man. On one occasion, as petals swirled around the veterans sitting in their wheelchairs, a man reached out his hand and caught one, and announced, 'That's my friend I left behind.'[55] Poppy petals and wreaths are also laid at Thiepval, the counterpart monument in France, and at the foot of the countless white Portland stone headstones that shine throughout the landscape, as well as at isolated spots across the old killing fields, where only the pilgrim knows what he or she is commemorating. Most graves are marked, but many poignantly assert that the remains below are only 'Known unto God'.

On the Somme every year, along the lip of the huge Lochnagar crater whose mine was blown by the British on 1 July 1916, a burgeoning crowd gathers around the gaping maw. Perched on the edge of the monstrous depression, a huge wooden cross stands guard, and around its base a pile of poppy wreaths is endlessly renewed. Children hand out poppy petals as the memorial service ends, and a shower of red is carried on the wind to cloak the sides and floor of the crater. This is the gift of Lochnagar to the spirit of those men who have lain there for almost a century.[56] Under a tree, by the narrow country road which winds past the crater, a middle-aged woman opens the boot of her car and reveals a display of ceramic and glass souvenirs, all hand-painted with the poppy flower. Their sale supports the upkeep of the crater, which was rescued by Richard Dunning, an Englishman who bought the land to avoid its being filled in by a French farmer for cultivation.[57] As we move further away in time from the terrible events of the First World War, each of us must endeavour to bring its memory back into focus, saving more of its old battlefields and making them a destination for historically minded tourism and reflective pilgrimage.

From its creation in Moina Michael's dreary office, and its quick uptake in Anna Guérin's entrepreneurial mind, the Remembrance Poppy balanced the poignant with the practical, respect for the dead with support for the living, commemoration with commercialisation. Today, as younger generations visit the old battlefields to remember family and history, they frequent hotels, guesthouses, cafés, museums and shops that, like the poppies themselves, spring up each year in order to cater to war tourists around meaningful anniversaries. Nowhere is this more visible than in the Ypres Salient in Belgian Flanders. It is fitting that a boom in Great War tourism centres on this area which saw so much fighting.

Walking through the city of Ypres, it is impossible to escape the poppy. It has become a marketing device, simultaneously a logo for war tourism and an emblem of remembrance. There are war-themed sweets packed in octagonal tins, red chocolate poppies, souvenir cups and glasses, and a 'Remembrance Beer' advertised on a pub wall. All of them sport the poppy.

Along with the poppy logo, every year John McCrae's poem is pressed into service to raise funds for war veterans. During Remembrance Week, one confectionery shop in the market square in Ypres mounts a special window display: a copy of McCrae's original handwritten text for 'In Flanders Fields' is joined by decorated shells and a rum jar from the battlefield, a soldier's uniform, wartime photographs and chocolates moulded in the shape of a Tommy's helmet – the last item available for purchase inside. The whole ensemble is showered with poppies, of course.[58] (Edible Remembrance Poppies are not confined to Belgian sweetshops; a chocolate poppy was introduced for ANZAC Day 2007, and was aimed at commemorating all New Zealanders who died in conflict, but particularly those who struggled ashore on Gallipoli in April 1915.)

The potency and ambiguity of the poppy is seen to greatest effect in the city's use of the flower as the emblem of its renowned First World War museum. Opened in 1997 and christened, perhaps inevitably, the 'In Flanders Fields Museum', the logo shows three poppies sprouting from barbed-wire stems – a remarkably effective image, which Lee Keedick might have wished to have invented in place of his Flanders Victory Memorial Flag. The museum aimed to incorporate multimedia displays of objects, voices, music and old film of the war landscapes into its exhibitions, allowing visitors to imagine the brutal landscape of war that once dominated these places of remembrance.[59] As the First and Second World Wars disappear from living memory, we enter a new era where emblems rather than living people or personal experience must stand for our common understanding of the costs of global war.

Evocative symbols such as McCrae's poem and the Remembrance Poppy are vital to this era, even as we witness ongoing conflicts in Afghanistan and Iraq and the debates that stir around them. Every year, millions of ordinary and well-known people alike buy and wear poppies, but some commentators insist that the emblem has lost its universal meaning: it has come to stand for whatever the wearer desires, including a desire to fit into the crowd. In 2004 David Aaronovitch observed: 'People now make what they want out of such institutions, choosing for themselves whether they are commemorating our glorious dead, or mourning the futility of war. It is a bit like wearing a one-minute silence. You can think what you like while you stand there, head bowed'.[60] Aaronovitch points out that, like the Christmas wreathes that start to appear in shops in mid-October, the poppy is now brought out to demonstrate memory and piety well before 11 November. Within a decade, he writes, tongue in cheek, 'we will be wearing poppies in June, building our own porch-cenotaphs and holding half-hour silences for those members of the Light Brigade who never returned'.[61]

This acute observation is ironically matched by what some see as pressure to wear a poppy against one's own wishes. Channel 4 newsreader Jon Snow refused to wear a poppy on air in 2006. Viewers complained, and Snow replied that while he wore a poppy in his private life, he didn't agree with wearing any emblems espousing a cause on air. He famously went on to say, 'There is a rather unpleasant poppy fascism out there'.[62] The issue is contentious and emotional for some people, as Snow himself admits:

I am begged to wear an Aids ribbon, a breast cancer ribbon, a Marie Curie flower ... You name it, from the Red Cross to the RNIB [Royal National Institute for the Blind], they send me stuff to wear to raise awareness, and I don't. And in those terms, and those terms alone, I do not and will not wear a poppy.[63]

Almost every year around 11 November, it seems that a new poppy 'scandal' erupts, demonstrating how controversial an emblem it is, and how deeply it is embedded in the moral sensibilities of British society. In 2009, the *Daily Mail* ran a campaign demanding that Premier League football teams wear an embroidered poppy on their shirts during matches over the weekend of Remembrance Sunday, in a year when casualties in Afghanistan appeared to be mounting. The football clubs eventually agreed, as did newsreaders on the BBC, ITV and Sky News, all of whom had previously received complaints when poppies were not worn. In 2011, the poppy once again became contentious among the football clubs when FIFA, the game's international administrative body, banned English players from wearing a poppy logo on their shirts during an international match against Spain on Saturday, 12 November. After Prime Minister David Cameron and Prince William wrote to FIFA in protest at the decision, a compromise was reached, whereby the English team instead wore poppy armbands. The incident was dubbed 'Poppygate' by the media.

One might say that wearing poppies is a risky business for politicians, as it is they who send the young to war, with inevitable consequences. They too are caught in the poppy trap – representing the nation by honouring its war dead on commemorative occasions, but bound also to take military action in what they regard as the country's strategic interests.

At a November 2004 meeting between President George W. Bush and Prime Minister Tony Blair, the symbolism was indicative of the different ways in which the Remembrance Poppy had evolved in America and Britain. Blair wore a blood-red poppy while Bush, despite being the US Military's commander-in-chief, sported a miniature Stars and Stripes badge, with no Buddy Poppy in sight.

Alongside the previous war dead, we add the names of recent casualties to the roll of the heroic warrior ancestors of the nation. Conjured up like a ghostly army on parade, they are collectively remembered by the same politicians who ostentatiously wear poppies (or flag badges) at public commemorations. For some this is as it should be; for others, particularly the bereaved, it can be seen as an unforgivable hypocrisy. Perhaps it was for this reason that the memorable American tradition which saw a Poppy Boy or Poppy Girl present the first Buddy Poppy to the President was discontinued long ago. The poppy, after all, is a badge of responsibility – not to the nation, but to her fallen soldiers.

The Remembrance Poppy is a sensitive flower. It is a barometer of feelings about conflict, and calibrates a nation's reactions to the dead of past wars as well of those still being played out. In times of peace, politicians can bask in the poppy-wearing pride of respecting the nation's war dead, but in times of war, the poppy is a jagged reminder of each day's casualties.

ANNA GUÉRIN and her French war widows sold millions of Remembrance Poppies around the world during the early 1920s. The money raised transformed the lives of families and orphans in the devastated battlefields. Yet, for all Guérin's success, the French did not embrace the poppy as the singular symbol of the war dead. The reason was simple. In France, luxuriant garlands of colourful, sweet-scented blooms had long been displayed at funerals.[64] These were unlikely to be displaced by the flimsy, odourless and weed-like corn poppy. And if any single flower in French culture is associated with death, tombs and remembrance, it is the chrysanthemum, the 'golden flower', which blossoms in the autumn, the time when death, in nature, is near. Each year, chrysanthemums adorn French cemeteries on All Saints' Day, 1 November[65] – and very few of the war dead would not be considered to be among our most hallowed souls.

The association of the chrysanthemum with the dead is seen across Catholic Europe, from France to Italy to southern Germany.[66] These nations' Protestant neighbours did not share such deathly associations with the autumnal flower, not least because the tradition of laying cut flowers on graves emerged in the Netherlands in the sixteenth century, after the Church had divided.[67] While flowers were displayed at their funerals, the English, despite the Victorian 'language of flowers', did not have a specific bloom tied to spirituality and the dead; the cypress tree held that honour. Thus, the poppy was perfectly placed to fill this void in Britain. For the Catholic French, however, the religious connotations of flowers were so deeply embedded in the national psyche that even the trauma of the First World War could not dislodge them.

While the poppy has no sentimental attachments and is devoid of any spiritual feelings for the French people, it has become a highly visible badge of remembrance for British and Commonwealth visitors to the Somme, and a commercially valuable logo for the local tourist economy. This may have influenced Pascal Truffaut's idea of a poppy-sown commemorative corridor from Calais to the battlefields, which was described in the first pages of this book.

The French possess their own distinctive flower to commemorate their war dead, the blue cornflower (*Centaurea cyanus*), which was adopted unofficially during the Great War as its colour matched the spotless uniforms of raw recruits newly arrived at the front. Those already in the trenches had long since seen their clothing stained by mud and filth, and so the young soldiers soon became known as *les Bleuets* ('the blues'). During and after the war, two women working at the Hôtel des Invalides in Paris organised a workshop where disabled French soldiers could make cloth versions of the cornflower to commemorate the dead and help support themselves financially. The cornflower became the official French flower of remembrance in 1920.[68]

In 2008, the towns and villages of northern France celebrated the ninetieth anniversary of the end of the First World War with a profusion of floral displays. The 'Campaign in Bloom' provided communities with seeds to be planted throughout the countryside, but there was neither a poppy nor a chrysanthemum in sight. Instead, 'From April to October all the war memorials and participating villages will be decorated with the cornflower as a symbol of the Great War'.[69] Perhaps the poppy remains invisible to French eyes because it has never managed to shake off its identity as an agricultural weed.

The French cleave to their own history and culture of flowers, as they do with many things. Despite all of her advocacy for the poppy, Anna Guérin could not change that national trait. In the passion for local rivals to the poppy, some wonderful discoveries have been made. Recently, a French botanist saved from oblivion the famous La Marne rose, named after the 1914 Allied victory at the Battle of the Marne, where a German advance on Paris was halted.[70] Thought to have been lost, a specimen was found in a rural garden and successfully propagated.

Though they share predominantly Protestant Anglo-Saxon origins with the British, the Germans have also ignored the poppy's powerful symbolism. Of course, it would have been incongruous for the German people to have adopted an American-invented commemorative flower inspired by a wartime Canadian poem, and it would surely have been an affront to the victorious Allies if they had done so.[71] There were also deeper and darker forces at play, however. Stretching back into the nineteenth century, the Germans had forged a self-image as a race with a romantic, almost spiritual connection to the primeval enchanted forests of their homeland.[72] Towering oak trees were deeply rooted in folklore and mythology; there was no room for the diminutive, frail poppy. In commemorating their war dead, the Germans welded together two icons of their identity – one natural, the other industrial. The oak tree (and its acorns) joined the distinctive steel helmet as symbols of the enduring strength of the Germanic nation.[73]

As we have seen in the case of the United States, the poppy's appeal is not universal in the English-speaking world. In Ceylon (modern Sri Lanka), the flower became entangled with anti-imperial senti-ment during the inter-war years. Despite its status as an international emblem of remembrance, the British decided that money raised by the sale of poppies was exclusively for the benefit of *British* ex-servicemen; money would not be given to support Sri Lankan veterans. In 1933, Doreen Young, a British teacher, wrote a newspaper article entitled 'The Battle of the Flowers', in which she ridiculed the idea that Sri Lankan schoolchildren were expected to buy poppies for British soldiers while ignoring their own war heroes.

Many Sri Lankans were outraged, and in response, Aelian Perera, one of Sri Lanka's many impoverished ex-soldiers, formed the 'Suriya-Mal Movement',[74] which promoted the selling of *suriya* flowers from the portia tree specifically to raise money for Sri Lankan ex-servicemen. Every year between the wars, suriya flowers were sold on Sri Lanka's streets on Armistice Day in direct competition with the Remembrance Poppy, which was dubbed an 'imperialist' flower. British short-sightedness about the poppy blew up in their faces when the Suriya-Mal Movement became a rallying point in anti-British campaigns in Sri Lanka.

As would be repeated decades later in Northern Ireland, when Catholics refused to wear the 'British Poppy' on 11 November, the poppy revealed its ability to mean the opposite of what Moina Michael and Anna Guérin had intended.

7

THE WHITE POPPY

THE SCARLET PETALS DID NOT TUG ON EVERYONE'S heartstrings. When confronted with the Remembrance Poppy each November, some veterans, bitter and unemployed, as well as many of the bereaved women of that lost generation, complained that the symbol was being hijacked. They blamed the politicians, who, they said, used the flower for the glorification of military might rather than for the memory of the dead. The trauma of the Great War was still raw.

The No More War movement grew out of a widespread and at times irrepressible desire for peaceful solutions to the world's problems. Founded in 1921, and emerging from the wartime No Conscription Fellowship, the organisation was socialist as well as pacifist in spirit, and soon became the British section of War Resisters International, which counted Albert Einstein among its supporters. Pacifism was popular. Popular enough that in 1926 one member suggested that the movement should make their own poppies – white ones – and that the black centre of the Remembrance Poppy should be inscribed with the motto 'No More War' rather than the prosaic 'Haig Fund'.

The red Remembrance Poppy was in full bloom, however, strewn along the nation's streets every year, and the suggestion came to nothing – until 1933. Then, a short taxi ride across New York City from where Moina Michael had first envisioned the red Flanders Poppy, Pastor Harry Fosdick, an ex-army chaplain, gave an inspirational sermon on the occasion of Armistice Day. He entitled it 'The Unknown Soldier':

> *If I blame anybody . . . it is men like myself who ought to have known better. We went out to the army and explained to these valiant men what a resplendent future they were preparing for their children by their heroic sacrifices. [I] . . . renounce war because of what it does to our own men [and] what it compels us to do to our enemies. I renounce war for its consequences, for the lies it lives on and propagates, for the undying hatred it arouses, for the dictatorships it puts in the place of democracy, for the starvation that strikes after it.*[1]

Fosdick, like Michael, wanted to speak to the dead, and his sermon was a powerful apology to those who had died in the Great War. Fosdick's words struck a powerful chord with Canon Dick Sheppard, the motivated and energetic vicar of St Martin-in-the-Fields, in London. Sheppard had long opposed the official Remembrance Day ceremony, which he considered to be overly militaristic. In October 1925 he argued in a letter to *The Times* that raucous victory balls on the evening of Armistice Day were inappropriate, irreligious and indecent.[2]

Many agreed with him, but the issue revealed a split in the nation. Some veterans thought the living should celebrate their delivery from the angels of death, while others regarded this as blasphemy. The leader pages of the newspapers fanned the flames of public opinion by targeting the gala dinners held in such well-heeled spots as London's Ritz and Savoy hotels; the editorials even attacked the extension of drinking hours at the capital's Old Comrades Association around Remembrance Day.[3] Sheppard won the argument when the Royal Albert Hall victory ball for 1925 was postponed and replaced by a solemn service of remembrance. The ball was moved to 12 November, which one might consider a somewhat hollow victory.

Still, with that one day's difference, Sheppard's campaign began to change the way in which Armistice Day is marked in Britain. The following year, a more sombre event was held, and in 1927 the first British Legion Festival of Remembrance took place at the Royal Albert Hall. The conscience of the nation was soothed in the press, because 'No future generation can charge us with having been neglectful of "Our Glorious Dead".'[4]

As support for the No More War movement mounted, Sheppard publicly declared himself to be a pacifist. Re-energised by Fosdick's New York sermon in 1934, Sheppard penned a letter to the press in which he urged people of like mind to come together to embrace the creed of non-violence. The *Manchester Guardian* and others published it on 16 October. Sheppard was acutely aware of the widespread view that only women were pacifists, and so aimed his appeal at men, asking them to reply to his 'call to arms' and pledge that they never support war again. The response was immediate: 135,000 men took the pledge, and in a mass meeting at the Royal Albert Hall on Armistice Day, they founded a new organisation, Dr H.R.L. Sheppard's Peace Movement.

Two years later, the name was changed to the Peace Pledge Union (PPU) and women were allowed to join. The remnants of the No More War movement combined with the PPU, and the PPU rolls topped 100,000. The group attracted major figures of British society, including Vera Brittain, Benjamin Britten, Aldous Huxley, George Lansbury,

Bertrand Russell and Siegfried Sassoon (who was a celebrity for his service as an officer in the Great War) as members.

THROUGHOUT THE 1930S, the value of the sacrifices made by those who died in the 'war to end all wars' was weighed. Anxieties were growing across Europe – a second global war seemed to be looming – and fewer people participated in Armistice Day services as a consequence. As public sentiment shifted and Hitler rearmed Germany, a new symbolic flower was proposed, one that would stand resolutely for peace.

The British Women's Co-operative Guild (WCG) began life in 1883 as a typically Victorian response to issues and problems concerning domestic family life. By 1914, it had focused its daily efforts on the war, first opposing hostilities and then providing relief to those who had men at the front. Indeed, at the International Women's Congress held at The Hague in late April, the Guild was a signatory to the resolution that 'the terrible method of war should never again be used to settle disputes between nations, and urge that a partnership of nations, with peace as its object, should be established and enforced by the people's will'. Exactly two months later, the world was at war. By the end of the war, many of the Guild's members counted themselves among the wives and mothers of the war dead. It was around this time that they turned wholesale to their work of campaigning for international peace.

In 1933, after watching more and more people don the red Remembrance Poppy each November, the members searched for their own emblem, something they could wear to display their passion to banish war and to embrace non-violence. They revived the No More War movement's long-dormant suggestion of adopting a rival flower: the White Poppy, its bleached petals representing purity of thought and deed. Initially the Guild's poppies were made by the Co-operative Wholesale Society, which had a long history of supporting social reform, and the revenue was used to support conscientious objectors in Britain and across the rest of Europe. As the White Poppy became a visual 'pledge to peace that war must not happen again', ever larger quantities were in demand.

The Guild made a point of stating that the White Poppy did not merely express the longing for a world without war but also commemorated the civilian as well as military victims of past conflicts. This was meant to complement the Remembrance Poppy's evocation of spilled blood, but it did not prevent either symbol from being politicised.

The British Legion regarded the new emblem with suspicion. The question was, would the White Poppy be an offence or insult to their members, or worse, a commercial threat? At their 1934 national conference, a motion was passed that Legion members should be 'discouraged by all possible means' from wearing the White Poppy.[5] The Guild quarrelled with the British Legion's position, and claimed that in the previous year they had offered the Legion the contract to make White Poppies, including the right to keep the money raised for Haig's Fund. The Legion would not bend, however, and refused any association with what it considered to be a morally dubious rival.

Desperate for help, the Guild turned to Sheppard's newly formed peace group, which adopted the White Poppy as its own in 1936. The PPU immediately began to produce and distribute the poppies, as it still does today.

THE PPU FOLLOWED Canon Sheppard's lead and took inspiration from Harry Fosdick's sermon. Every member took the pledge: 'I renounce war and will never support or sanction another'. Such sentiments were common among the Women's Co-operative Guild, not least because their members were the distraught mothers, wives, sisters and sweethearts of men who had been killed or maimed during the war. They were natural compatriots.

The mood was for peace. As early as October 1933, the famous 'peace by-election' returned a pacifist Labour MP in the previously safe Tory seat of East Fulham. In 1934–5, Lord Robert Cecil and the League of Nations Union had surveyed 11.6 million British households (thirty-eight per cent of the population), and the overwhelming majority supported armament reductions and 'economic and non-military measures' in order to quash aggression and further war.[6] The Great Depression was strangling job opportunities across Europe, making it ever harder for wounded veterans to find a living. Most people wanted to show respect for the war dead and to support the wounded, and everyone wanted an end to all wars. The White Poppy encapsulated the British public's ambivalence towards the legacy of the Great War, and its obvious and unpalatable consequences. Wearing the red Remembrance Poppy alone did not seem to convey all that needed to be said – at least, not for everyone.

Then, on 7 March 1936, Hitler sent troops into the Rhineland in violation of the Treaty of Versailles and the Locarno Pact, which had demilitarised the area; on 17 July civil war broke out in Spain. As the Second World War grew from vague threat to reality, the White Poppy was entangled in the volatile debates over patriotism, the Depression, international sovereignty, appeasement, respect for the dead and the place of commemoration. Some resolved these dilemmas by wearing both the white and the red, as Thomas Summerbell, the mayor of

Sunderland and a 'prominent member' of the Sunderland and District Peace Council had done when he not only wore both poppies but his war medals as well on Remembrance Sunday 1936.[7] A White Poppy was worn by the lord mayor and the lady mayoress at Leeds war memorial that year, and in subsequent years White Poppy wreaths were laid on cenotaphs across the country. In many cases, they were immediately thrown off the memorials and jumped upon by angry crowds.[8]

Tensions ran deep, and the white and the red had become the opposing poles of opinion. The year 1937 saw the sale of White Poppies soar to 85,000, though this was still far below the figure for the Remembrance Poppy, and the General Secretary of the Women's Co-operative Guild felt moved to publish a pamphlet recounting the persecution of those who wore the white flower as a sign of their support for peace.[9] Here were tragic but typical tales: a woman who had patriotically toiled in a munitions factory between 1914 and 1918, who had lost a husband in the war and had worn the red Remembrance Poppy for eighteen years to honour him, could lose her job for wearing a White Poppy as a sign of her hopes that no other woman would be widowed by war. As the war machine built up on the continent, the red inevitably dominated lapels.

For Remembrance Sunday 1937, Dick Sheppard had organised an alternative ceremony in London's Regent's Park (he died unexpectedly in October and others took up the campaign). Its slogan, interestingly, was 'not peace at any price but love at all costs',[10] and the large crowd 'wore white "peace" poppies as well as the scarlet poppies of Earl Haig's Fund' according to The Times.[11] The crowd marched on Whitehall, where, with Scotland Yard's permission, several wreaths of White Poppies were laid at the Cenotaph. Considering what had occurred at the official Armistice Day ceremony earlier in the day, this was perhaps an unexpected act of leniency by the authorities.

Prime Minister Neville Chamberlain had stood perfectly still as the two-minute silence ticked away. Suddenly, a lone figure broke through a line of sailors and charged towards him. In what the *Manchester Guardian* reported as a 'high tormented voice', the man shouted 'All this hypocrisy!' before being felled by police just two yards from the prime minister.[12] Stanley Storey was a veteran, forty-three years old, and, to the government's relief, was found to have escaped from a lunatic asylum. Insane or not, Storey's outburst voiced what many must have pondered as they commemorated Armistice Day while the nation prepared for what was likely to be war. It took a deranged mind to break through the code of silence and speak the words that the sane would not.

Storey, however, was not representative of the views of his fellow veterans. Most saw the White Poppy as an insult to the sacrifice made by so many of their comrades, a silly emblem that called to mind the white feather of cowardice (used so potently to shame conscientious objectors in the Great War) and the white flag of surrender. For old soldiers, the red poppy was a peace flower, born out of suffering and loss, and avowedly non-political. To their mind, the White Poppy was too closely connected to the Labour Party.[13]

By 1938, with the *Anschluss*, the Munich Agreement, Chamberlain's appeasement over the Sudetenland and Kristallnacht vividly in the public consciousness, the battle of the poppies became more stark. Even John McCrae's poem, which had so inspired Moina Michael and Anna Guérin, gained a rival. A hymn to the White Poppy was composed, and began with the words:

> *White poppy, white poppy, you signify peace,*
> *On this day of Remembrance all war will cease;*
> *The red one beside you for memory is laid,*
> *To honour the millions who sacrifice made.*[14]

Most of those who championed the White Poppy saw it as a symbolic companion to the red one, not a replacement. The Remembrance Poppy was too hearty and vital to be extirpated as the Third Reich marched across Europe.

Just months before Britain declared war on Germany in September 1939, Prime Minister Chamberlain received a letter from a Guild mother. Her plea embodied all that the White Poppy stood for. She had not, she said, raised her twenty-year-old son 'for you to claim him now to be a cog in the wheels of a military machine which threatens mankind . . . I hope I have behind me all the mothers of sons, and the mothers of sons who have already made the supreme sacrifice to show us that war is not the way to transform the world'.[15] Hundreds of thousands did stand behind her, joining the PPU, and when war was declared most of them wore the White Poppy with a combination of pride and despair.

The British Legion, not the proponents of the White Poppy, caused some of the friction. Back in 1930, Dick Sheppard had written an article in which he demanded that 'we must never give in to the belief that the sacrifice of countless lives given with no thought of self has been in vain'.[16] This was an argument with which the Legion could not have disagreed. Occasionally, the Legion and the authorities displayed compassion to the wearers of the White Poppy. When Sheppard died, a cross was planted for him in the Field of Remembrance at Westminster Abbey by the British Legion – a meaningful gesture. Sometimes, too, a police guard was mounted on White Poppy wreaths at war memorials.[17] Yet the pendulum could easily swing the other way. The Peace Pledge Union approached the Legion on the eve of war, renewing its offer to have the Legion produce the White Poppy emblem as part of its campaigning – but to no avail.

The White Poppy was less than pure in the eyes of those opposed to Hitler's rise in Germany. Many believed that pacifist elements in

Britain had not distanced themselves sufficiently from the Nazis. In August 1940, for example, the editor of the pacifist *Peace News*, John Middleton Murry, wrote, 'Personally I don't believe that a Hitlerian Europe would be quite so terrible as most people believe it would be'.[18] In 1943, at the height of the war, the Marquess of Tavistock won election to the Peace Pledge Union council despite having founded the pro-Nazi British People's Party. He too had taken the side of the Germans in the pages of *Peace News*, referring to 'the very serious provocation which many Jews have given by their avarice and arrogance when exploiting Germany's financial difficulties [and] by their associations with commercialised vice'. The groundswell of moral outrage at such pronouncements did nothing to enhance the White Poppy's cause of peace and freedom for all.

Vera Brittain, author of the famous First World War book *Testament of Youth*, was branded by some to be a virtual apologist for the Nazis at this time. In a letter to her fellow-campaigners, on 3 May 1945, she argued that the gas chambers were being publicised by the Allies 'partly, at least, in order to divert attention from the havoc produced in German cities by Allied obliteration bombing'.[19]

Such moral failings and naivety tainted the White Poppy's purity. Throughout the inter-war years, the flower seemed to become more of a symbol of division and confusion. What is the true meaning of remembrance? Is it possible to commemorate those who have sacrificed their lives in a time of war without the politics of the conflict intruding? Would those who have fallen in the past have championed pacifism if they had survived? In raising these questions, the White Poppy became as contentious and potentially toxic as the Remembrance Poppy had been in the eyes of the Peace Pledge Union and the Women's Co-operative Guild.

AFTER THE SECOND WORLD WAR, Armistice Day became Remembrance Day in Britain, and was observed on the nearest Sunday to 11 November. New lists of the dead and wounded reinvigorated the event as an occasion for honouring and remembering the fallen. The sufferings of 1939–45, especially among civilians, meant that there was no longer the naive expectation that all war had been banished. No one called this the war to end all wars.

The White Poppy lingered in the background from the 1940s through to the 1970s, just as the Remembrance Poppy faded from among the younger generations of the 1950s and 1960s. A resurrection for the peace emblem came about during a period of dramatic political change. In the 1980s British society was polarised by mass unemployment and the forthright politics of Prime Minister Margaret Thatcher. This political swing to the right also sparked a new notoriety for the White Poppy. On the afternoon of Remembrance Sunday 1980, a silent procession walked from Trafalgar Square to the Cenotaph and laid a wreath of white flowers, to which the following dedication was attached:

> *For all those who have died or are dying in wars*
> *For all those who have died or are dying as resources*
> *to feed or house them have gone to war preparations*
> *For all those who will die until we learn to live in peace*
> *When shall we ever learn?*

The silent walk became an annual event, and the White Poppy was revived, with sales perceptibly increasing during the Falklands War of 1982. The Peace Pledge Union argued at the time that rejecting the war was not meant to support the Argentinian junta – though the British government, they said, had been happy to supply it with arms until those arms were turned on British territory.

As incendiary as that contention may have been, it was another six years before the blanched flower again grabbed the headlines in Thatcher's Britain – and more contentiously than at any other time in the previous half-century. The chain of events began in 1986, when John Baker, the Bishop of Salisbury, told the nation that the White Poppy was not an insult or provocation to the memory of the nation's war dead. 'There is space for red and white to bloom side by side', he said even-handedly. Robert Key, the local Conservative member of parliament, used the Prime Minister's question time on 28 October to offer Thatcher an open goal:

> On Sunday week, my right hon. friend the Prime Minister and other party leaders will represent us at the annual Cenotaph service. Does my right hon. friend share my deep distaste at the proposals of the so-called peace movement to substitute white poppies for red poppies? This causes deep offence to the vast majority of people and, incidentally, reduces the income of the Royal British Legion.

Thatcher replied, 'I share my hon. friend's deep distaste. The Cenotaph service is a national occasion. It brings help and comfort to all our citizens'.[20] While the Iron Lady eagerly condemned the White Poppy, it is unclear whether she knew what it represented to its supporters.

By coincidence, the PPU had just published a book for schools on the theme of 'war, peace, and remembrance'. This proved too combustible a target for the British media to resist, and they gleefully crowed about it, knowing that the Royal British Legion would react. All publicity is good publicity, however, and sales of White Poppies soared. The PPU's schoolbook was more popular than expected, and in a rekindling of the old rivalry between the American Legion and the VFW, as well as between the British Legion and PPU, the Royal British Legion refused to appear on any radio and television programme that featured PPU supporters.

On Remembrance Day old soldiers shouted abuse at two hundred anti-war protestors who proceeded to lay a wreath of White Poppies at the Cenotaph. For those with long memories, it was a rerun of the confrontations that had occurred during the inter-war years.

The White Poppy was dangerous again. It became the focus of passions in newspapers, homes and pubs up and down the nation. The furore involved the Peace Pledge Union's position that while Remembrance Day appropriately comforted the bereaved, it was also used to justify the state's decision to embark on war – any war. The government employed the red poppy to bolster the idea that war always has a valuable purpose, a 'lie', in the view of the PPU, that was 'repeated sanctimoniously every day of remembrance since 1918'.[21] 'The White Poppy symbolises the belief that there are better ways to resolve conflicts than killing strangers'.[22] They believed Remembrance Day was being hijacked, with the government and the British Legion reaffirming the noble and heroic purpose of the military rather than expressing regret about the cruel waste of lives. Their remarks fuelled an uproar.

The arguments between supporters of the White and the Red rage on. From his church in Ipswich, the Reverend Andrew Kleissner announced in November 2005 that White Poppies could be worn alongside or instead of red ones. Local war veterans said this was disgraceful. Dunkirk survivor Bernard Sharp said: 'The red poppy is a symbol of help and to remember those who've died. I lost lots of friends in the war . . . I don't recognise the white poppy.' Kleissner himself said, 'I didn't mean to cause offence, it's just something I've done for years. Christ said, "Blessed are the peacemakers".' He continued, 'I don't want to detract from the sale of red poppies and I don't want to decry the memory of those who fought, but I want to look to the future and there are ways of solving problems that don't involve conflict.'[23] The local chairman of the Royal British Legion felt obliged to restate that 'The red poppy doesn't promote war in any way. It's red for blood and has a black centre for grief'.[24]

For those who favour the Remembrance Poppy, it is sobering to discover that Kleissner's father came to England from Germany, where in the late 1930s he was involved in the student anti-Nazi movement. So committed was he that he took up arms against the Nazis by serving in the British army during the Second World War.[25] Like those Great War veterans who had known what it was to kill for their country and then became pacifists – including Siegfried Sassoon – wearing the White Poppy is an act based on personal experiences and emotions. As with any symbol, the poppy exhibits a seemingly never-ending capacity to shift and to change, to evoke slippery meanings and excite violently opposed attitudes.

Such ambivalence and bitterness is not limited to Britain. In Canada, the White Poppy has long been eyed with suspicion. In November 2006, Canadian veterans in Edmonton threatened legal action against those who sold White Poppies during Remembrance Week. Michael Kalmanovitch, a shop owner, protested that he should have the right to offer the White Poppy to his customers who wanted to display a symbol of their hope for peace. The Royal Canadian Legion wasn't buying that argument. In an echo of the fight over the adoption of Anna Guérin's Remembrance Poppy in Canada, the Legion announced that White Poppies were an insult to veterans and appeared to infringe the Legion's trademark. The RCL's local spokesman, displaying an ignorance of history and a lack of judgement, stated, 'The use of the poppy in any colour other than in blood red is a disservice and dishonour to all our fallen dead, the past and our latest veterans.' Kalmanovitch replied with devastating clarity and honesty. 'I mean it's a little bit un-Canadian that somebody has a trademark on the poppy. It would be like having a trademark on the rose in Alberta or the beaver . . . It's just bizarre.'[26]

It was an old argument, stretching back to the beginnings of Vetcraft's Remembrance Poppy production in the 1920s, when commemoration was commercialised in order to raise money for maimed veterans. While no one would deny financial help to the broken men of war, framing the issue in terms of trademarks and copyright sits uneasily with many.

Perhaps for this reason the White Poppy, almost despite itself, continues to inspire heartfelt support and provoke strong reactions. The religious think tank Ekklesia proposes that White Poppies are more Christian than red ones, because the latter imply that redemption can come through war – a forthright but contentious interpretation. Of course, the Christian value of non-violence stands at the heart of their argument, but they also suggest that the Remembrance Poppy has become a badge of political correctness as much as of commemoration, and that churches should at the very least promote the wearing of both emblems. Jonathan Bartley, co-director of Ekklesia, believes that individuals should not be vilified for wearing the White Poppy. His pronouncements stirred heated responses, with the Royal British Legion accusing Bartley of wilfully misunderstanding the Remembrance Poppy, which they see as 'a symbol of the need to reflect on the human cost of war'.[27]

For his part, Bartley is unconvinced. He says the red poppy shares much in common with the crucifix: they are both symbols of violence, bloodshed and sacrifice. He argues that while wearing the cross in public is at times frowned upon by officialdom, everyone is encouraged to wear a poppy come Remembrance Day. The Legion believes that there is a real risk that people will be confused if they are presented with both red and white emblems and will forget why it is important to buy them. If the White Poppy implies peace, they say, then the public will come to associate the red Remembrance Poppy with war. It may be a simplistic assertion, but propaganda typically is.

WHEN MOINA MICHAEL and Anna Guérin invented the Remembrance Poppy, they fashioned a symbol to inspire the generations. What would they have thought of the rivals and offshoots that have been invented in the decades since?

The Black Poppy was created by Reverend Simon Topping of Birmingham in 2001 to symbolise the problems of world poverty.[28] Playing on the phrase inscribed on countless war memorials across Britain, Topping's campaign slogan was 'Lest we forget the victims of debt'. Some in the Royal British Legion worried that the public would confuse the black emblem with the red one, following on the decades-long concern about the rival White Poppy. Topping's rebuttal: 'I shall certainly be wearing both a red and black poppy'.

During the 1960s and 1970s, antelope and water buffalo became opium addicts during the conflicts in Vietnam and Cambodia. In normal times, the animals consume just enough of the opium poppy to numb pain or relieve tiredness, but the intensity of modern warfare, incessant bombing and barrages and machine-gun fire drove them to eat more and more of the world's most ancient euphoric plant.[29] It had a deadly effect. 'Water buffalo within earshot of combat zones were . . . observed browsing opium poppies, showing signs of addiction and withdrawal'.[30]

These were far from the only animals devastated by war. In July 2006, London's Imperial War Museum launched *The Animals' War*, a special exhibition to commemorate animals that suffered and died during the human conflicts of the twentieth century. The First World War had seen dogs employed as front-line messengers, bomb and poison-gas detectors, and scouts and rescuers. Horses and donkeys were beasts of burden in battlefields, their charred and bloated carcasses caught for ever on black-and-white photographs taken above the trenches. The Belgians burned alive 2,500 messenger pigeons to avoid them being used by the advancing Germans. As an experiment, sea lions were used by the British in their efforts to detect German submarines. Other creatures served as wartime mascots, or were kept for companionship in the dark days of war. In the Second World War, the Royal Air Force bombed elephant convoys carrying Japanese war materiel. More recently, dolphins and seals have been trained by the US military to detect underwater mines. According to the animal rights charity Animal Aid, these aquatic spies are called 'advanced biological weapons systems'.[31]

At the time of the exhibition Animal Aid commented that the bravery of animals is in the human imagination – the reality is that animals are victims, not heroes.[32] Today, the charity campaigns against the use of animals in weapons testing in Britain. Pigs, mice, dogs and rats are all sacrificed by the British Ministry of Defence to test the killing power of biological and chemical weapons and the effectiveness of antidotes. As new wars flare and rage, the number of animals dying has soared. Between 2000 and 2005, their number has doubled from 11,985 to 21,118 in Britain alone.[33]

Just as traumatised Cambodian water buffalo had turned to the opium poppy in time of war, so Animal Aid decided to call upon the Remembrance Poppy to commemorate the animal victims of conflict.[34] Kate Fowler-Reeves, the charity's head of campaigns, said:

> *For years we have commemorated the human victims of*
> *war and overlooked the impact that worldwide conflicts*

have had on animals. Now, it's time to redress the bal-
ance. By wearing a purple poppy – alongside the tradi-
tional red one – we will finally be acknowledging that
millions of animals have been drafted into conflicts
not of their making and have lost their lives as a result.
Remembering them is the least we can do.[35]

Ever and again, the poppy endures as an emblem, adapting in extraordinary ways.

AMONG ALL OF THESE MUTATIONS and reinventions, one
thing is clear: the White Poppy expresses the universal human hope
for peace and no war, while the red Remembrance Poppy honours and
commemorates those who have died when war occurs. As all wars
begin with politics, it should not be surprising that competing political agendas around the two poppies can at times become venomous.
The rivalry between the supporters of the white and the red says more
about politicians, money and egos than it does about the importance
of memory to the human condition. Ironically, perhaps, the struggle
between the two poppies for the memory of the war dead guarantees
that they are not forgotten.

The Stop the War Coalition, which opposes the British military
presence in Iraq and Afghanistan as well as the so-called War on Terror,
has embraced the White Poppy as its own. Lindsey German, the coalition's convenor, accused Tony Blair of taking Britain into illegal wars
and using the Remembrance Poppy for his own ends while Blair laid
wreaths at the Cenotaph on Remembrance Sunday 2011. She refused

to wear the red poppy and adopted the white instead. In an instant, the clock seemed to turn back to 1937, when Stanley Storey broke free of the crowd to shout 'hypocrisy' at Neville Chamberlain.

German's outburst was a gross oversimplification to some – a misguided ethical objection to war that was wholly indifferent to tyranny and genocide and ignored the moral imperative of combating evil.[36] German quoted Siegfried Sassoon's 'Aftermath' for her side:

> *For the world's events have rumbled on since those*
> *gagged days,*
> *Like traffic checked while at the crossing of city-ways:*
> *And the haunted gap in your mind has filled with*
> *thoughts that flow*
> *Like clouds in the lit heaven of life; and you're a man*
> *reprieved to go,*
> *Taking your peaceful share of Time, with joy to spare.*
> *But the past is just the same – and War's a bloody*
> *game . . .*
> *Look down, and swear by the slain of the War that*
> *you'll never forget.*[37]

The obvious solution, that both poppies might be sold and worn, too often gets lost in the rhetoric and debates surrounding the politics of our most recent wars. The rise, fall and resurrection of the White Poppy during the past decade, in particular, has chained the symbolism of the Remembrance Poppy to the narcotic powers of the opium poppy, a linkage that might last for a generation. For, in a deadly twist, the kinship of the White and the Red has most bluntly struck the public's feelings through the events of the white-petalled opium fields of Helmand Province, Afghanistan.

Take, for instance, the case of Captain Nichola Goddard, Canada's highest-ranking and only woman soldier to die in Afghanistan. In May 2006 she was killed while directing artillery fire at enemy positions. Her father, whose relatives had fought on the Somme ninety years before, said he would be happy for her to be remembered with the White Poppy, not just the red one. 'Peacekeepers or peacemakers, they're all worthy of our respect', he said, arguing that all deaths – be they civilian or military – should be commemorated equally. If this was the meaning of the White Poppy, then he had no objections to it. Perhaps, he added, it would help bring an end to the war so that his daughter's death would not have been in vain.[38]

The irony is that the opium poppies cultivated in Afghanistan, those whose cultivation has bankrolled the insurgency there, are mainly pure white or purple, and vastly outnumber the red varieties of the flower. It was white poppies – real ones – that helped to support the forces that killed Nichola Goddard in battle, while artificial ones commemorate her.

8

THE NARCOTIC GRASP
ON HELMAND

THE EVENTS OF 11 SEPTEMBER 2001 BROUGHT THE
dark side of the poppy back into the public eye. Out of the blue, it
seemed, two passenger jets passed above New York's streets, just miles
from where Moina Michael had bought her first poppies in 1918 and
experienced her very Christian revelation. As the World Trade Center
burst into flames and then collapsed into a billowing shroud of dust
and debris, and as two more planes crashed into the Pentagon and a
field in Pennsylvania, 2,977 people were killed in what would soon be
christened the 'War on Terror'.

In the immediate aftermath of the terrorist attacks, the Veterans
of Foreign Wars did what it had always done: it established a tribute
to the dead and the missing. The 9/11 Memorial Poppy did not replace
the venerable Buddy Poppy, but renewed the contract between respect
and remembrance – between the living and the dead.[1] It was an irony
worthy of the scarlet bloom that the birthplace of the Remembrance

Poppy saw the invention of the 9/11 Poppy, whose purpose was to commemorate the deaths that would lead to a vicious war dictated by the opium poppy.

According to America's leaders, the 'axis of the evil' could be found in the network of terrorist training camps that had been built in the remotest regions of Afghanistan over the previous decade. When Afghanistan's fundamentalist Taliban regime refused to hand over Osama bin Laden, the self-proclaimed head of al-Qaeda ('The Base'), the US response was to invade the country. The Americans were joined by a coalition of allied nations, including Britain and other Coalition partners in Operation Enduring Freedom. The nightmare of the Great War returned, as soon American and British soldiers were dying in the poppy fields of war once again.

FOR THE BRITISH, there was more than a whiff of nineteenth-century imperialism in the fearsome battles that followed the Coalition invasion. They had last fought in Afghanistan's opium winds during the summer of 1880, when an entire British army force was all but annihilated by Pashtun tribesmen at the Battle of Maiwand on the banks of Helmand River. It was one of the worst military disasters of British colonial history, at a time when the British Empire was the undisputed superpower of the world. Famously, Arthur Conan Doyle made Sherlock Holmes's faithful companion Dr Watson a survivor of Maiwand – and an outspoken critic of Holmes's habitual use of morphine. Afghanistan's opium cost Britain too dearly. History made Britain the worst possible choice of nations to police Helmand Province, and it remains a mystery as to how this decision was made[2] – but in

2004 the G8 nations elected Britain to spearhead the fight against narcotics in Afghanistan.

Invaders have received shrill warnings from the natives of Helmand throughout history. Alexander the Great was forced to fortify the region – then a province of the Persian Empire – more heavily than any of the other vast areas that he conquered. He spent years of his short life, and unrivalled amounts of energy and manpower, in his attempts to subdue Afghanistan. During the 1400s, Genghis Khan similarly waged bloody battles in Helmand, feeding his seemingly insatiable desire for vengeance against the unruly natives by devastating their land and murdering the entire populations of the medieval cities of Herat and Balkh. Empire after empire arrived and withdrew, each leaving a legacy of struggles and rubble. Then in the nineteenth century the British came onto the scene and tried to make Afghanistan their pawn in the 'Great Game'.

This geopolitical struggle with Russia led to the first two Anglo-Afghan Wars (1839–42 and 1878–80), the first of which saw 4,500 British soldiers and 12,000 camp followers perish in a disastrous retreat from Kabul in January 1842. After a series of alternating victories and defeats between the British and Afghans, the second war ended in May 1879 with the signing of the Treaty of Gandmak, under which the Emir of Afghanistan, Mohammad Yaqub Khan, granted control of his country's foreign policy and strategic border territories to Britain. The Third Anglo-Afghan War lasted just a few months (May to August 1919), and while it was deemed to be a minor tactical success for the British, they suffered 1,751 casualties, almost double those of the Afghans. The Afghans subsequently regained control of their foreign policy and became independent with the signing of the Treaty of Rawalpindi on 19 August 1919. The British left in disarray.

One might think these repeated lessons would have made modern empire-makers a bit shy when it came to the land of the Afghans, but the Soviet Union was also drawn into its lethal trap. After months of ignoring the pleas for military support from Afghanistan's Communist government, Soviet premier Leonid Brezhnev sent several hundred troops into Kabul on 27 December 1979 to begin the campaign against 'Islamic warriors' – the *mujahideen*. Within a few weeks, more than one hundred thousand troops had flooded into the country; eventually half a million would serve there. By the time the Soviets gave up the fight in 1989, 14,453 Soviet personnel had been killed and some US $60 billion had been spent. Here was yet another empire conquered by hubris.

History, however, is too often ignored before it is even written.

HELMAND PROVINCE SPRAWLS across 58,584 square kilometres of southern Afghanistan and is home to over a million people, who are predominantly ethnic Pashtun. Fatefully, its main products are wheat, maize and opium, with the last crop having been smuggled across the nation's unstable borders for centuries, particularly through networks of ethnic kin in what is today Pakistan and Iran and with whom they share political, economic and family allegiances. Helmand means 'many dams', and before the Russian invasion, much of the region was criss-crossed by elaborate networks of canals that irrigated the fields and yielded a rich harvest of crops. War would destroy this subtle hydraulic regime.

Natural disasters too have helped to make Helmand a terrorists' paradise. Severe droughts regularly cripple the region, and in 2001 ninety-five per cent of all crops were destroyed, displacing three quarters of the population. Around the town of Now Zad, in northern Helmand, workable agricultural land was reduced from 80,000 hectares

(200,000 acres) to 5,000 hectares (12,000 acres) between 2000 and 2003 due to lack of rainfall and the disrepair of canals.[3] British forces would eventually move into this seething cauldron of geography, history, religion and opium.[4]

During the 1950s, the region was known as 'Little America', because it was the focus of a massive irrigation project – the Helmand Valley Authority, modelled on America's Great Depression-era Tennessee Valley Authority and exported to Afghanistan by the TVA's director David Lilienthal. The centrepiece of the programme was the construction of a hydroelectric dam, paid for by the American taxpayer. This expensive and backbreaking work paid off handsomely, opening up the desert to agriculture and settlement, and transforming Helmand into a thriving hub of the Afghan economy. Fifty years later, US taxpayers were financing the wholesale destruction of the dazzling infrastructure that their parents and grandparents had paid for – all to remove the opium-funded Taliban from every corner of Afghanistan.

The irony of the American response to the Taliban is epitomised in the fate of Lashkar Gah, Helmand's capital. The city's name derives from the Persian for 'army barracks', and for a thousand years its mud-brick monuments have stood as the strategic foundation stone of the region. The modern city was built during the 1950s to serve as a headquarters for the engineers working on a massive irrigation project. Recreating provincial Americana in the wilds of southern Afghanistan, the planners laid out broad, tree-lined streets and threw up reassuringly solid brick houses which had no need for walls to separate them from the road. Areas were designated across the city as pleasant and well-irrigated green parks.

Everything ended with the Soviet invasion in 1979. When the Americans left, the trees came down and garden walls went up. During the decade of conflict that followed, Lashkar Gah and its economic hinterland were ravaged and unemployment rocketed. The only growth, it seemed, was in the countryside, where opium-poppy cultivation became a barometer of cultural change and the road sign to a troubled future.

Today Lashkar Gah is the scene of a deadly insurgency carried out in the shell of a facsimile America. The once stately avenues are frequently haunted by suicide bombers, strapped up and ready to hit 'detonate' should a Coalition soldier appear. Over the years of the war, the Taliban have scored many successes, with dozens of British soldiers killed and wounded while patrolling the city's streets. In response, the British army abandoned regular patrols as too tempting a target.

The danger threshold oscillates, however, with lulls in the violence coming with the opium-poppy harvest. Each year as the poppy crops matured, Taliban commanders would promise to suspend fighting. It stands to reason, since the poppy has supplied the Taliban with millions of dollars in funds to launch their attacks.[5] More recently, the Taliban called the region's farmers to a *shura* or 'consultation', and ordered them to grow opium. The poppy, it seems, rules the countryside and the city, as shown in November 2007 with the seizure by Afghan and British forces of one hundred kilograms of opium in the city's District Centre. A drop in the ocean of Helmand's narcotic bounty, it nevertheless had a street value of one million US dollars.

War is the catalyst for the proliferation of the poppy. Since 2001, many farmers in Afghanistan have abandoned traditional crops and now grow opium instead. The poppy is the ideal low-risk crop in a high-risk environment[6] – a perfect product for the insurgents and the farmers alike because of its high commercial value, low shipping weight and seemingly endless global consumer demand. The United Nations recently announced that more than half of the country's poppy farmers only began planting opium after the 2001 invasion, and in Helmand seventy per cent of poppy growing is new to the land since 2005.[7] So-called narco-farmers find it economically attractive to irrigate the barren desert to grow opium, particularly near towns and alongside the remnants of the old American canal system – but not to grow anything else.

Opium is not a naturally rare commodity of great value, but a product whose supply and demand depends on fashion. Historically its price has been set on the winds of diplomacy and conflict, as during the Chinese Opium Wars, and the battle over Afghanistan and its opium trade has proved to be no exception. Underwriting the Coalition's invasion was a US narcotics policy that, since the First World War, had demonised opium and its derivatives. History repeats itself in unexpected ways.

In June 1965, as hostilities in Vietnam escalated, the Chinese Premier Zhou Enlai met Egyptian President Gamal Abdel Nasser in Alexandria, on Egypt's Mediterranean coast. The two men discussed America's involvement in South-East Asia. Zhou was reported to have said:

> the more troops they send to Vietnam, the happier we will be, for we feel that we will have them in our power, we can have their blood . . . Some of them are trying opium. And we are helping them. We are planting the best kinds of opium especially for the American soldiers in Vietnam. Do you remember when the West imposed opium on us? They fought us with opium. And we are going to fight them with their own weapons.[8]

Zhou's hope came true. A 1973 US government report revealed that in 1971,[9] the year in which President Richard Nixon first officially declared an American 'War on Drugs', forty-two per cent of American military personnel serving in Vietnam had used opiates, and half of them had become addicts. Despite mandatory testing for heroin among servicemen starting in 1971, many veterans brought their habit home, and this contributed to the explosion of heroin use across the United States over the next decade.

Throughout the 1970s and 1980s, American domestic and foreign policy encompassed anti-drug trafficking measures. Near the end of President Ronald Reagan's tenure in office, the US Congress passed the National Narcotics Leadership Act of 1988, establishing the US Office of National Drug Control Policy headed by the so-called drug czar. The US government approved military operations in a number of Latin American countries in an effort to stop drug trafficking.

So perhaps it is not a surprise that the US military commanders and other Coalition leaders came to Afghanistan somewhat obsessed with destroying the opium crop. This would prove to be a calamitous mistake. The fundamentalist Taliban had initially outlawed the growing of opium poppies as 'un-Islamic'. According to the *Ahadith*, the official account of the life of the Prophet Muhammad, 'If a large amount of anything causes intoxication, a small amount of it is prohibited.'[10] Between 2000 and 2001, the Taliban government had, with the help of the United Nations, all but eradicated poppy growing in many areas. There was a ninety-four per cent fall in opium production, with only 184 tons being harvested in the months preceding the 9/11 attacks. The programme was widely described as 'the largest single cutback in illicit drug production ever',[11] but it was a sham.

The Taliban had co-operated with the UN in the hopes of obtaining recognition for their regime – and millions of dollars in international aid. Hedging their bets, they purchased vast amounts of opium on the side. When the price of the drug soared after the ban – from £20 ($28) to £275 ($400) a kilogram – the Taliban cashed in spectacularly.[12]

Despite this double-dealing coup, it is still a bitter truth that the

2001 American-led invasion increased opium production thirty-three fold, to some 6,100 tons. The reason was as simple as it was deadly: military action brought chaos to rural Afghan society, and peasant farmers were forced to abandon their traditional wheat crop. The switch was lucrative – wheat brought in about £85 per hectare ($300 per acre), the opium poppy £200 per hectare ($700 per acre). The consequences were predictable.

In 2006, when Abdul Ghani, a greying Afghan farmer, cast his eye over a field carpeted with opium poppies, he reported that he was torn between his desire to feed his family and to combat the Taliban insurgency. The meagre rewards for growing wheat and tomatoes simply could not compete with the money that came from opium. Opium 'isn't something we can eat and we're not opium addicts', he said with a sigh of resignation. 'We're very poor people. To feed our families we grow poppies'.[13] Another farmer approached some American soldiers who were burning a poppy field. 'We're poor – we're not with the Taliban or anything,' he said. 'You've made a big mistake. Now we'll grow more [poppies] against you . . . I have to feed my children.'[14] Such statements sounded a vital warning to politicians in Washington and London. As the US ambassador at the time remarked, 'There is more linkage here in Helmand between the drug trade and the Taliban and terrorism than there is anywhere else in Afghanistan'.[15] Yet the warnings went unheeded, and the Coalition missed its chance to control the poppy – though perhaps the poppy is uncontrollable.

The Taliban were quicker. They changed their minds, capitalised on the Coalition's error of judgement and openly accepted the poppy. Taliban commanders gained sympathy and support by offering protection to impoverished local farmers against Coalition forces that were targeting their opium fields. The Taliban levied an 'opium tax' for this service, turning events to their own tactical advantage. Not only was the protection money used to buy weapons and pay for suicide bomb-ings, but the insurgents started booby-trapping the opium fields with explosives, making the poppies themselves a weapon against intrusions from American and British soldiers. The opium poppy was literally a 'flower of death', planted in a different No Man's Land.

Vast quantities of opium began to be produced in Afghanistan, accelerated by the new relationship between impoverished farmers, the Taliban and drug-traffickers, and aided by the Coalition's alienation of local people. The statistics are as staggering as they are depressing. In the 1980s, thirty per cent of the world's illegal opium came from Afghanistan, yet by 2006 this had risen to ninety-two per cent in a busi-ness worth $3.1 billion (£1.8 billion). By the time this hit the streets of cities such as London and Paris, usually as heroin, the total had leapt to an astonishing $38 billion.[16]

Afghanistan's total opium harvest was 193,000 hectares (480,000 acres) by 2007 – some ninety-three per cent of the world's supply.[17] A deadly shift had occurred by this time, as the number of poppy-free Afghan provinces jumped from six to thirteen. Opium growing had relocated to the insecure south and west of the country, and now seventy per cent of Afghanistan's opium came from the region most affected by resistance to the Coalition forces.[18] It was a marriage of extraordinary convenience for the insurgents, and a nightmare for the Afghan government and its international allies.

Helmand became the new focus for opium production. In 2003, it produced nineteen per cent of Afghanistan's total poppy crop, and by 2005 it was twenty-five per cent. The UN's *Afghanistan Opium Survey 2005* sharply defined the issues for the province. One third of wheat fields were given over to opium growing, and the total opium yield was one thousand metric tons, worth about £3,000 per hectare (or $2,200 per acre) – more than ten times the price for an equivalent haul in wheat.[19] In other words, 'the total value of opium produced in Helmand reached a staggering US $143 million, compared to the total value of wheat produced at only US $44 million'.[20] The nightmare grew exponentially, and by 2007 the province's output had soared to $528 million (about £270 million).[21]

When wheat hit twenty cents (ten pence) per kilo, and opium $141 (£70), the blowback was obvious. A farmer's ability to feed his family was determined increasingly by whether or not he chose to cultivate the poppy. Equally persuasive in this decision was the 'poppy credit' offered by middlemen – an almost irresistible payoff to poor farmers who supplied raw opium. This inducement became so widespread that land rental values were often calculated according to poppy production estimates rather than probable wheat yield. Life and death in Helmand was traded in the weight of opium poppies.

Swiftly, Helmand Province grew to be the source of more opium than entire countries, such as Myanmar (Burma), supplying about fifty per cent of the world's production in 2008. While only four per cent of Afghanistan was under poppy cultivation, Afghanistan's overall poppy production had jumped significantly in each of the two years previous. Around 380,000 people – a third of the region's population – relied on poppy growing for their daily bread. Astronomical revenues were siphoned off by the insurgents, who bankrolled increasingly deadly attacks on Coalition forces and even fellow Afghans with their narco-wealth. By March 2008 the situation had become so critical that it prompted an official communiqué issued jointly by the US State Department, the British Foreign Office, the Afghan government, the International Security Assistance Force (ISAF, formerly the Coalition) and the United Nations Office on Drugs and Crime.[22]

Such documents often put a gloss on the tarnished policies of the past by being partial and selective. This communiqué did not break that tradition. Counter-narcotics activities, the statement suggested, were currently focused on destroying the opium crops belonging to major landowners, who were in league with the major traffickers, corrupt officials and Taliban sympathisers. Poor farmers, who were merely trying to eke out a living, were not their target. Yet it is after all farmers, not landowners, who grow and harvest crops, and while it may be true that many farmers in Helmand live on about one US dollar a day, it's wrong to imply that opium profits were not reaching the region's poor. When poppies were ripe, seasonal harvesters could earn fifteen dollars a day, and tenant farmers could receive $15,000 (£7,500) for growing one hundred square metres of poppies[23] – princely sums that put a lie to the idea that ordinary farmers were not part of the opium trade. The conclusions are, alas, inescapable. Years of ISAF initiatives led to an increase, not a decrease, in Helmand's opium-poppy cultivation, resulting in a flood of cheap heroin on the international market, mostly in Europe, where more than ninety-two per cent of the drug ends up.

Beginning in the summer of 2009, the drug wealth was extracting its levy, as Helmand became an ever more lethal killing field for American and British troops. The ISAF had put additional forces into the region as part of the 'Panther's Claw' operation, a pre-election offensive aimed at pushing the insurgents out of central Helmand in order to enable the province's eighty thousand residents to vote. A litany of casualties ensued, including the death of ten British soldiers. Within days of the election it was announced that turnout was estimated to have been between five per cent and eight per cent of the population – and possibly far lower – and that only 150 Afghans who had been made safe by Panther's Claw had cast a ballot. Ten British soldiers had died for 150 Afghan votes.[24]

Poppy wealth was employed to acquire more sophisticated weaponry and tactics against the ISAF. The use of improvised explosive devices, or IEDs, was imported from the insurgency in Iraq, and proved a deadly addition to the Taliban's arsenal. The term 'improvised' is misleading, however, as it gives the impression of a ragtag army grop- ing for any weapon available to kill the infidel invaders. In fact, poppy money was being ploughed into the research and development of new versions of these weapons, as with the introduction in 2009 of roadside IEDs made of carbon and glass that could thwart metal detectors. Their effectiveness was shown to deadly effect in July of that year, when the first nineteen British soldiers were killed by the bombs.[25] Scores more have been injured and killed by the innovative IEDs in the past few years.

When such weapons are combined with opium-fuelled corruption, not least among the Afghan police, they are certainly deadly. In August 2009, after a presumed tip-off from local police, a Taliban hit squad detonated an IED underneath a vehicle carrying three British Special Forces soldiers near Lashkar Gah. Once the bomb had exploded, the Taliban ambushed the soldiers with rocket-propelled grenades and machine guns.[26] One nefarious variation is the so-called daisy-chain tactic, an ambush where one soldier is wounded by an IED and, when others go to help, they are wounded or killed by a second bomb. A daisy-chain attack was responsible for the deaths of three other British soldiers in August 2009 in Sangin, a major centre of the opium trade,[27] and many more have lost their lives in similar attacks since.

There was, of course, a surge in Taliban attacks leading up to the 2009 Afghan elections, but the relationship between the poppy and the insurgency's violence had long been clear. In December 2007, ISAF soldiers retook the Taliban stronghold of Musa Qala (the 'Fortress of Moses') in Helmand, taking some eleven thousand kilograms of opium and thirty-two kilograms of heroin, along with the equipment used to manufacture the processed drug. The haul – totalling eighty-five sacks of narcotics – had a street value of £150 million.[28] In the tradition of the corn poppy emerging from the bloody trenches of the Great War, the opium poppy can at times take on a metaphysical identity that is rooted in its physical reality. As ISAF General Dan McNeill put it: 'When I see a poppy field, I see it turning into money and then into IEDs, AKs [assault rifles], and RPGs [rocket propelled grenades]'.[29]

McNeill's words, in their own way, are a modern recasting of Moina Michael's vision, albeit phrased in military language. The poppy, Michael had said after the First World War, was the frailest of flowers, yet it somehow signified that the blood of heroes never dies – that it was eternal. After 1918, the corn poppy lent its appearance to the Remembrance Poppy, the badge whose proud display was a measure of societal reconstruction in those countries devastated by the war. Afghanistan or Iraq has replaced France, the poppy's colour has changed and the politics are more contorted, but for the men and women who daily risk their lives, little has changed in ninety years.

Today, when we think of war, it is often the opium poppy that comes to mind. It is the herald of a distinctly twenty-first-century catastrophe, just as the scarlet corn poppy stands for the terrible leap into the modern age that came with the Great War. It is the cruellest irony that the tragedies of Helmand were financed by a tax levied to protect the opium poppy from American and British soldiers.

It is difficult to think of a purer example of the ambiguous but often lethal relationship between the poppy and human suffering – yet there is one. A startling reverse trade has begun, which harks back to the dawn of civilisation in the Fertile Crescent of Mesopotamia. The sweet, heavy scent of opium poppies may hang heavily above the killing fields of Helmand, but that has not kept it from travelling westwards on the winds of war.

Beginning in 2007, if not earlier, rice farmers along the banks of the River Euphrates south of the Iraqi capital of Baghdad were growing opium poppies for the first time in thousands of years.[30] As we saw earlier, the first known written mention of opium was inscribed on wet clay tablets found at the Sumerian city of Nippur and dated to 3400BCE. Nippur is just to the east of Diwaniya, the centre of Iraq's renewed cultivation.

Hot and humid, the low-lying plains of Diwaniya are not a natural home for the opium poppy, and growers are having difficulties. (In ancient times, it is likely that most opium came from the nearby highlands to the east.) The area remains a dangerous place, controlled by Shia militias whose bitter rivalry during the last years of US occupation may have been sparked by a fight over the rewards expected from the anticipated opium harvest. If the terrain and climate allow, the crop is poised to make its way swiftly into the international heroin market, since drug smugglers have long used Iraq as a transit point for Afghan heroin; indeed, trade was once controlled by Saddam Hussein's secret police based in Basra.

The likelihood of southern Iraq becoming a major opium and heroin supplier is lessened, however, by the fact that Iraqis themselves have not historically consumed significant quantities of the drug, even though their ninth-century leaders were ardent champions of its medical and recreational value.[31] But the threat remains. Opium profits in Afghanistan have been so astronomical that there must be a great temptation among the gangs that control the Diwaniya region's fields to turn them over to the poppy. And, as with wheat in Helmand, rice growing in Iraq cannot compete with the narcotic dream, in terms of financial reward or potential for stirring conflict. For the ancient Sumerians, opium was *Hul Gil*, the 'joy plant' – a quality entirely absent in modern cultivation.

AMERICAN, BRITISH, CANADIAN and other Coalition forces came to Afghanistan to hunt down Osama bin Laden and his Taliban protectors. They cited too a desire to build a democratic future for the nation – though controlling the strategic oil corridor that runs from central Asia to the Indian Ocean also played its part. But the invaders were soon drawn to the poppy fields, with all their dangers and contradictions – sometimes destroying the crops, and at other times compromised into protecting them, whatever the official policy at home was at the time.

Confusion reigned in the Coalition's attitudes towards the poppy from the start. Should opium fields be eradicated, and if so, who should do it, and how? One suggested policy seemed to involve a grotesque entanglement with the poppy, then and now – adopting chemical warfare, not much different to that conducted just days before John McCrae wrote his famous poem in April 1915 outside Ypres in Belgium.

Recalling the American military's experience using Agent Orange in Vietnam, in March 2006 the US House of Representatives passed a bill requiring the American government to research the use of myco-herbicides (fungus-based herbicides) to eradicate illicit heroin crops in both South America and Afghanistan. The bill was sent to the Senate for debate, where an all-out spraying programme was considered, but only an initial study of the idea was passed as part of the law. According to *Forbes* magazine, however, the study was never con-ducted,[32] though that hasn't stopped commentators from pushing the Bush administration and later the Obama White House to adopt the scheme. This despite the fact that decades of research had shown the herbicides' unsuitability by virtue of 'indiscriminately destroying fruit and vegetable crops, causing open sores and feminisation in reptiles and other animals, and sickening humans' as well as contaminating the soil for years.[33]

The Afghan government appeared split, with President Hamid Karzai preferring to offer sweeteners and alternatives to the farmers to wean them off the narcotic, while Vice-President Ahmad Zia Massoud supported some sort of chemical intervention. A counter-narcotics expert at the British embassy in Kabul expressed his country's view that aerial spraying would be handing the insurgents a propaganda coup. 'Every subsequent birth defect, or "two-headed cow"', he said, would be blamed on the spraying.[34]

The power of opium was not foreseen by the Coalition. Destroying poppy fields did not feature in the British army's original plan, and they had neither the time nor the resources to pursue the strategy at the beginning of the war. When they first entered the town of Sangin, they had no answer to the burning question that seemed to be on everybody's lips: 'Will you ban poppies?'[35] When the UN and the Afghan government called for help from ISAF, they were told that this was not their responsibility.[36] Yet in January 2006 the British defence secretary John Reid announced that British troops in Helmand will 'support international efforts to counter the narcotics trade which poisons the economy in Afghanistan and poisons so many young people in this country'.[37]

In 2009, the British House of Commons Foreign Affairs Committee issued a critical report concerning the nation's objectives in Afghanistan. Too many decisions had been dominated, the authors said, by incoherence and 'mission creep'. Instead of focusing on military matters, British soldiers had been sucked into poppy eradication, nation building and human rights causes.[38] The opium poppy had become irresistible, and had diverted precious resources away from the British mission. Whatever politicians said, soldiers on the ground inhabited a very different world.

HAMBURGER HILL is a thirty-metre-high sandy dune near the deserted town of Garmser, another major centre for the opium trade, in the badlands of southern Helmand.[39] In April 2008 it was fortified by a contingent of Scottish soldiers armed with machine guns. Here, the struggle against the Taliban takes precedence over the destruction of opium.

Contradictions rule the hilltop bunker, whose location affords an apprentice's training in the opium-poppy trade. Poppy fields are watered by the remnants of the irrigation canals built by the Americans during the 1950s. That leaves the hill floating like an island in a sea of pink poppies, with the Coalition soldiers posted at its summit separated from the insurgents by a measly strip of barbed wire. 'As you can see, we are surrounded 360 degrees by poppy,' said Sergeant Brian Russell of 5 Scots A Company as he stood behind a Javelin rocket launcher. Just beyond the wire, turbaned men hunched over each poppy bloom in turn, expertly slicing the bulbous pod and collecting the oily, creamy resin that oozed out. Sergeant Russell noted, 'They start after dawn and don't finish till last light.' The British forces even had a bird's-eye view, provided by a surveillance camera suspended from a balloon, which recorded the comings and goings at the local drug lord's enclave.

Thousands of workers travelled thirty-three miles from Lashkar Gah to attend to the fields. They were well paid for their work. After being collected into glass jars, the resin would be handed off to a man on a motorcycle and smuggled across the 'Desert of Death' to the Pakistani border, 120 miles away. While the riders were probably Taliban – and it was an open secret that this opium funded the insurgency – the Scottish soldiers would sometimes chat with the workers, and would give their children sweets; they would even lend the occasional hand. When one poppy worker arrived at the camp gate suffering from heat exhaustion, he was referred to the main British base in Garmser town, less than a mile away, and was treated by a military doctor. 'We're not much interested in what they are doing with the poppy,' said Sergeant Russell. 'We know it's going on but we're soldiers, not politicians. And we're here to do a good job.'[40]

The British have had to be pragmatic. That has usually meant not interfering with the opium harvest. As Major Neil Den-McKay, the commanding officer of A Company, said in 2008, 'Right now we cannot set the conditions where counter-narcotics operations would be beneficial to British forces in Garmser. And let's face it, if we cannot provide an alternative livelihood to people, we must just accept it.' Wrestling with economic and moral issues beyond his control, he added, 'Before we start banging a drum about what is right and wrong, we should reduce the demand in the UK.'[41]

This is a brave man's view born of experience, not ideology, and it is at one with the opinions of the Afghan farmers themselves. 'We're sorry if opium causes sadness for people, but we don't make them eat it or smoke it . . . Besides, it's not us who turn it into heroin,' the farmers say.[42] Ordinary soldiers also see the contradictions – both in Afghanistan and at home. Fusilier Matt Seal observed, 'I go back to England, I live in the city of Birmingham where the heroin problem is outrageous – and ninety per cent of it comes from here.'[43]

Despite such statements, poppy propaganda hijacked much of the political debate and most of the attention of the invasion forces in the south of Afghanistan – what has been called 'Helmandcentricity'. The default excuse for the continuing military sacrifices in Helmand almost always comes down to the fight against opium.[44] For those nations devoted to annual Remembrance Poppy Appeals, the rhetoric can at times be hard to swallow, as ever more commemorative wreaths of red paper poppies are placed on memorials for men and women whose deaths have been in response to the 'narco-terror threat'. As if in a cruel dream, British and Coalition forces now lay innumerable Remembrance Poppies in army bases across Helmand to commemorate their fallen comrades.[45] The corn poppy and the opium poppy were once again locked in a deadly embrace.

THICK OPIUM FUMES escape into the cold dawn air through the door of Islam Beg's house in the hamlet of Sarab, north-east of Kabul. The curse of opium strikes everywhere, not just at Coalition soldiers and Western drug addicts. Here, even the newborn are not immune. Beg puffs out a cloud of smoke, and then his wife passes the pipe to their daughter, who promptly blows it into the mouth of her one-year-old baby boy. Their faces are drawn and wan. They are slaves to the narcosis.[46]

Beg's addiction has long since turned his home into a hovel. He has sold every one of his possessions to feed the family habit. 'I am ashamed of what I have become,' he said, gesturing towards his five-year-old grandson with sorrow. 'I've lost my self-respect . . . I take the food from this child to pay for my opium. He just stays hungry.'[47]

It wasn't always like this, either for Beg and his family, or the thousands like them who live in remote communities scattered across Afghanistan's inaccessible mountain ranges. The Soviet invasion and the War on Terror have impoverished whole villages. It is war, as ever, that has transformed the opium poppy from folk-medicine painkiller to destroyer of communities. In Sarab, where once only a single family smoked opium, about half the village – some nine hundred people – are now addicted. The place is drowning in opium. The nearest drug clinic boasts two thousand people on its waiting list, yet has only thirty beds for patients. Despite the millions of dollars pumped into Afghanistan over the past decade, relief from this addiction, pain and despair seems as far away as ever. 'Once you're hooked, it's over. You're finished,' Beg said.[48]

Opium stories often freeze the blood with their cold cruelty. Consider the tale of a teenage addict who was 'rescued' from his addiction – and brought to work on a poppy farm.[49] Throughout the country, perhaps as many as 3 million of the 28 million Afghans are involved to some degree in opium growing, with farms serviced by an additional 225,000 traders, all of whom have easy access to the drug. The UN calculated in 2005 that there were almost 1 million drug users in the country,[50] of whom perhaps 150,000 were addicted to opium and 50,000 to heroin,[51] for a combined total of 200,000 addicts. Compare this to the 150,000 addicts in the United States, with a total population of 307 million. Criminalising the behaviour of such a large percentage of the Afghan population is not an option, and would only drive them further into the arms of the Taliban.[52] To make matters worse, in Helmand the police force is said to be riddled with addicts. Abdul Rahman Jan, a major figure in the opium trade, was the provincial police chief until 2006. More worrying still is the general level of drug-related corruption in Afghan government circles and the building of so-called poppy palaces, often referred to as 'narcotecture', in the upmarket Sherpa neighbourhood of Kabul. These garish and grandiose mansions cost hundreds of thousands of dollars to build and are funded by the illegal proceeds of opium production.[53]

Alternatives to the poppy are urgently needed but problematic.[54] Numerous attempts to wean farmers off opium by offering them financial compensation to return to wheat and other crops were mishandled. The British promised to pay Helmand farmers £200 ($350) for destroying every fifth of a hectare of their opium poppies in 2005. The farmers honoured their side of the agreement, but the British did not – at least in the view of the Afghans. A year later, no payments had been made, and anger and frustration boiled over among farmers.[55] At the same time, over three thousand British soldiers were about to be deployed in Helmand Province to protect anti-drug activities.

After more than three thousand years, the poppy's hold on the region may be loosening. Botanists have discovered that there are more varieties of pomegranate tree in Afghanistan than anywhere else in the world, and that it may be the birthplace of the fruit. With demand for 'anti-oxidant'-rich pomegranate juice rising in the West, a seedless variety has been identified as a potential 'billion-dollar project' that could be a lucrative agricultural alternative to the poppy.[56] One early adopter, twenty-eight-year-old farmer Mushtaq Rahman from Kapisa Province, reported that he was growing more pomegranates than ever. 'It's good for the blood and these pomegranates are the best in the world,' he said.[57]

It has been difficult to create alternative livelihoods in Helmand, despite the international community's best intentions and one of the largest investments of foreign aid. In a classic case of mistaken priorities, the US Agency for International Development (USAID) earmarked $84 million for Afghanistan in 2005–6 but committed its budget to building infrastructure and promoting business services. This included funding for the river and irrigation systems of the old Helmand Valley project, which repairs canals, water gates and riverbank structures that have been deteriorating over the decades.[58] Despite the huge cash injection, Helmand received one of the lowest cash payments for replacing the poppy crop. At the same time, poppy growers were more than grateful for the improved irrigation that they did receive.

Disasters are perhaps inevitable, but not all efforts to eradicate the poppy failed. Poppy-free areas in Afghanistan increased from six to thirteen of the country's twenty-eight provinces in 2007, though sometimes less by a troubled eradication programme than the seductive call of political power. In south-east Nangarhar province, previously the country's second most productive poppy-growing region, production shrank almost to zero in 2008 because the local governor wanted to contest the presidential elections in 2009.[59] (He lost.) Nevertheless, opium's cash value to the Taliban and others is so great that the problem simply moves to another hot spot, and so today Afghanistan is still awash with opium.

AS A RESULT OF VARIOUS POLITICAL SHIFTS, Helmand emerged as the key opium-growing region, and the focus for Coalition eradication initiatives. In 2008, attempts to destroy the poppy crop with tractors and sticks yielded meagre results. Several workers were killed and dozens more were injured, but only four thousand hectares (ten thousand acres) of opium were destroyed – including just one fifth of the crop belonging to the notorious Abdul Rahman Jan.

A new initiative was launched in 2009, when Helmand's governor Gulab Mangal created a £3.5 million (£6 million) 'food zone' and the first realistic alternative for the area's 32,000 farmers. British taxpayers donated £2 million worth of fertilisers to replenish the nutrients taken by the poppy from the soil, and then tendered wheat seeds as a replacement crop, with the aim of restoring Helmand to its former position as the bread basket of Afghanistan. Grateful farmers were caught in the crossfire between the Coalition and the Taliban, and many remained wary of the offer, having become as dependent on opium in their own way as any heroin addict on the streets of London, Paris or New York.

A farmer named Hoomayoon typified the ambivalent response. He was supporting an extended family of sixty on eighteen hectares of land cultivated with opium poppies. 'The money we [previously] got for the poppy was good,' he said, 'but the Taliban took taxes on it.' He and his two brothers had previously tried to break the narcotic chain by growing melons and carrots, but it had simply not been enough to feed their families. 'It will be good not to worry about feeding my family, and not to pay money to the Taliban . . . Opium is a forbidden crop and I've seen its effects on young people in Afghanistan. It makes people sleepy and lazy. I'm glad not to be growing it any more.'[60] Foremost in his reasoning was the fact that farmers and their families can't eat opium. He was appreciative of the British initiative.

While he may prefer the extra money brought by poppy growing, that wealth could only be obtained by dealing with the hostile world of the Taliban and their drug-trafficking enablers, and that inevitably attracted the attention of Coalition troops. Mustafa, a thirty-year-old farmer, agreed. 'If we cultivate poppy and store the opium, we can't eat it. But we can store and eat the wheat, and my family will not be hungry. And if there's some left over, I'll sell it. The government has agreed to buy our wheat at a good price.'[61]

On the Somme and in Flanders between 1914 and 1918, corn poppies sprung up among the rolling wheat fields, while today in Helmand the relationship between wheat and opium is being rearranged by money and war. Wheat, one of humankind's greatest inventions, enabled and sustained civilised life for thousands of years. Growing side by side with poppies, the two crops forged a potent intimacy between eating and dreaming, action and lassitude. The war in Afghanistan has turned that millennia-old marriage upside down.

OPIUM CONFUSES THE MINDS of governments as well as those of addicts. There is, it seems, no end to the narcotic poppy's ambiguity, and the moral confusion which surrounds it. While the British government ordered its troops to burn Helmand's opium fields, it simultaneously permitted British farmers to grow the narcotic in rural English fields. The logic was eminently bureaucratic: there was a shortage of morphine in Britain.[62] But a surrealist with a dark mindset might imagine a British soldier wounded while destroying poppies near Lashkar Gah, then flown home for medical treatment and given morphine extracted from locally grown opium.[63]

Just a few miles away from these not-so-secret fields of English opium, a deeper grief from the war flourishes in a hitherto unremarkable place. Throughout the course of the war in Afghanistan, the Wiltshire village of Wootton Bassett has commemorated each killed soldier repatriated in a public display of honour and respect.[64] Relatives of the bereaved join the people of Wootton Bassett to line the high street as a cortège drives slowly by, on its way from RAF Lyneham where the dead are flown in, to the mortuary in nearby Oxford. Flowers are thrown as the hearse passes through the town, and Remembrance Poppy wreaths adorn the local war memorial, newly built.[65] Here, in the heart of rural England, the three poppies flourish, caught in a web of international war and domestic controversy.[66] The corn poppy, opium poppy and Remembrance Poppy circle each other, bringing grief, financial gain, respect and relief from pain in random and unequal measure.

For English farmers, the opium trade is more lucrative and safer than it is for their impoverished Afghan counterparts. Licensed by the British Home Office, the Edinburgh-based pharmaceutical company Macfarlan Smith now grows opium poppies in farms spread across the counties of Oxfordshire, Northamptonshire and Lincolnshire.[67] One farmer, Guy Hildred, reports that he has turned forty hectares (one hundred acres) of his Oxfordshire farm over to opium-poppy cultivation. 'It is worthwhile from a farmer's point of view and it's an expanding market,' he said.[68]

In a twist of history, Macfarlan Smith – which claims to be 'one of the oldest pharmaceutical companies in the world' and the 'world leader' in alkaloid opiate production – was founded in 1815, the year of Wellington's defeat of Napoleon at Waterloo. This too was the year that the legend of red poppies nourished by the blood of the fallen was born, and the year that the emperor attempted suicide by opium at Versailles. During the First World War, Macfarlan Smith thrived, supplying morphine as a painkiller to soldiers wounded on the battlefields of the Western Front and beyond.[69]

Almost a century later, a company spokesman announced: 'We have a number of [English] farmers under contract to grow poppies, which we then harvest. You can extract morphine and codeine from the poppies' capsules.' He added, with no trace of irony, 'We are the only company processing poppies in this way in the UK. The same crop is grown in Afghanistan, India and Turkey for illegitimate reasons.'[70] This was not the entire picture, however, as India and Turkey are licensed to grow opium for medicinal purposes. Furthermore, this legal trade was part of a bold strategic alternative to otherwise rampant and uncontrolled opium trafficking.[71]

The British government's position was clarified by a Home Office spokeswoman, who said, 'The poppies in question, *Papaver somniferum*, can be grown without a licence . . . the people who work to produce the drugs have to be licensed . . . the Home Office receives information about where the poppy farmers are and how much they are growing from the pharmaceutical companies. We then send growers a letter that they are encouraged to show to local police to make them aware of their activities'.[72] This somewhat disengaged announcement could easily be read as an open invitation for any member of the public to grow opium. An equally tangled statement, quickly denied, was issued by the then Foreign Office minister Lord Malloch-Brown, who observed that the morphine shortage was so severe that legalising opium growing in Afghanistan might be considered.

The idea that Afghanistan's entire opium crop could be bought by Coalition governments and then sold on to pharmaceutical multi-nationals may have appeared to be outrageous to some, but it was common sense to many. In 2006, for instance, the *Washington Quarterly* published an article arguing that the international community should establish a pilot project and investigate a licensing scheme to start the production of morphine and codeine as a way of subverting the evils of the illegal opium trade.[73]

Medical experts in Britain went even further. Two leading doctors from the British Medical Association (BMA) suggested that Afghan opium, refined into the pharmaceutical diamorphine, could be used to circumvent the National Health System's shortage.[74] Dr Vivienne Nathanson, the head of science and ethics at the BMA said, 'If we were harvesting this drug from Afghanistan rather than destroying it, we'd be benefiting the population of Afghanistan as well as helping patients.'[75] Her view was supported by another leading physician, Dr Jonathan Fielden, a consultant anaesthetist and intensive care specialist. 'Over the past year the availability of diamorphine has dramatically reduced. It has got to the stage where it is almost impossible in some hospitals to get hold of this drug'.[76] The response from the UK Department of Health was that diamorphine shortages were due to problems with production, not a shortage of raw opium.

Throughout the debate, confusion and disagreement reigned. On 12 September 2007, the European Parliament's Committee on Foreign Affairs issued a report advising the European Council to propose to the Afghan government that part of the opium crop should be acquired for the licensed production of morphine and codeine.[77] This idea was championed by a non-governmental organisation known as the Senlis Council – an international think tank which had its own 'Poppy for Medicine' programme and an office in Kabul, and which now works under the name International Council on Security and Development (ICOS).[78] At the time the Senlis Council pointed to the success of the similar schemes in India and Turkey as a possible model for Afghanistan. A Nobel laureate and the leader of Canada's Liberal Party endorsed the idea.

The issue of legalising opium involves a murky world of commandeering local groups and influential international bodies, few of which are actually criminal, and the arguments for and against legalisation brim with moral hazards and unforeseen consequences. The UN had argued against legalisation because, despite the recent morphine shortage in Britain, it said that the world's illegal opium exceeded the global demand for medicinal opiates by more than three thousand tonnes.[79] Legalisation would open the floodgates to more cultivation rather than deal with a relatively small medical crisis. And Susan Pittman of the US State Department's Bureau of Narcotics announced in 2007 that 'Legalizing is not an option', closing the door on American sanction of such a policy.

In contrast, a British embassy spokesperson in Kabul stressed the need for law and order if legalised opium production was going to work. Otherwise, he said, 'You'd be putting the Afghanistan government in competition with the narcotics traders'.[80] Confusing strategic aims, morality and economics, he noted that legalising opium might be unprofitable because traditional Afghan techniques could not compete with the cheap fertilisers and automated systems used in other countries.[81] He might have added, but didn't, that the legal market in medicinal painkillers is worth more than about £4 billion ($6.5 billion) a year.[82]

Most Afghan farmers simply want peace and a living wage for their crops. If they received a fair and guaranteed sum for 'legal' opium, as well as for wheat and other agricultural products, then the high prices paid by the drug-traffickers might prove little temptation. This assessment chimes with the view of the Senlis Council, which argued that in its scheme, groups of farmers would sell their morphine to the Afghan government for $3,100 (about £1,800) per kilogram – a significant mark-up on the farm-gate price of opium – and the government could then sell it on for $4,300 per kilogram.[83] This strategy, or something like it, might break the chain of dependence between farmers, Taliban leaders and the drug-traffickers. It could also staunch the flow of cheap heroin, and plug the gap in the global shortage of medicinal opiates, not least in Afghanistan itself.

But the question must be asked: is there a morphine shortage at the same time as a heroin glut? The Senlis Council has argued persuasively that painkillers are a rich person's prerogative but should be available to all, regardless of their economic status or nationality. Rather than approach these issues of fairness, the British government has countered that there is no morphine shortage, just issues with appropriate supply. Indeed, Vienna's International Narcotic Control Board (INCB) has bolstered this position, claiming that there is enough morphine to satisfy global demand from currently legal sources, including the twenty-five per cent of medicinal opiates produced by GlaxoSmithKline in Tasmania. It seems as though Senlis has little chance to make their case, even if they could point to a statistical mirage, whereby many countries under-prescribe and under-report their morphine use for ideological reasons.[84]

Legalising Afghanistan's opium for medicinal purposes may not be an easy option politically, but the deadly linkage of narcotics, cash and insurgency continues to demand bold new thinking. Richard Holbrooke, President Obama's special envoy to Pakistan and Afghanistan, took up his post with honesty in March 2009. 'The United States alone is spending $800 million [£550 million] a year on counter-narcotics. We have gotten nothing out of it, nothing,' he admitted then.[85] He went further, saying that: 'It is the most wasteful and ineffective programme I have seen in forty years'. Not only was this huge investment not hurting the Taliban 'one iota', in Holbrooke's view, but as production had soared beyond demand in recent years, the drug barons had stockpiled enough opium to ensure years of heroin supply even if opium production slowed.[86]

Holbrooke's appraisal was damning of President George W. Bush's strategy, yet coolly realistic. Events on the ground soon accelerated, and by the end of June 2009, after two weeks in Helmand and Kandahar provinces, Holbrooke tore up the old policy. 'Eradication is a waste of money,' he told a meeting of the G8 foreign ministers in Trieste, Italy.[87] 'It might destroy some acreage, but it didn't reduce the amount of money the Taliban got by one dollar'.[88] 'All we did was alienate' poor farmers, driving them into the arms of the Taliban.[89]

The figures spoke for themselves. In 2003, 21,000 hectares (51,900 acres) of poppies were destroyed, but only 5,500 hectares (13,500 acres) were destroyed in 2008. This meagre victory amounted to 3.5% of Afghanistan's total opium yield of 157,000 hectares, and was due to teams being attacked or bribed by drug lords and drug-traffickers. Despite the overall 19% drop in the opium harvest for the year, the crop still earned the insurgents over $50 million.[90] Rather than spending an estimated $44,000 per hectare on poppy eradication, Holbrooke announced that US aid for agriculture would soar from tens of millions of dollars to hundreds of millions. 'The Afghans are great farmers,' the diplomat added, 'but they need help.'[91]

The new policy was interdiction. The aim was to stop opium and heroin from leaving the country, and to target dealers and traders rather than peasant farmers. Antonio Maria Costa, the chief of the UN Office on Drugs and Crime (UNODC), explained the issue in colourful language: 'We want to create a flood of drugs within Afghanistan. There will be so much opium inside Afghanistan unable to go out that the price will go down.'[92] American and British troops were now commanded to search and destroy so-called drug bazaars – 'marketplaces which sell drug paraphernalia, precursor chemicals [and] laboratory equipment', as well as opium and poppy seeds. Holbrooke was enthusiastic about the shift in approach. One week of interdiction was probably worth two years of eradication, in his view.[93]

Change is often born of desperation, and the Obama administration's dramatic rethink may or may not have altered the opium poppy's fortunes, especially after Holbrooke's death in 2010. Long overdue common sense is not a silver bullet. In 2012 three times more opium was grown in Helmand than when the British arrived in 2006, and the UNODC forecasts that 2013 will see an even bigger crop with more than 75,000 hectares under cultivation.[94] Afghan farmers who had been persuaded to grow cotton abandoned it when no market could be found, and returned to the lucrative poppy. Afghanistan's border regions remain poorly policed, and poverty will continue to push unemployed youth into the arms of the well-paying Taliban for the foreseeable future.

The dead clamour ever more loudly. July 2009 saw not only the new policy on opium poppies, but also a record forty-four US troops killed. The following month saw another increase, to an all-time high of forty-seven American dead. American public support is elusive, and opinion polls show a clear majority against the war. Admiral Mike Mullen, chairman of the US Joint Chiefs of Staff went public in August: 'I think this is serious and it is deteriorating . . .'[95] As if to prove Admiral Mullen's point, a Taliban suicide bomber blew himself up outside a Kabul mosque in early September, killing Afghanistan's second-highest ranking intelligence officer and twenty-two others.[96] The insurgents were using opium money to improve their tactics, buy better intelligence and strike at the heart of the nation.

In Helmand, and in the eastern border areas with Pakistan, American commanders could see evidence of more sophisticated military training in Taliban attacks. Opium money was almost certainly behind this, paying, for example, for professional mercenaries to come to Afghanistan from around the world. 'These embedded trainers . . . [American] officers said, play almost the same role as US military training teams that live with and mentor Afghan government forces'.[97] So it came as no surprise when General Stanley McChrystal, newly appointed as President Obama's military commander in Afghanistan, announced that the Coalition was losing the war, and that ever greater numbers of troops were needed on the ground. Towards the end of 2009, the US president responded by announcing that an extra thirty thousand troops would be sent, bringing the total American forces to 100,000.

Yet another nightmare hovered in the wings. Jean-Luc Lemahieu, the UNODC's country chief, warned that Chinese drug dealers would soon capitalise on falling opium prices caused by Afghanistan's overproduction. While China's heroin users currently feed their addiction on opium grown in the 'Golden Triangle' of Myanmar (Burma), Thailand, Vietnam and Laos, Lemahieu believed it was only a matter of time 'before the Chinese pick up on the Afghan market'.[98] And here the spectre of the nineteenth-century Opium Wars haunted the scarred battlefields of Afghanistan.

THE REMEMBRANCE POPPY bloomed in a multitude of forms after 1918, though there were always the tangled threads of money and memory woven into its paper petals. In the wake of the 2001 attack on the World Trade Center, another commemorative floral tribute was made to the dead: the 9/11 Poppy. Despite this rejuvenation of the memorial flower in the United States, it was the opium poppy that gripped the American public. The opium poppy defined the war in Afghanistan, and soon found unique artistic expression.

Among the traditional crafts of the region are woven Afghan rugs. Nomads have carried such handiwork along Asia's ancient Silk Road for centuries, the 'Pazyryk', a 2,500-year-old rug on display in the Hermitage Museum in St Petersburg, Russia being the oldest-known specimen. For the largely non-literate peoples of the area, woven textiles remain a vivid – and sometimes the only – record of tribal history. The slender, deft fingers of women and children are most often employed to weave the rugs on home looms, giving a voice to many who are not otherwise heard in traditional Afghan society. Natural dyes are used to make the rugs' blue, ivory and reddish-brown hues. Today, perhaps six million Afghans are involved in some way with the textile business, each year producing 200 million square metres of rugs and carpets valued at about $170 million.[99]

Burkha-wearing Afghan women have recently begun making a new and unusual poppy textile, however. In an initiative started by the Belgian Mothers for Peace organisation, they embroider bright red Remembrance Poppies (not the more traditional opium poppies) onto small hand towels.[100] The towels are shipped to Belgium and sold in Ypres' 'In Flanders Fields' museum shop to raise money for these impoverished rural communities.

Yet the opium poppy casts its dark shadow even in this domestic sphere. Long hours and hard work, together with poor nutrition and little access to health services, lead weavers to take opium as a pain-killer – it is the only way they can avert fatigue and continue working to make a living.[101] Many women become addicts, and so do their children. 'When my children are restless and cry, I cannot work properly,' said Feroza, a carpet weaver and mother of six. 'When I give them a small piece of opium they become calm and fall asleep, allowing us to work.'[102] Nobody knows how many women use opium in this way, but in 2005 the UNODC estimated that 120,000 women used drugs across Afghanistan. This may not be the same tale told by the widows buying and selling Remembrance Poppies after the First World War, but the pain and grief of conflict are evident nonetheless.

Before the Soviet invasion, rugs were decorated with the age-old motifs of flowers, birds and other traditional symbols. But since 1979, these natural forms have taken on a distinctly modern and mechanical appearance. After the invasion, Sunni Muslim weavers of the Baluchi tribe began to create textiles incorporating the materiel of modern war, from AK-47 assault rifles and bombs to fighter jets and tanks.[103] Terrible suffering was portrayed, including blood-red images of *mujahideen* and Pashtun tribesmen whose limbs were blown off by Russian landmines. In some scenes woven into the rugs, maimed women and children are stalked by helicopter gunships.[104] Images of animals morph with those of tanks and armoured personnel carriers, and many typical symbols – such as the elephant's footprint – were replaced with bullets and mines.

Rugs also celebrated the Soviet withdrawal in 1989. Military convoys were depicted against a map of the route of their humiliating retreat. Some of these rugs had opium-poppy images woven into them – a reflection of the belief that the narcotic played a subtle but critical role in the USSR's defeat, because of the number of Russian soldiers who became addicted during their tours of Afghanistan.[105]

Al-Qaeda's attack on the United States, and the American response, inevitably inspired new scenes of death and destruction to be woven into Afghan rugs. The poppy became a recurring motif; its actual seeds are sometimes woven into the carpets. The most startling and controversial of this latest generation of rugs show passenger planes crashing into the World Trade Center, and tiny figures falling to earth from the Twin Towers. Despite the traumatic effect of these events on the American public, 'After 9/11, people's interest in war rugs went up dramatically,' says Kevin Sudeith, who began selling the Soviet-era rugs in a New York flea market long before 2001.[106] The new rugs became a way of remembering the dead of 9/11, and, with hindsight, were a herald of more deaths and suffering to come.

Woven histories soon portrayed the arrival of Coalition troops, and their attempts to hunt down al-Qaeda and eradicate the opium poppy. Some rugs depicted hand grenades disguised as white opium poppies. Soviet war machines were replaced by US-made Abrams tanks, F-16 fighter jets and M-16 rifles. Even the unforgiving landscape of Tora Bora – site of the US assault on Osama bin Laden's cave hideouts in March 2002 – was commemorated in textiles.[107]

As with many other aspects of the war, money became part of the story. In 2005 the Esso Gallery in New York City had a show of war rugs by a collector, and many dealers have been trading in war rugs since not long after the Soviet invasion. One war rug, showing a tank rolling across the desert with F-14 fighter jets, a Blackhawk helicopter and a predator drone flying overhead alongside the inscription 'War Against Terror', recently sold for $1,250.[108]

'In its purest form the war rug is more than a trinket made for tourists,' writes textile expert J. Barry O'Connell Jr.[109] 'The true war rug is a cry of expression from those who have no other voice. Will anyone listen? Will anyone care?' The questions echo along the rugged valleys of Afghanistan and the cold corridors of power in the West.

THE INVASION OF AFGHANISTAN breathed new life into opium, and made the narcotic poppy blossom a powerful emblem of Afghan survival and resistance – as well as of poverty, corruption and addiction. This poppy is a peerless generator of wealth, funding a deadly insurgency and acting as a midwife to heroin dependency in the West. The war against terror incorporated a war against nature, and destroying the poppy became a key but failed aim of the Coalition strategy, as is now widely conceded.

A century after the British humiliation at Maiwand, British soldiers are back in Helmand, dying not for some forgotten imperial contest with czarist Russia, but for a local solution to the global threat of fundamentalist and terror-minded Islamists. The world and the poppy may have moved on since the nineteenth-century 'Great Game', but the poppy retains it deadly ambivalence. More than ten years on, after multiple promises to remove Coalition forces from the country, the bodies of British and Canadian soldiers killed among the opium fields of Afghanistan return home to be honoured with Remembrance Poppy wreaths.[110] The first months of 2013 seemed on track to being one of the deadliest years since the United States and its allies arrived.

Ignoring the lessons of history, Coalition forces created the very disaster they aimed to avert, and propelled the opium poppy into a new and lethal dimension. The poppy is no longer merely a symbol of the war; it has become a reason for continuing conflict.

The clock has been turned back a century and more, from the

commemorative poppy of the First World War, to the Opium Wars between the British and the Chinese. The opium poppy is still the prize, but instead of fighting for the right to enslave a nation to narcotic addiction, the British (and others) have switched sides, now seeking to 'free' the world from its consuming evils. Opium wealth, which once helped finance the British Empire's conquests and colonisations, now supports insurgent forces, who see themselves as combating neocolonialism.

On 11 November 2012, sixty thousand poppy crosses were planted in the Field of Remembrance outside Westminster Abbey in London, many of them put there in memory of men and women lost in Iraq and Afghanistan. And as is always the case, each bore the photograph of someone too young to die.[111]

9

THE LIVING LEGACY

BLOOD-RED AND FRAGILE, HUNDREDS OF PAPER PETALS
flutter in the chill wind. The war dead seem briefly to walk among the
crowd once again. On this typically cold November morning in 1987,
poppy wreaths are lying on the war memorial in Enniskillen, Northern
Ireland, men and women gathering round, children clutching their
parents' hands. All wait for the eleventh hour to strike; the seconds
tick away. None of those present imagine they are about to be victims
of what will become known as 'The Poppy Day Massacre'.[1]

The Provisional Irish Republican Army detonated the bomb without
warning, killing eleven and injuring sixty-three. The stories of personal
loss are heart-rending, but the attack was sectarian murder, and all
who died were Protestants. More than this, it was an assault by Irish
Republicans on the Protestant heritage of Unionist Northern Ireland,
as represented by the Remembrance Poppy's origins as the memorial
flower of the First World War.[2] For the Protestant Irish, as for millions
of others, the poppy was a symbol of respect for the war dead, but it
was also a strident emblem of their Britishness. As a result, for many

Catholic Irish Republicans the flower stood for imperial oppression and British occupation.

The roots of this divide are found on the poppy-strewn battlefields of France in 1916, where on 1 July the 36th (Ulster) Division climbed out of their trenches as the Battle of the Somme began.[3] In the Ulster imagination, the memory of their heroic action at the Somme was freely mixed with Unionism, and subsequently associated with the Battle of the Boyne in 1690, which had sealed the future of Protestant English control of Ireland.[4] Soon after the war, the Protestant paramilitary organisation known as the Ulster Volunteer Force (UVF) painted a giant mural to commemorate one of its murdered fighters in north Belfast. In the painting, masked gunmen pose in emulation of the guard of honour that attends Armistice Day commemorations, drawing visceral connections between the two events. Two more gunmen crouch at the base of the mural alongside an inscription: 'In memory of the 36th Ulster Division'. The meaning is clear, as is the presence of the blood-red poppy painted nearby.[5] The Remembrance Poppy was a *Protestant* flower, cherished by Unionists and loathed by Nationalists.

The Ulster poet Michael Longley captured the poppy's power to crystallise the divisions of history and identity on either side of the political divide.

> *Some people tried to stop other people wearing poppies*
> *And ripped them from lapels as though uprooting poppies*
> *From Flanders fields, but the others hid inside their poppies*
> *Razor blades and added to their poppies more red poppies*[6]

After the Enniskillen bombing there was an outpouring of public sympathy for the bereaved and wounded, but the divide did not heal. A decade later, on the anniversary of the atrocity, the Irish president-elect, Mary McAleese, announced that she would not wear the Remembrance Poppy on her Armistice Day inauguration. For McAleese and her supporters and advisers, the flower 'was still too firmly entangled in the briar of Northern Ireland politics'.[7] The Royal British Legion petitioned her to wear the poppy, but after long deliberation she determined that apart from the shamrock, 'the president should not wear emblems or symbols of any kind'.[8]

The response was predictable. Andrew Mackay, the Conservative spokesman on Northern Ireland, said, 'It's obscene for Mary McAleese to confuse the poppy with any sectarian issues. It's a mark of respect for the millions of people who gave their lives in both world wars, including many thousands of Irish men and women.'[9] The British government's reaction was a lame platitude, devoid of any sense of history or sensitivity: it was hoped, the communiqué said, that the poppy was not going to become a 'political football'.[10] In a reversal of the usual politics of colour, McAleese's decision made the headlines not long after workers at a factory in Londonderry had been suspended for wearing the flower against a company ruling – in much the same way that women had lost jobs in the 1930s for wearing the White Poppy of peace.

President McAleese's dilemma over the poppy returned in the following year, when she attended the opening ceremony for the Irish Peace Park outside Mesen (Messines) in Belgium. The new memorial was to commemorate the memory of all Irishmen who have died in combat. Alongside Queen Elizabeth II and King Albert II of Belgium, both of whom laid poppy wreaths at the base of the Irish Round Tower, McAleese placed a laurel wreath.

Arguments over who should wear the Remembrance Poppy and in what circumstances are not new, however much the tragedy of

Enniskillen polarised the issue. Rendered down to its essence, the question became: What is the proper use of the poppy symbol?

BRITISH WAR VETERANS were horrified in 1993 when the software company Amiga appropriated the Remembrance Poppy to illustrate a new computer game, and, in a total lack of sensitivity, to launch its product on Remembrance Sunday. The name of the game rubbed salt in the wound: *Cannon Fodder.* The manufacturers were even so tone deaf that they announced that: 'War has never been so much fun'.[11] The poppy was scheduled to feature on the cover of the computer magazine *Amiga Power*, which would publicise the game's debut when it hit newsstands on Armistice Day.

The Royal British Legion were understandably appalled. 'This will offend millions at a time when they remember loved ones who gave their lives in war', their press release said. Viscount Montgomery of Alamein, the son of Britain's famous Second World War Field Marshal, added, 'It is very unfortunate that anyone should see fit to detract from the poppy's place as a symbol of remembrance'.[12]

Virgin Interactive Entertainment, which was marketing the game, issued a tortuous response: 'The poppy is there to remind consumers war is no joke'. The *Daily Star*, which broke the story, called Virgin's response a 'publicity writer's hypocrisy. Computer-game designers compete to glorify war and viciousness'.[13] It was a rare lapse of judgement by a brand whose guiding genius, Richard Branson, normally had his finger on the pulse of the nation.

Amiga Power changed its cover art after a storm of protest,[14] but acting editor Stuart Campbell would not back down entirely. In an editorial, he wrote, 'Old soldiers? I wish them all dead'. The revamped December issue included a spread in which the Royal British Legion were labelled as 'conscientious objectors'. An enraged Royal British Legion spokesman stormed: 'Good God. It leaves you speechless. If it was not for the old soldiers who stood up during the wars he might not be alive.'

Despite an apology from the magazine's publishing director, the Legion turned to its solicitors, who issued a formal warning to the game's manufacturers. Outlining the suspect morality, the contentious launch date and most especially the unauthorised use of the poppy logo, their lawyer warned, 'The use of a Royal British Legion Poppy in this way is unlawful and inter alia defamatory. The undoubted impression conveyed to the general public is that this particular game has received the endorsement of our clients, which, being a war game, is directly contrary to the Legion's principal aims and objectives'.[15] Legal action would follow if Amiga didn't respond within twenty-four hours with an undertaking to apologise, compensate the Royal British Legion for its legal costs and remove the poppy logo from the game and all other promotional materials immediately. Both the magazine and the game eventually debuted without a Remembrance Poppy in sight.[16]

IT CANNOT BE ARGUED that Remembrance Day is devoid of commercialism. The Poppy Day Appeal is a vast fundraising oper- ation for the Royal British Legion, raising around thirty million pounds annually, even at a time when the Legion's membership is in decline. Veterans of war, having suffered terrible injuries, have been given hope and help by the proceeds of the campaign for more than eighty years.

But in 2003, the Legion felt forced to bow to pressures brought by an increasingly risk-averse and money-conscious society: the Legion stopped supplying pins with its poppies because of fears about compensation claims from the public who might 'injure' themselves with a pinprick.[17] The change in policy overturned an almost century-old tradition of manufacturing. At first, Legion branches provided stickers instead of poppies, then plastic alternatives. It wasn't long, however, before all Remembrance Poppies came with an ultra-safe green plastic fastener. The new 'health and safety' line was summed up by Malcolm Gainard, the chairman of a local Somerset branch of the Legion. 'I think we should use something else. I'm worried about the safety aspect. People can easily stab themselves with a pin and there is always the worry of litigation. We do supply poppies without pins. For instance, the Cadbury Schweppes factory in Keynsham will not allow any metal into the premises for fear that the pins could fall into the machinery.'[18]

Not everybody agreed. The wittiest comment came from Peter Westwell, the Shropshire Legion branch secretary, who called the no-pin rule 'poppycock'. 'It is compensation culture gone mad,' he said.[19] The Legion itself had to be more circumspect, but a spokesman commented that it was a sad reflection on British society. Two years later, in 2005, a group of war veterans was banned from selling poppies in a shopping centre because their stall was considered a fire-risk hazard.[20] The cotton-wool path of health and safety was assured.

If a society chooses paranoia over common sense, it can easily lose its way. In late October 2009, as Remembrance Day approached, every library in Derbyshire was ordered to stop selling poppies, so as to ensure neutrality and equality by not favouring one charity over another.[21] The decision, demonstrating ignorance of local history, proved a public-relations disaster. During the First World War, 140,000 men had served in the county regiment, of whom some 11,409 were killed;

in the Second World War, 1,520 of the nearly 27,000 who served had lost their lives; and almost every night, it seemed, came more news of casualties from Afghanistan.[22] Seventy-nine-year-old Dorothy Reynolds, whose husband had served in the Second World War, could not contain her disbelief. 'My husband would walk five miles to make five pence for the Poppy Appeal. Now he would want to know why on earth the library cannot sell poppies.'[23] Another resident responded angrily: 'Poppies raise money for the families of our war dead and our injured soldiers. By buying one we are honouring their memory.' The decision was quickly overturned in the face of the outcry. In his retreat, the council leader, Andrew Lewis, announced: 'We are wholehearted supporters of the Armed Forces and I am very happy for libraries to sell poppies on behalf of the British Legion.'

But no sooner had the poppy been reinstated in Derbyshire's public libraries than they were banned from the forecourts of one thousand Shell petrol stations across Britain.[24] In a triumph of multinational corporate hubris, Shell ignored the debate that had swirled in the Midlands as well as a timely reminder from the Royal British Legion Scotland that the company's North Sea Oil platforms had been protected for decades by the armed forces. Shell UK's chairman, James Smith, issued an apology, which his PR team optimistically called an 'endorsement' of the Poppy Appeal. 'I am very sorry we got it wrong,' he said in a brief statement.[25]

More insults to the Remembrance Poppy followed, however. The Royal British Legion's poppy sellers were banned from shaking their collection tins and asking people to buy a poppy as it was deemed a 'public menace' that could lead to prosecution.[26] While other charity volunteers could ask for donations, poppy sellers were told that it was illegal for them to 'harass people' or act in an 'aggressive way'. It seemed they had to remain still and silent.

To many this was the latest example of political correctness spinning out of control. Ann Widdecombe, then the Conservative MP for Maidstone and the Weald, Kent, said: 'It's absolutely ludicrous and people have been rattling tins while selling poppies for years.' The military historian Correlli Barnett agreed, saying that it was ridiculous that other charity workers 'are allowed to come up to you and hassle you on the street but these veterans can't even offer you a poppy'.

The poppy has lost none of its power to incite conflicting opinions, even in that hearth of traditional British society, the pub. When former RAF serviceman David Marchant, then seventy-seven, walked into his local pub, The Windmill, in the Weald, he was told by landlady Bernice Walsh that there was no room for his Remembrance Poppy collection tray on the bar. People could buy their poppies 'somewhere else'.[27] Marchant's father had fought in the First World War, his older brother had fought in the Second, and his cousin had been killed flying a Spitfire.[28]

Shocked and upset by the landlady's decision, the villagers started a boycott, even though the pub had been supported by the locals when it had recently reopened. One villager commented, 'Everybody supports the poppy campaign, and I can't think for one minute why she refused to have the tray on the bar.'[29] The answer is unknown but might be quite simple: Walsh comes originally from County Mayo, in the Irish Republic, where the Remembrance Poppy resonates in a very different way than it does for the patriotic pub-goers of south-eastern England.

While many Legion initiatives have helped the wounded and bereaved, new conflicts have proved troublesome to the Poppy Appeal's public image. While the Legion is highly regarded by the British public, the current wars in Iraq and Afghanistan have not been popular, particularly in recent years.

In October 2007, a new charity was launched to raise money to support the men and women wounded in these two conflicts, apparently in an attempt to pull politics out of the equation.[30] No poppies bloom for the Help for Heroes campaign, and the nearest equivalent is a three-coloured wristband on sale for two pounds. Formed by Bryn and Emma Parry after a visit to Birmingham's Sellyoak Hospital, where many of the seriously wounded are treated, H4H carries none of the burden of the poppy's history. The charity cuts to the quick on its website: 'It's about Derek, a rugby player who has lost both his legs . . . It's about Richard who was handed a mobile phone as he lay on the stretcher so he could say goodbye to his wife'.[31] The contrast with the Legion's website is stark and immediate: there are no pensioners, and Iraq and Afghanistan are the focus – not all wars. Most of all, the site is bedecked in blue, not red, and there is no sign of the Remembrance Poppy. In their first two years, and without any flower to serve as their logo, Help For Heroes (H4H) raised thirty million pounds.

Is H4H the beginning of a new direction for raising money for the war wounded, one that does not look back to the Great War and the poppy that grew from it? Might the two merge in the future – just as the British Legion came together from four charities – or will H4H remain dedicated to these more recent contentious conflicts? Could President George W. Bush's self-proclaimed War on Terror – caught up so treacherously with Afghanistan's opium poppy – be the war that ultimately sees the Remembrance Poppy fade away?

PERHAPS MORE THAN ANY OTHER, the Canadian experience of the poppy embodies the wild fluctuations in the flower's fortunes, and the ways in which the emblem reflects changing attitudes and ideas about the military and about war. It was only in 2005 that representatives of the country's First Nations officially took part in the annual remembrance ceremony at Belgium's Menin Gate for those who were listed as missing after the Battle of Ypres. Joseph Clement, a Métis veteran, lost an uncle in the Battle of Passchendaele in July 1917. 'Before, we didn't know where he was killed. But now we know,' he said. 'We found his name up in the wall of Menin Gate. It was emotional. It was very, very emotional.'[32]

Tears streamed down the cheeks of Clement and other descendants as a rain of poppies, released from skylights in the monument's ceiling, fluttered through the cold evening air. 'I can honestly tell you, when the poppies came down, everybody cried,' he said. 'There was one poppy for every name on that wall.'[33] Eddy Wabie, an Algonquin veteran, was also in attendance. 'It was amazing. I didn't know what was happening at first. The road itself leading into the archway turned red as you walked in. And I was thinking of all the blood the soldiers shed.'[34] The spirits of long-lost warriors were called home at last.

Across the Atlantic, the Remembrance Poppy's narcotic cousin gripped the nation in a quite different way. Every year, a report revealed, Canadians consume a staggering 28,000 kilograms of legal opiates in the form of codeine – billion dollars' worth of the drug. The land whose most famous son had inspired the Remembrance Poppy with his poetry had become the number one consumer of the poppy's pain-killing effects. Most of these narcotics are imported, yet on the rolling plains of Alberta, Hutterite farmers cultivate poppies to supply the seeds to the confectionery and bagel market. Peter Facchini, a leading expert on the opium poppy, believes that Canada could build its own pharmaceutical industry around a domestic poppy crop. The poppy flourishes in southern Alberta, he said, so, 'Why are we importing this stuff?'[35] While politicians and health experts ponder this provocative question, the poppy remains a potent symbol in Canada. McCrae's moving poem appears on ten-dollar notes, passing from hand to hand in countless daily transactions, a never-ending circulation of tangible commemoration of the war dead – if the bearer takes the time to note the text. Imagine: one hundred million poppy poems are exchanged for codeine annually.

The popularity of the notes inspired the Royal Canadian Mint to issue a remembrance coin. On 21 October 2004 a quarter-dollar (25 cent) piece, with a red-painted poppy at its centre and 'Canada 2004' and 'Remember / Souvenir' emblazoned below, was released to general circulation. Almost thirty million 'poppy quarters' were minted in total.[36] Bureaucrats hoped that the coin would help people to remember the veterans of the Second World War, many of whom were passing away. With a 'poppy' in their pocket, the public would 'never forget' the sacrifices of this generation – or so it was hoped. The official government statement on the release of the coin was far broader, citing the nation's 117,000 war dead, from the First World War to Iraq and Afghanistan.

But the poppy could never be a stable object, even when minted in metal. Nature's poppy has always been fragile. This was part of its appropriateness to serve as a symbol of commemoration for the dead – a metaphor for frail human bodies shattered and maimed by the weapons of modern war. Now the poppy itself had become metal, jingling in pockets, and unselfconsciously referred to by the younger generation as 'shrapnel'. And, like all good symbols, the poppy could change its form and meaning in an instant.

IN EARLY 2007, with nerves frayed by the ongoing mission against al-Qaeda, the US Department of Defense issued a public warning. Suspicious 'spy coins' had appeared, adorned with red-painted flowers that concealed secret radio transmitters.[37]

The episode was an unlikely concoction of post-9/11 paranoia and confusion. Some US army contractors were travelling across Canada in a hired car when one noticed a poppy coin in the cup holder. His initial assessment – straight from the pages of a Robert Ludlum thriller – was that: 'It did not appear to be electronic (analog) in nature or have a power source'.[38] Nevertheless, the contractors decided to subject the coin to further analysis. 'Under high power [sic] microscope, it appeared to be a complex consisting of several layers of clear, but different material, with a wire-like mesh suspended on top.'[39] And thus a conspiracy was born.

Soon after, the Defense Security Service, an agency of the US Defense Department, announced that 'mysterious coins with radio frequency transmitters were found planted on American contractors with classified security clearances on at least three separate occasions between October 2005 and January 2006 as the contractors travelled through Canada'.[40] The protective coating applied by the Royal Canadian Mint to ensure that the poppy's scarlet did not rub off was interpreted as a sinister application of cutting-edge nanotechnology. Arguably more worrying was that army contractors seemed totally oblivious to numerous bits of intelligence that would have cleared up the confusion, including billboards posted along Canada's highways and car number plates emblazoned with the red poppy logo and the word 'veteran' that had been issued to those who had fought in Canada's foreign wars.

Coin specialists quickly guessed the embarrassing truth, but there was nothing like a good story to generate hysterical headlines. Fuelled by non-attributable leaks and emails, the 'poppy war' developed its own momentum. One of the contractors went so far as to claim that an unidentified person had surreptitiously slipped two of the poppy coins into his coat pocket. The pocket was empty that morning, he reckoned, but yet, later in the day, he discovered the mysterious quarters. For those with a grasp of military history, it recalled similar – and equally wild – tales that had circulated during the First World War, where objects and even strangers with odd accents appeared and disappeared from trenches.

The investigation descended into farce when US government papers concerning the events were classified so that America's allies would not be allowed to see them. Perhaps Britain and other Commonwealth countries were so devoted to their Remembrance Poppy that they were in on 'the plot' with Canada. Intelligence officers around the world were left speechless. Luc Portelance, deputy director of the Canadian Security Intelligence Service, was forced to quiz a subordinate to find out what was going on. The most memorable comment came from H. Keith Melton, a leading intelligence expert: 'I thought the whole thing was preposterous, to think you could tag an individual with a coin and think they wouldn't give it away or spend it.'[41] (Some of the classified papers were finally released under a US Freedom of Information Act request, but only after heavy censorship.)

The Americans eventually admitted to an unfortunate case of mistaken identity, made possible because no one at the Defense Department recognised or recalled the Remembrance Poppy, despite the emblem being an American invention – and despite the department dedicating a page to the nation's official 'commemorative flower' on its own website. Forgetfulness had struck at the heart of the institution.

The 'spy coin' affair revealed how far the United States' own Buddy Poppy had slipped beneath the radar of everyday life. Such an episode would have been as impossible for previous generations of Americans as it currently was to the Canadians, British, Australians and others. The little red stamp was not seen as a memorial to the dead but as a reference to the eradication of the opium poppy from Afghanistan, and the loss of lives of so many Coalition soldiers.

Sometimes in history, random events come together to reveal deeper truths. It is tempting to construe the poppy-coin affair as a sign of long-standing American neuroses. An obsession with the opium poppy has been mainlined through the veins of the nation's history: from the opiate addiction which struck down the veterans of the Civil War, to the draconian narcotics laws of the 1970s, to the tragic explosion of cheap heroin within the United States in the wake of the invasion of Afghanistan in October 2001. Even the legacy of one of the hallowed fathers of American independence, Thomas Jefferson, wasn't safe from the curse of opium. The medical poppies that Jefferson planted in his garden bloomed for two hundred years until the directors of Monticello, panicked by a US Drug Enforcement Agency raid on the nearby University of Virginia, uprooted the subversive plants and burned them in 1991.[42]

The Monticello estate was apparently later told that it could continue growing the narcotic plants, despite it being illegal to do so in the United States – an indication of how history can trump all when it comes to the opium poppy. What we make of the poppy depends entirely on context.

BRITAIN'S NATIONAL COLLECTION of oriental poppies is held on the estate of the Scottish Agricultural College at Auchincruive, near Ayr. Among the dazzling ranks of multicoloured flowers, a gorgeous red and white hybrid flutters in the breeze. It is called the 'Victoria Cross Poppy', and its deep red petals carry a pure white cross at their heart.

Nobody knows its origins, though it was most likely created sometime between 1856, when the Victoria Cross medal was first cast at the end of the Crimean War, and 1890, when the flower was first given the name. After languishing in obscurity for over a century, until festivities for the 150th anniversary of the VC medal granted the VC Poppy a new lease of life,[43] it is today a living tribute to valour of the highest rank and yet another manifestation of the Remembrance Poppy's enigma.

Unlike such famous ornamental varieties as the Shirley Poppy and the Mother of Pearl, the VC Poppy is not a hybrid of the scarlet corn poppy (*Papaver rhoeas*), as its Latin name *Papaver somniferum* reveals.[44] Instead it is a crossed variety of the opium poppy. It is lovingly cared for not only by professional gardeners, but also by former military personnel mentally tormented by their experiences in recent wars.[45]

Anna Baker Cresswell set up the Gardening Leave programme in 2007 to provide horticultural therapy for those with post-traumatic stress disorder, those who suffer flashbacks, depression or anxiety from their time on the front lines. Described as a 'life saver' by some of the participants, the programme augments the standard clinical and non-clinical therapies organised by Combat Stress, a welfare society to help ex-service members in Britain.[46] For ex-soldiers who served in Afghanistan, there is an irony in the therapy: once, they burned fields of opium poppies and suffered attacks funded by the Taliban's opium harvest; now they find peace of mind by growing their own variety of opium poppy in a quiet corner of Scotland.

The poppy follows these veterans when they leave Auchincruive. VC Poppy seeds are gathered up by the staff and given to Gardening Leave volunteers to take home and plant in their own back gardens. Through this strange invasion into family life, the poppy soothes the wounds inflicted during war.

IN 2001, Stephen Mulqueen of New Zealand journeyed to the imposing memorial to the missing at Tyne Cot Cemetery, near Passchendaele in Belgium's historic battlefields. He has been called an artist, an archaeologist, an alchemist and, more grandly, a 'postmodern surveyor of the Dominion of signs'.[47] Inspired to create sculptures exploring the tensions between nature and culture, and the contradictions between ancient artefacts and anonymous products of the industrial age, he has been particularly drawn to the battlefields of the First World War as a subject and a source for his art.

For years Mulqueen has collected the recycled debris of war known as trench art, and as he cast his artist's eye on the ranks of white gravestones, he was stunned by the sheer scale of the slaughter. He wandered around war memorials, museums and bookshops seeking genuine First World War .303-inch brass cartridge cases to take home to his workshop in Dunedin. He recalls how 'I began playing and created a hybrid between the casings and the poppy emblem, a conjunction where "terror meets beauty" as a memory and a commemoration of young New Zealand men who had fought and died in the nation's twentieth-century wars'.[48] It was a fusion of symbols that would have memorable consequences.

The .303 cartridge was instrumental in the killing or wounding of thousands of men during the First World War. Crushing one is a symbolic act in itself. Transforming the contorted metal into a poppy with brass petals is a flight of imaginative commemoration, a transformation of war into peace.[49] Mulqueen says each one 'carries its own in-built ironies and poetic resonance and is at once a signifier for death, mourning and new life'.[50] Mulqueen's cartridge-case poppies are sold as presentation pieces to families who want to commemorate a relative who has fallen during war. Each artwork bears a legend inscribed inside the petals which gives the name, rank, serial number and theatres of war of the soldier to be remembered. Mulqueen turns cartridges into poppies, but each takes a full day to make, and can never be more than a personal item.

Memorials are more often public in nature. The huge Poppy Man towered over astonished passengers travelling through London's Heathrow airport in 2008. Five metres tall, swathed in eight thousand red paper poppies, he appeared like a figure from English folklore, a relative perhaps of the Wicker Man, which Julius Caesar said the Druids burned in effigy as part of a human sacrifice to the gods. This Poppy Man was a gargantuan version of a life-sized figure built for the Royal British Legion the previous year as a mascot of sorts. The conduct of war changes, and public opinion shifts, with each generation, and the statue was designed to connect with young people in a more meaningful way than previous campaigns that had relied on recruiting celebrities, such as the Spice Girls, to support poppy sales. It proved a public-relations coup, and a singularly poignant monument. Although hollow, this void is filled metaphorically with the loved one lost in war. The effigy captures the fleeting transience of life, linking the dead and the maimed with the figures who stand alongside the statue, as well the thousands of poppy sellers who throng the streets in the weeks before 11 November.[51]

And the effigy moves through time and space. The Legion launched its 2008 Poppy Day Appeal by taking Poppy Man to the war zone of southern Iraq, where it was posed alongside British soldiers.[52] Here, in the land where Sumerian scribes first wrote down the name of the opium poppy nearly five thousand years ago, and where insurgents today are battling to grow the narcotic flower again amid the chaos, Poppy Man stood calm and surreal, reminding everyone of a century and more of war. Later, the statue stood alongside soldiers in Basra at a service to dedicate a memorial wall for British soldiers who have fallen in Iraq. It even was taken on a tour of the troops' barracks.[53]

As much as these ceremonies are full of tradition, Poppy Man was also thoroughly modern. The project has a page on Facebook, and a blog that tracked the statue's travels.[54] No matter the extent of disquiet about the wars in Iraq and Afghanistan, he tapped into the core of the Remembrance Poppy – honouring the past but also the young men and women who die and are wounded on battlefields far from home. War still produces a heartbreaking litany of loss, and Poppy Man was born so that we would not forget.

WALKING THROUGH A FIELD of opium poppies in the early light of dawn, one cannot escape the assault on the senses. The bleeding heads ooze their sap, and the area is suffused with the heavy, sweet scent that dissolves time itself. Gazing on a field of corn poppies, too, can overwhelm the senses, but in a different way. To be changed by the scarlet, one has to know the stories – tales of death, destruction, sacrifice and grief that are mixed with bravery, hope and the memory of those who have gone. Fields of white opium ease the troubles of the living and calm the mind; the crimson sea requires knowledge and understanding of history.

Tracking the poppy's meaning is a journey through time, a voyage through what makes a civilisation and what makes a war. A kaleidoscope of images is seared into our memory – of poppy fields burning across Helmand, and of peaceful Oxfordshire ablaze with white and red; of bonnet-capped women harvesting opium as a folk medicine and of crude morphine injections administered on the battlefields of the American Civil War; of poppy badges collected in a keep-sake box year after year, and of traumatised veterans calmed as they plant a VC

Poppy in their back garden. This flower represents our hopes, fears and aspirations – the best of what we are, as well as our darkest hours. The Remembrance Poppy's story captures these – a botanical hybrid of the human imagination, where two poppies have mingled with sentiment and science, bending and bowing in the winds that blow across battle-fields from Flanders to Helmand.

Foretold by a man, invented by two women, the Remembrance Poppy has been brought to life by generations of sacrifice and sorrow. It has the power to conjure the dead, to distil memories into tears and to comfort the worst pains. It is in the poppy fields that souls linger, mortality fades and the afterlife is glimpsed.

NOTES

1. Genesis

1   Lichfield, J. 1999. The idea of this memorial was that for six weeks every year, from June to July, this stretch of French countryside would be carpeted with tens of millions of corn poppies.

2   Lloyd, D. 1998: 24

3   The exact number of poppy species reported in different sources is given variously as 120, 200, and 250. The latter figure is adopted here (along with other botanical information on poppies) as it appears in the definitive book *Poppies: The Poppy Family in the Wild and in Cultivation* by Christopher Grey-Wilson (2005: 21), who was formerly a principal scientific officer at the Royal Botanic Gardens, Kew, in London. Globally, the poppy family (*Papaveraceae*) has about 23 genera, of which the *Papaver* genus is the largest (Grey-Wilson 2005: 71). It is to this genus that the corn poppy (*Papaver rhoeas*) and the opium poppy (*Papaver somniferum*) belong.

4   Nikiforuk, A. 2008; and see note 5 below

5   *Papaver setigerum* grows wild in the Mediterranean region, especially in south-western Europe. It is closely related to the opium poppy (*Papaver somniferum*), so much so that it is widely regarded as a variety or sub-species of that species. *P. setigerum* produces only a small amount of morphine compared to *P. somniferum* (Farmilo, C.G., et al. 1953). Also, *P. setigerum* has twice as many chromosomes as *P. somniferum*, which means for some scientists that it cannot be considered the wild ancestral species of the opium poppy (Farmilo, C.G., et al. 1953), while others argue against this view (Hammer and Fristch 1977).

6   Kapoor, L.D. 1995; and see PBS; Chouvy, P-A. 2002; Schiff Jr, P.L. 2002

7   Merlin, M.D. 1984: 78–9

8   Merlin, M.D. 2003: 298–9

9   Solecki, R. 1971; Merlin, M.D. 1984: 82; 2003: 303; the site, known as Shanidar
     Cave, is located in Iraq's Zagros Mountains. Solecki's view that flowers were
     deliberately placed with the dead brought widespread publicity in the 1960s,
     not least because of the hippy 'Flower Power' phenomenon of that time. The
     archaeological evidence was seen by many as indicating some kind of spiritual/
     commemorative activity by Neanderthals.

10   Rottoli, M. and A. Pessina. 2007: 147

2. The Flower of Forgetfulness

1   Merlin, M.D. 1984: 153

2   Terry, C.E. and M. Pellens [1928] 1970: 55

3   Krikorian, A.D. 1975. Krikorian is especially critical of this view, and his 1975
     essay is a masterful and influential argument against the identification of opium
     as the 'joy plant'. He concludes his investigation by saying that 'No case whatever
     can be based on cuneiform sources to the effect that the opium poppy and/or
     opium were known to, cultivated by, or used by the Sumerians, Babylonians, or
     Assyrians. . . . [and that] . . . no seeds identifiable as those of the opium poppy
     have yet been found among the many plant materials uncovered in numerous
     important archaeological "digs" in the area concerned' (Krikorian 1975: 113).
     This view is a sober antidote to speculation, and highlights the difference between
     botanical identification gained from literary sources and that obtained – or in this
     case not obtained – from archaeological investigation. Krikorian himself avoids
     saying that it is impossible that opium was not known or used in Mesopotamia,
     adding only that judgement be reserved. And see Merlin, M.D. 1984: 157.

4   Collins, P. 2003

5   Nidaba. n.d. Wikipedia. http://en.wikipedia.org/wiki/Nidaba

6   Quoted in Merlin, M.D. 1984: 154

7   Thompson, R.C. 1949: 226

8   Such was Thompson's reputation as a scholar that his translations and
     interpretations were often adopted uncritically. For instance, in the report on
     one of his painstaking investigations, he quoted how the poppy was harvested:
     'Early in the morning old women, boys and girls collect juice by scraping it off
     the wounds [of the poppies] with a small iron scoop, and deposit the whole in

an earthen pot, where it is worked by hand in the open sunshine until it becomes of considerable thickness.' In an instant, it seemed, millennia had slipped away, and we see a scene which fades in and out between ancient Mesopotamia and the poppy fields of the Golden Triangle and Afghanistan today. The problem was that Thompson was describing a contemporary scene. He had merely reproduced a report of opium harvesting in India from 1817 to illustrate more graphically a translated Assyrian text which refers to women and children scraping the juice off a unidentified plant (Merlin, M.D. 1984: 156).

9   Albenda, P. and E. Guralnick 1986

10 Kilgour, F.G. 1960: 19

11 Krikorian, A.D. 1975: 104–6

12 Ibid.

13 Scurlock and Andersen 2005: 27

14 Budge, E.A.W. 1926: 199

15 Merrillees, R. 1974: 7

16 Merrillees, R. 1968: 157

17 Sjoqvist, E. 1940: 79; Holmes, Y.L. 1975: 93; Krikorian, A.D. personal communication 1976 to M.D. Merlin. Merlin, M.D. 1984: 254

18 Amar, Z. 2006: 21. Amar notes that these distinctive small containers have been found in the Bronze Age levels of several sites, including Jerusalem and Megiddo. (The page reference here belongs to an English translation of the original Hebrew publication, which Amar kindly supplied to the author in July 2011. The bibliographic reference is to the Hebrew version.)

19 Similarly inconclusive is a report that opium traces were found in an alabaster jar of the Egyptian priest Cha, in the necropolis of Thebes (Merlin, M.D. 1984: 256–8).

20 Merrillees, R. 1962: 290; 1968: 160; and Merlin, M.D. 1984: 254–7

21 Merlin, M.D. 1984: 261

22 Martin, G.T. 1974: 79; and see Merlin, M.D. 1984: 263

23 Gabra, S. 1956: 42; and Merlin, M.D. 1984: 268–9

24 Gabra, S. (1956: 40–2) reviews this issue, listing reasons why in his opinion these earrings are opium poppies not pomegranates, and includes an artistic comparison of the ways in which ancient Egyptians depicted pomegranates compared to poppies.

25 Quibell, J.E. and A.G.K. Hayter 1927: 37–8; and see Merlin, M.D. 1984: 264–5

26 Touregypt.net. n.d.a 'The Tutankhamun Exhibit: Jewellery and Ornamentation. Pectoral with Solar and Lunar Emblems'.

27   The *udjat-* (or *wedjat-*) eye is known as the 'eye of Horus'(Shaw, I. and P. Nicholson 1995:133–4), its design representing the appearance of the peregrine falcon's eye – Horus himself often being depicted as that bird of prey. The term *udjat/wedjat* derives from the hieroglyphic terms for the colours green, possibly in relation to green of the papyrus plant. The 'eye' is also personified as *udjat/ wedjat* – originally a goddess in her own right during earlier, pre-dynastic times in Lower Egypt. Her protective symbolism subsequently became associated with other Egyptian deities with whom she shared her name, and later during dynastic times with Horus.

28   Touregypt.net. n.d.b 'The Tutankhamun Exhibit: Jewellery and Ornamentation. Rigid *Udjat* Eye Bracelet'

29   Touregypt.net. n.d.c 'The Tutankhamun Exhibit: Basic Funeral Equipment. Golden Shrine'. And see Eaton-Krause, M. and E. Graefe 1985.

30   Laurent-Tackholm, V. 1951: 102; and see Merlin, M.D. 1984: 270–1

31   Wilkinson, A. 1998: 52–3; poppies also appear as decoration around the lid of the casket, Hepper (2009): 10

32   Scholl, R. 2002; and see Merlin, M.D. 1984: 274

33   Gabra, S. 1956: 48, 50–2. R. Merrillees (1968: 196) believes that *shepen* was the opium-poppy plant, and *shepenn* the opium-bearing capsule, and agrees with Gabra that it was widely used as a painkiller and had been introduced into Egypt around 1500BCE.

34   Gabra, S. 1956: 53. This prescription clearly shows the nature of ancient Egyptian medicine as a mix of real pharmacological knowledge (represented by the calming effects of opium), and superstition (the fly dirt). This did not change for millennia, as shown by a similar concoction found in a much later Coptic Christian remedy; see note 94 below.

35   Ibid.; Gabra, as a knowledgeable Egyptian, also reports that an ancient prescription for abscesses found in the Smith Papyrus recommends a poultice made from red poppy flowers, and that this concoction is still used today – 3,500 years later – by Egyptian agricultural workers, with the red poppy flowers being replaced by the opium-poppy capsule (Gabra 1956: 51).

36   Bietak, M. 2000

37   Linear A was the official script of the royal Minoan palaces and society in pre-Mycenaean times and was used from c. 1900–1450BCE

38   Blegen, E.P. 1936: 372

39   Merlin, M.D. 1984: 245–6; Karageorghis, V. 1976

40   Bucholz, H-G. and V. Karageorghis 1973: 165

41   Budge, E.A.W. [1930] 1978: 310

42   Kritikos, P.G. and S.P. Papadaki 1967: 23

43   Marinatos, S. and M. Hirmer 1960: 153

44   Zervos, C. 1956: 47

45   Merlin, M.D. 1984: 265

46   Personal communication to M.D. Merlin 12 April 1977. Quoted in Merlin, M.D. 1984: 267–8

47   Merlin, M.D. 1984: 265–6

48   John Chadwick, personal communication to M.D. Merlin. Quoted in Merlin, M.D. 1984: 198

49   Merlin, M.D. 1984: 204–5

50   The site of Troy (modern Hisarlik) in what is today north-west Turkey was excavated by Heinrich Schliemann between 1871–3 and again in 1878–9. The site has nine distinct levels ranging from 3000BCE to the fourth century CE. Schliemann identified Troy 1 then Troy 2 as the Homeric city, but today the majority opinion is that Troy 7, dated to 1300–1190BCE, is the most likely candidate, not least because it was a large and well-fortified settlement, had been destroyed by war and thus matches closely Homer's account of the city's destruction by the Greeks.

51   Homer's *Odyssey* 4. 219–32. (transl. Rouse, W.H.D. 1937: 43–4), quoted in Merlin, M.D. 1984: 214

52   Kritikos, P.G. and S.P. Papadaki 1967

53   Merlin, M.D. 1984: 215

54   The well-respected expert Professor Manfred Hesse of the Institute of Organic Chemistry at Zurich University regards nepenthes as possibly being opium dissolved in wine (Hesse, M. 2002: 338).

55   Wace, A.J.B. et al, 1908–9: 108,133; and see Merlin, M.D. 1984: 213–4

56   Kritikos, P.G. and S.P. Papadaki 1967: 30

57   Plutarch, *Theseus* 30, 31. Quoted in Merlin, M.D. 1984: 213

58   Brewer, E.C. [1894] 1993: 637

59   Virgil, *Georgica* 1.78, quoted in Merlin, M.D. 1984: 233

60   Merlin, M.D. 1984: 159–63

61   The original early Greek term for the opium poppy is *mekon*, and may be of Indo-European origin. In Old German it is *mage* or *maga,* and in Ancient Slav, *maki*. The modern term opium derives from Latin, and its Greek inspiration,

opion (poppy juice), is a diminutive of *opos*, meaning vegetable juice (Merlin, M.D. 1984: 148–50; and see Veselovskaya, M.A. [1933] 1976: 12).

62   Skalet, C.H. 1928: 41; Kerényi, C. 1963: 42

63   Gow, A.S.F (ed.) 1965, quoted in Merlin, M.D. 1984: 220

64   Amar, Z. 2006: 23. The page reference here is to an English translation of the original Hebrew publication which Amar kindly supplied to the author in July 2011. The bibliographic reference is to the Hebrew version. Interestingly, the Jewish scholar Abraham Ofir Shemesh mentions that children from villages in this area were put to sleep with 'pills' made from opium, honey and dough (Shemesh 2009).

65   Pausanias 2.19.4ff, quoted in Merlin, M.D. 1984: 212. Aphrodite, while usually identified as the goddess of love, was also associated with flowers and springtime and thus related to the Earth Mother and fertility deities (ibid. and see Seyfert, O. 1956:39).

66   Two thousand years later, the botanist Carl Linnaeus reportedly counted 32,000 seeds in a single poppy capsule (Perry, F. 1972: 221).

67   Merlin, M.D. 1984: 221

68   Ibid.: 230–1

69   The Inner Gate (Propylaia) at Eleusis, was built around 40BCE by the Roman Consul Appius Claudius Pulcher, a contemporary of Cicero. The architraves which rested on two Corinthian columns were decorated with triglyphs and metopes which carried the images of items associated with the Eleusinian Mysteries. These included sheaves of grain, sacrificed bull skulls and distinctive rosettes. The rosettes had four petals that corresponded to the poppy, and were often reduplicated as eight-petal motifs (Kerényi, C., 1967: 74–5, and figure 21:b).

70   Taylor, T. [1791] 1891: 107

71   Valencic, I. 1994; Wasson, R.G., et al 1978

72   Cicero, *Laws* II, xiv.36

73   Merlin, M.D. 1984: 212

74   Reflecting the ancient symbolic associations of the poppy with the pine cone and, to a certain extent, the pomegranate, Hera's sanctuary has preserved the seeds of all of these. The seeds of the poppy and pomegranate are of course both edible and symbolic. The ivory representations are especially significant inasmuch as ivory itself was commercially valuable and ritually significant, and thus ivory poppies compounded this dual symbolism. See Pedley, J. 2005: 165–6.

75   There are thirteen references to opium and the opium poppy in Hippocrates' work (Scarborough, J. 1995: 5).

76   Kritikos, P.G. and S.P. Papadakis 1967

77   Ibid.

78   Theophrastus, quoted in Kritikos, P.G. and S.P. Papadaki 1967

79   Herakleides, *On Government*, quoted in Kritikos and Papadaki 1967. Other Greek peoples used the poppy in euthanasia, often with hemlock, and also to ease the pains of old age (Kritikos and Papadaki 1967: notes 23, 24, 25).

80   Booth, M. 1996: 20. The exact year of Hannibal's death is debated; Atticus and Livy suggest he died in 183BCE, but others indicate it was 182BCE or 181BCE.

81   Booth, M. 1996: 20

82   Dioscorides, *De Materia Medica*, [2000], 4–64

83   Ibid. Quoted in Kritikos, P.G. and S.P. Papadaki 1967

84   Scarborough, J. 1996: 48

85   Kritikos, P.G. 1960: 61; 13.273; Kritikos, P.G. and S.P. Papadaki 1967. It appears also that Marcus Aurelius took opium as an ingredient in the drug mithridatium (arguably the ultimate designer drug of antiquity, which had perhaps sixty-five components and was supposed to protect against poison and fortify the body). The percentage of opium was adjusted according to the emperor's mood, and contrary to some opinions, Marcus Aurelius does not seem to have been addicted to opium (Scarborough, J. 1995: 17–8).

86   Ciaraldi, M. 2003

87   Ciaraldi, M. 2000

88   Jashemski, W.M.F. and F.G. Meyer 2002: 138–9

89   Dioscorides (I.64.6), quoted in Kritikos and Papadakis 1967. Some sources mention that Egyptian opium in Alexandria was adulterated (presumably to weaken its deadlier effects), and was referred to in later times as Cyrenaic and Theban opium (Kritikos and Papadaki 1967, especially note 30).

90   Crawford, D.J. 1973

91   Ibid.: 238

92   Kritikos, P.G. and S.P. Papadaki 1967

93   Crawford, D.J. 1973: 232; the Oxyrhynchus papyri preserved several fragments of medical remedies for a variety of ailments, a number including opium, such as one for use as a soporific (henbane, anise and opium), and another for quartan fever – malaria – (hemlock, henbane, opium, castor and black hellebore) (Hunt, A.S. 1911).

94   Crawford, D.J. 1973: 232; and see Chassinat 1921, which deals with a Coptic Christian medical papyrus and contains about twenty-two mentions of opium.

As with ancient Egyptian remedies, the mix of real and imagined properties of ingredients is evident in prescriptions for ailments of the uterus, in which opium is mixed with the 'oil of small rats' to effect a cure (Gabra 1956: 54).

95   Another important opium-poppy growing area during Islamic times was around the town of Abu Tig in Upper Egypt. Interestingly, its Arabic name derived from the Greek word *apotheke*, meaning 'shop' or 'warehouse', but which later inspired the Latin word 'apothecary' from which the term 'chemist' was derived.

96   Tibi, S. 2006. Early Islamic medicinal knowledge of opium may have been influenced by the large number of Hellenistic Greek treatises which were available in Alexandria and elsewhere in the decades following the seventh century Muslim conquests, and which were avidly collected, translated and read by Muslim scholars in Baghdad during the eighth, ninth and tenth centuries. This phenomenon, often called the 'Translation Movement', is one of the most extraordinary, and, in the West, under-acknowledged, intellectual achievements in history. Ironically, the Byzantine successors to Greek/Hellenistic civilisation cared little for this vast storehouse of documents as they had been produced by pre-Christian pagan scholars. See Gutas, D. 1998.

97   Emboden, W. 1979

98   Booth, M. 1996: 25

99   Ibid.: 32–3

100   Ibid.: 26–7

101   Ibid.: 33; Dover's precise measurements of ingredients in his Dover's Powder produced a relatively reliable and consistent potion at a time when there was neither regulation nor standardisation in the preparation and prescription of medications.

3. Opium Dreams

1   Goebel, S. 2007: 13. The influence on the First World War of earlier nineteenth-century literary and cultural fashions, and the resulting emergence of 'modernity', is explored in Paul Fussell's landmark book *The Great War and Modern Memory* [1975] (2000). Stefan Goebel plays on the title of Fussell's book, and goes back to medieval times to identify and trace complex aspects of culture that, in a reconfigured form, resurfaced before, during and after the world's first industrialised war. In particular, he explores the role of medievalism in post-1918 war commemoration, drawing parallels between the soldiers of the First World

War and medieval knights, and showing how the nineteenth century's fascination with medieval values of chivalry were reshaped between 1914 and 1918, but did not survive the Second World War as an appropriate way of representing conflict.

2   Thisteleton, T. H. 1889: 372

3   Alkaline properties refer to a substance (often a natural salt) which is soluble in water. Alkaloids are naturally occurring chemical compounds, many of which have mind-altering effects on humans and animals. The term was invented in 1819 by the German chemist Carl Meissner, and applied to Sertürner's morphium/morphine – the first alkaloid to be isolated in chemical terms.

4   Throughout the discussion of the Opium Wars, I have used the Wade-Giles system for Mandarin Chinese, following the usage in many of the works consulted and cited below.

5   Anon. 1850: 147–59

6   Today Lintin Island is more familiarly known as Nei Lingding Island.

7   Chrastina, P. n.d.

8   Savoie, C. 2004

9   Under the Wade-Giles system, the city – today Nanjing – was called Nan-ching. However, the agreement made there is universally known as the Treaty of Nanking, and so I have retained that style here.

10   Now known as the Hai River, it flows from Peking (Beijing) to T'ien-ching (Tianjin), then on to the Yellow Sea.

11   Chinese women as well as men were opium addicts, but while figures are readily available for the latter, they are more difficult to assess for the former. This may well be due to the increased sensitivities concerning the social stigma attached to women addicts, itself exacerbated by the fact that many female addicts were forced to become prostitutes and died of disease.

12   Savoie, C. 2004

13   Booth, M. 1998: 35; Hayter, A. 1968

14   This influence reached into literature beyond poetry. Mary Shelley knew Coleridge well, and referred to *The Rime of the Ancient Mariner* twice in her Gothic novel *Frankenstein* of 1818. This tale of a human-like creature made from spare body parts was eerily prophetic of limbless veterans fitted with prosthetic arms and legs who would haunt European streets in the aftermath of the Great War.

15   High, B., 2005

16   De Quincey, T. 1897

17 De Quincey's problematical and overemotional relationship with, and reaction to the death of, Catherine is explored by Thron, E.M. 1988

18 Allingham, P.V. 2006

19 Ibid.

20 In 1860, the French poet Charles Baudelaire translated and adapted *The Confessions*, spreading the artistic reputation of opium further still.

21 Barrett Browning, E. 1843

22 Ward Fay, P. 1975: 6

23 Booth, M. 1996: 191

24 Ibid.: 190

25 Inciardi, J.A. 1990: 1

26 http://www.encyclopedia.com/topic/opium.aspx; Aldrich, M.R (n.d.) http://www.cnsproductions.com/pdf/Aldrich.pdf; different pharmacists in different states and cities returned varying percentages, which ranged between sixty and eighty per cent. Kandall, S.R. (1999): 16,18

27 Inciardi, J.A. 1990: 2

28 Heroes of the time, such as Ernest Shackleton and Captain Scott, fortified themselves with cocaine tablets on their expeditions to Antarctica.

29 See, for example, ARU 2001

30 US surgeon-general, 1870: 645, cited in Mandel, Jerry. n.d.

31 Starkey, G. 1971: 482–4

32 Booth, M. 1998: 73

33 Ibid.: 73; and see Courtwright, D. 1978: 106–7, and 1982

34 Ibid.: 73

35 Koznarsky, M. 2007; and see Hasegawa, G.R. and F. Terry Hambrecht 2003

36 Starkey, G. 1971: 482–4

37 Brooks, S. 1966: 127

38 Mandel, J. n.d.

39 Whitmen, Wait. 1895, cited in Mandel, J. n.d.

40 Adams, George Worthington. 1952: 138; see also 50–1, 116–9, 228–9

41 Courtwright, D. 1982

42 Anon. 1867: 572–4

43 Day, H. 1868; Oliver, F.E. 1872; Anon, 1876

44 Terry, C.E. and M. Pellens [1928] (1970): 15

45 Russell, I. 1887; Keeley 1881

46 Starkey, G. 1971: 482–4

47   Day, H. 1861: 1 (emphasis added); see also Booth, M. 1998: 73

48   Moore, J.H. 1997: 111

49   Ibid.: 111

50   Anon. 2004

51   'How did we get here?: History has a habit of repeating itself', *The Economist*, 26 July 2001, http://www.economist.com/node/706583?story_id=E1_SDGVRP

52   Brecher, E. 1972

53   The signatory nations were China, France, Germany, Italy, Japan, the Netherlands, Persia, Portugal, Russia, Siam, the United Kingdom and the United States, and the agreement was later incorporated into the Treaty of Versailles, which set the terms for peace after the Great War.

54   International Opium Convention, The Hague, 23 January 1912, http://www. worldlii.org/int/other/LNTSer/1922/29.html

55   Booth, M. 1998: 74

56   Hodgson, B. 2001: 85

57   Ruskin, J. 1875: 79

58   Ibid.: 86

4. Barbed-wire Battlefields

1   Cecil Lewis, quoted in Fussell, P. [1975] (2000): 254

2   Ibid.

3   Feilding, R. 1929: 21, 23

4   Hodges, F.J. 1988: 84

5   Martin, J. 2009: 220. Sapper Jack Martin's diary is one of several recently published First World War accounts that had lain undiscovered for decades, or whose significance has only recently been realised. Diary keeping, by British soldiers at least, was against military law during the 1914–18 conflict, partly because the militarily useful details they might contain could fall into enemy hands if the soldier was captured (dead or alive). Severe punishments could be inflicted on diary keepers if discovered, yet despite this, it now seems that more soldiers wrote daily accounts of their experiences than had hitherto been realised. Some of these diaries are substantial enough to have been published as books, as with Martin (2009) and Smith (2009), while others have appeared as articles/chapters in the academic literature (see Schofield, J. 2009; Bagwell, M. 2012, and Leonard, M. 2012 for recent examples).

6   Smith, L. 2009

7   Ibid. Private Len Smith's diary is another example of a recently discovered and published First World War account. What makes it unusual is that it is highly illustrated with the author-artist's own sketches and paintings, as well as contemporary postcards, posters, cartoons and newspaper clippings which he acquired during the war. The recent publication of this extraordinary document reproduces the diary and its illustrations in typescript but with some of the author's original longhand comments in unpaginated form.

8   Elias, A. 2007

9   Ibid.

10   Paul Fussell, quoted in Elias, A. 2007. Back in Australia, the soldiers' womenfolk placed flowers on memorials and special places such as the gates of Woolloomooloo in Sydney, and included handwritten messages for those who would never return. (Luckins, T. and J. Damousi, quoted in Elias, A. 2007)

11   Stidger, W.L. 1918

12   Verleyen, H. 2004: 13–4

13   Ibid.: 22

14   Prescott, J.F. 1985: 98

15   Graves, D. 1997: 200–2

16   http://greatwar.nl/poppies/orderofburial.html

17   http://shelllibrary.com/samples/11551s.pdf

18   Graves, D. 1997: 202

19   Preminger, A. [1965] (1969): 311; de Sola Pinto, V. [1951] (1965): 130

20   Art nouveau was especially fashionable in Europe, though arguably less so in Great Britain, which favoured the work of the Arts and Crafts movement.

21   Chambless, S. 2004. This article, appearing on the First World War website, Hellfire Corner, focuses on the Remembrance Poppy's relationship with poetry, literature and memory. While written for the general public (albeit one with an interest in the First World War), it identifies and explores many important issues and connections.

22   Hart, L. 2000

23   Broadway, Lisa. 1992/2007

24   Fussell, P. [1975] (2000): 243

25   The decline of the rose and the rise of the poppy were gradual, with, perhaps, the poppy not totally displacing the rose until around 1921. Physical evidence supporting this view takes the form of ephemera in the shape of paper souvenirs

for Armistice/Remembrance Day events during the early 1920s that show the rose, not the poppy (James Brazier, personal communication to the author 12 February 2010). It is also worth noting that the (recently ended) modern phenomenon of throwing flowers onto the passing hearses containing the repatriated dead from Afghanistan at the Wiltshire village of Wootton Bassett, involved mainly roses and other flowers rather than the poppy. And see chapter 8, note 65.

26   Frye, N. 1957: 144, cited in Fussell, P. [1975] 2000: 244. The poet David Jones explained the literary connections of the rose with Englishness when he said, 'If the dog-rose moves something in the Englishman at a deeper level than the Union flag it is . . . because the poetry of England, drawing upon the intrinsic qualities of the familiar and common June rose, by a single image of a rose, managed to recall and evoke, for the English, a June-England association.' (Quoted in Iles, J. 2008: 202)

27   Mosse, G.L. 1990: 109

28   Ibid.: 107

29   The image of men being sacrificed in war as Christ was a recurring visual and literary trope during and after the war, and was reinforced by the landscapes of battle. In 1916, for example, at the height of the Battle of the Somme, countless men marched past Crucifix Corner, with its medieval calvary showing Christ on the cross. Hours later, they were rushing to oblivion across poppy-strewn battlefields. By the early 1920s, millions of poppies were being laid annually at the foot of calvaries, crosses and memorials across the world, identifying the wartime sacrifices of men, women and children with that of Christ two millennia earlier (Saunders 2003a).

30   Fussell, P. [1975] 2000: 159

31   Dyer, G. 1995: 18

32   Broadway, L. 1992/2007

33   Fussell, P. [1975] (2000): 250

34   Isaac Rosenberg quoted Fussell, P. [1975] (2000): 77, 251

35   Chambless, S. 2004

36   Silkin, J. 1972: 280

37   Ireland, Maj. Gen. M.W. 1923: 943

38   Ireland, Maj. Gen. M.W. 1927: 1018

39   Ibid.

40   Dunn, J.C. [1938] 1997: 369

41   Amar, Z. 2006; this unusual event has another interesting dimension, because the British, attacking Gaza from their base in Egypt, had to source large quantities of opium from somewhere. And, while *Papaver somniferum* had been grown in Egypt for millennia, its cultivation had been outlawed by the British at the beginning of the war in 1914 as a result of the Harrison Narcotics Act (Gabra 1956: 40, 50). This law was probably flouted at the local village level, whose piecemeal opium production may have provided the British with sufficient quantities of the drug for their ingenious plan, and they may also have held quantities of opium which had been confiscated since 1914.

42   Robinson, B. 2000: 388

43   Ibid.: 391

44   Editorial. *New York Medical Journal* 1915, cited in Brecher, E.M. 1972

45   Editorial. *American Medicine* 1915, cited in Brecher, E.M. 197

46   Marks, J. 1915: 315

47   These figures come from the US Department of Justice and were published by the television network PBS at http://www.pbs.org/greatwar/resources/casdeath_pop.html.

48   Terry, C.E. and M. Pellens 1928: 69; Waldorf, D., M. Orlick and C. Reinarman 1974. Riddled with legends, half-truths and political agendas, the extent of opiate addiction remains confused. It has been called a Civil War myth, and part of a fabricated past used by the US government to justify its draconian anti-drug laws during the 1950s and 60s. Such laws were needed, it was argued, to avoid the dangers of narcotic addiction so plainly visible in America's most iconic conflict – its own Civil War. Yet prohibition was to prove a double-edged sword, as Rufus King, chairman of the American Bar Association's committee on narcotics wrote in the *Yale Law Journal* in 1953:

> The true addict . . . is totally enslaved to his habit . . . So long as society will not traffic with him on any terms, he must remain the abject servitor of his vicious nemesis, the peddler . . . All the billions our society has spent enforcing criminal measures against the addict have had the sole practical result of protecting the peddler's market, artificially inflating his prices, and keeping his profits fantastically high.

49   Verleyen, H. 1997: 27

50   Chambless, S. 2004

51   Ibid.

52   Fussell, P. [1975] (2000): 250

53   Graves, D. 1997: 247

54   Ibid.: 250

55   Verleyen, H. 2004: 56–7

56   RCL 2007

57   This new flower – the 'almost Remembrance Poppy' – had so changed its nature that it would be used commemoratively, emblazoned in scarlet on the bible-black cover of a specially bound 2001 limited edition of Brooke's *Collected Poems*. When George Woodbury wrote the introduction in 1916, he was seemingly only half aware of the change in both poppy and poetry which had occurred: 'There is a grave in Scyros, amid the white and pinkish marble of the isle, the wild thyme and the poppies, near the green and blue waters. There Rupert Brooke was buried.'

58   Chambless, S. 2004

59   Chinese peasants from Shandong Province were attracted by pay rates four times greater than they received at home. They were initially employed on general labouring duties, especially repairing roads, during the war. The British began using them from mid-1917. After hostilities ended, they were widely used to clear the battlefields and locate human remains for burial. During these immediate postwar years, some British women drivers were employed to transport Chinese labourers around the old battlefields, and bought souvenirs which the Chinese had made from the scrap metal they had acquired while carrying out their duties (see Summerscale, K. 1998: 49–53). Altogether, the British would command about 95,000 Chinese men by 1920, and the French 44,000. For recent overviews of the Chinese Labour Corps (CLC), see Bailey, P. 2000; Dendooven, D. and P. Chielens (eds). 2008: 137–51

5. The Poppy Lady

1   Toland, J. 1976: XIX, 71, 72

2   Goodrick-Clarke, N. 1992: 145

3   Ibid.

4   Michael, M. 1941: 27

5   Ibid.: 47

6   Ibid.: 48

7   Ibid.: 79

8   Ibid.

9   Ibid.: 48

10   Ibid.: 49

11   http://www.powys-lannion.net/Powys/America/Keedick.htm

12   Lee Keedick said that Howard Carter, the discoverer of Tutankhamun's tomb, was 'the most quarrelsome and cantankerous of men'. (James, T.G.H. 2001: 370)

13   http://query.nytimes.com/gst/abstract.html?res=F30C10FB3B5910738DDDA00 A94DF405B808EF1D3

14   Michael, M. 1941: 69

15   Ibid.: 72

16   Ibid.: 76

17   In yet another fascinating but incidental way, Memorial Day has an origin which collides with poppy history. It began as 'Decoration Day', when flowers were placed on the graves of the American Civil War dead. General John A. Logan, commander-in-chief of the 'Grand Army of the Republic' (the Union's veterans' association), followed the Confederate practice of laying flowers on their soldiers' graves by announcing that 30 May 1868 would be the first official Decoration Day, and would see flowers laid on the graves of Union soldiers at Virginia's Arlington National Cemetery, outside Washington, DC. In 1873, Decoration Day became an official holiday in New York State, and from 1882 gradually came to be called Memorial Day, though this name change was only made official by a 1954 Act of Congress.

      The cemetery had been the site of a pre-war home of Confederate General Robert E. Lee, and became a national cemetery in 1864 when the Union started burying its dead on the property. It is said that the decision was made partly in retaliation for Lee joining his state of Virginia in seceding from the Union. (He had been a top graduate of the US Military Academy and a hero of the Mexican-American War.)

      Bitterness between the former Confederate states and the Union states lingered on well after the American Civil War, and it was only after the First World War Armistice that Decoration Day/Memorial Day shifted from honouring the Union dead to honouring all of the Civil War dead – and eventually all Americans who have died in wartime.

18   ALA, 2009

19   Michael, M. 1941: 80

20   Graves, D. 1997: 267–8

21   Ibid.: 268

22 Ibid.

23 The Legion became the Royal British Legion in 1971.

24 Brazier, J. 1996: 34

25 Harding, B. 2001: 122

26 Anon. ('The Wayfarer') n.d.

27 The Thin Red Line had an evocative military association in the British public's imagination. It related to the red-coated Sutherland Highlanders at the Battle of Balaclava on 25 October 1854 during the Crimean War. The small force of Sutherland Highlanders stood firm against a superior number of Russian cavalry, and the phrase The Thin Red Line became an English figure of speech for any thinly spread force holding out against enemy attack. The use of this term in the 'Wayfarer' leaflet was designed to recall such heroic imagery.

28 Anon. ('The Wayfarer') n.d.

29 Ibid.

30 Ibid.

31 Ibid.

32 *The Times*, 14 November 1921: 5, quoted in Bushaway, B. 1993: 155.

33 Grey-Wilson, C. 2005: 72, 127, 133–4

34 Porter, E.M. 1958: 117

35 Ibid.

36 London, M., T. O'Reagan, P. Aust, and A. Stockford. 1990: 1345; Booth, M. 1996: 57

37 Dunn, J.C. [1938] (1997): 199

38 Booth, M. 1996: 57–8

39 Brazier, J. 1996: 35

40 Harding, B. 2001: 123

41 Ibid.: 125

42 The Gallipoli campaign had profound political consequences for New Zealand and Australia, where the bravery and sacrifices of the ANZACs engendered a strong sense of national identity in both countries. ANZAC Day was announced as a public holiday in Australia in 1921, and was first observed by all Australian states in 1927. (Clarke, S. 2006)

The importance of ANZAC day in New Zealand continues, and was thrown into sharp relief in 2008 when thieves stole six thousand ANZAC Day poppies from the 'Takapuna Returned Services Association' in Auckland. It is alleged that they stole the poppies in order to sell them as though they were legitimate

ANZAC Day collectors, and planned to keep the proceeds for themselves (Ritchie, K. 2008). The thieves also took official collectors' badges and donation buckets. The theft was covered by local radio, which interviewed people on the city's streets about the news. Almost everyone was appalled at the theft. The shocked included Lilly Schmidt, a young German woman backpacking her way around New Zealand. Schmidt was wearing a poppy – a tradition unknown in Germany. She said, 'I think it's pretty important because I wish we had something like that in Germany as well.' When the reporter asked Schmidt how young Germans felt about countrymen who had died during war, she replied, 'Yeah, we still feel quite responsible for what happened even if people say OK, it is a long time ago, but we still feel responsible. So I think it's pretty important to keep this alive and to have remembrance days like this.' (Ritchie, K. 2008)

43 Clarke, S. 2006
44 Graves, D. 1997: 269
45 Michael, M. 1941: 81
46 Ibid.
47 Anon. 1919
48 Anon. 1921b
49 Anon. 1921a
50 Michael, M. 1941: 82; ALA 2009
51 Ibid.: 82
52 Ibid.: 83
53 Goody, J. 1994: 292–4
54 Michael, M. 1941: 84
55 Ibid.
56 Anon. 1921c
57 Delano, R. 2002.
58 Dyhouse, T. 1997: 13
59 Ibid.
60 Anon. 1922; Roan, L. 1941: 129
61 Anon. 1922
62 Hoover, H. 1931
63 Michael, M. 1941: 79, 80, 81
64 Ibid.: 90
65 Ibid.: 81
66 USWPA/FWP 1939

67   Ibid.

68   Ibid.

69   Hanlon, M.E. n.d.

6. Souvenir of War

1   The red poppies are situated in the cornfield foreground of this famous painting, and were used by the artist to conjure memories of Remembrance Poppies as well as bloody battlefields. See AWM (Australian War Memorial), n.d.b.

2   Pearl was a Tasmanian who served with the Australian Imperial Force (AIF). He enlisted on 9 November 1915 and returned to Australia in May 1918. He is an exception to the rule that most soldiers who made such souvenir trench-art objects did not keep notes on their manufacture (or, if they did, these have not survived). His written testimonies are held in the Australian War Memorial at Canberra (AWM n.d.). Trench-art objects, mainly though not exclusively the reworked metal detritus of war, were made during the conflict by both soldiers and refugees. During the inter-war years of 1919–39, civilians deprived of their livelihoods made similar items as souvenirs for the bereaved who made pilgrimages to the battlefields. Once regarded merely as kitsch ephemera of war, they are now valued as important three-dimensional memory objects, and often as remarkable works of art (see Saunders, N.J. 2002a, 2003b).

3   Wenzel, M. and J. Cornish 1980: 8

4   Derez, M. 1997: 441. The floral 'aftermath' of the First World War in Belgian Flanders has only recently drawn the attention of scholars, yet is a fascinating topic associated with postwar commemoration and landscape rejuvenation. While many foreign species appeared during and after the war itself, few alien species managed to establish themselves permanently in the area – other than those deliberately planted around war memorials and war cemeteries (Stubbe, L. n.d.).

5   Pedlow 2004. Many American towns claimed to have invented Memorial Day, but in May 1966, President Lyndon B. Johnson retrospectively declared that the official birthplace was the fatefully named town of Waterloo, New York, because it had observed the day for the first time on 5 May 1866. When Charles Lindbergh cast his poppies over America's war dead at Waregem, he was not that far from the Napoleonic battlefield of Waterloo, where poppies growing on freshly dug graves had caused such comment a century before, and in memory of which New York State's Waterloo had been named.

6   Verleyen, H. 2004: 49

7   Royal British Legion website article 28 October 2004

8   O'Neill, B. 2008; Friedman, D.M. 2008

9   Brown, A. 1971: 85

10   Harding, B. 2001: 123

11   Ibid.: 136

12   See a selection of these stories at the Poppy Factory website: http://www.
     poppyfactory.org/our-stories-2.html. Today, alongside the 100,000 wooden crosses
     with poppies attached, the Poppy Factory workers also make wooden Stars of
     David, crescents and a 'stick' for atheists (Hudson, R. 2008).

13   Quoted in Gregory, A. 1994: 103

14   Newall, V. 1976: 227

15   It became the Royal Canadian Legion in 1959.

16   Quoted on Canadian War Museum website, CWM (Canadian War Museum)
     n.d.

17   The extraordinary variety of items bearing the Royal Canadian Legion's poppy
     logo can be seen in the latest Legion Branch Catalogue: http://legion.ca/_PDF/
     Supply/Catalogue_Fall_11_Web_e.pdf

18   Gaddo, R. 2006

19   Michael, M. 1941: 113–4; and see, Penney, J. 2006, and Shannon-Martin, L.
     2007

20   Gregory, A. 1994: 103

21   Brown, A. 1971: 81

22   Gregory, A. 1994: 103

23   Ibid.: 107

24   Ibid.

25   Ibid.: 105

26   Ibid.

27   Ibid.: 102

28   Ibid.: 101

29   Ibid.: 101

30   Harding, B. 2001: 127

31   Ibid.: 132. The Field of Remembrance at Westminster Abbey was originally
     known as the 'Empire Field of Remembrance'. The tenth anniversary of the 1918
     Armistice – Poppy Day 1928 – fell on a Sunday, providing for an especially evocative
     Remembrance Sunday event. The following day's report in The Times said,

One of the most attractive features of the day was the effort of a number of disabled ex-servicemen from the poppy factory at Richmond, who were engaged in transforming a portion of the grass plot near the north door of Westminster Abbey into a miniature 'field of remembrance.' A roughly constructed wooden cross was set in the turf, and passers-by were invited to hand their poppies to the disabled men who reverently placed them around and near the cross. As the day wore on the spread of blooms increased until the ground was aglow with the scarlet emblems and the little wooden cross stood out in relief. The thousands who yesterday passed this simple representation of a Flanders poppy field on their way to pay homage to the memory of the fallen at the grave of the Unknown Warrior must have been stirred by its poignant appeal.

The wooden cross was likely dedicated 'In Memory of Thomas Atkins' – the symbolic 'everyman' of the British forces, and presumably also identified as the Unknown Warrior. By 1933, this practice had become widely accepted. *The Times* of 13 November 1933 reported, 'Many thousands also went to Westminster Abbey to file past the Grave of the Unknown Warrior and to plant a cross or a poppy in the Empire Field of Remembrance which for another year has been arranged in the shadow of the Abbey. The wearing of poppies on Saturday was general.' I am very grateful to James Brazier for bringing this fascinating sequence of events to my attention.

32   Gregory, A. 1994: 100–1, 115
33   Quoted in Ibid.: 101
34   Ibid.: 111
35   Dyhouse, T. 1997: 13
36   Ibid.: 16; Mason Jr., H. M. 1999: 59
37   Ibid.: 16
38   Read, H. 1966: 136–43
39   Gregory, A. 1994: 102
40   Michael, M. 1941: 87
41   Ibid.: 88
42   Gregory, A. 1994: 114
43   Ibid.: 172
44   Ibid.: 172
45   Harding, B. 2001: 138

46   Summerby, J. 2005

47   INAC 2008. First Nation veterans were at a serious disadvantage for a variety of reasons, including the iniquities of soldier settlement land purchases, a restrictive clause of the Indian Act concerning prairie homesteads and the limited approval of loan applications. Despite their patriotism and bravery during the war, First Nation Canadians often experienced appalling prejudice. When Duncan Campbell Scott, the deputy superintendent general of Indian affairs, appeared before a parliamentary committee concerned with amending the Indian Act in 1920, he testified: 'I want to get rid of the Indian problem . . . Our objective is to continue until there is not a single Indian in Canada that has not been absorbed into the body politic and there is no Indian question, and no Indian Department . . .' (INAC 2008).

48   Summerby, J. 2005: 10–1. Pegahmagabow was an extraordinary man. One of only thirty-nine men of the Canadian Expeditionary Force who received bars to their military medals, he was a fireman when the war began, but joined up in August 1914 and soon won a reputation for his iron nerves, patience and superb marksmanship. He earned his first military medal during the final Canadian assault on the village of Passchendaele between 5 and 6 November 1917, and his bar sometime later, possibly for taking three hundred German prisoners. He was invalided home in 1919 and became chief of the Parry Island Ojibwa Band. The list of names and accomplishments of First Nation Canadian troops is impressive and includes Henry Louis Norwest, who achieved a sharpshooting record of 115 fatal shots. A fellow soldier wrote of Norwest, 'Our famous sniper no doubt understood better than most of us the terrible cost of life and the price of death'. Norwest was awarded the Military Medal in 1917 during the Canadian assault on Vimy Ridge (Summerby J. 2005: 11–2).

49   INAC 2008

50   First Nation Canadians commemorate wars dating back into the nineteenth century with displays of the Remembrance Poppy. The war memorial on the Chippawas of Nawash Unceded First Nation on the Bruce Peninsula in Ontario presents a warrior dressed in First World War uniform standing guard over a plinth inscribed with the names of the dead from the conflicts of 1812, 1914–18, 1939–45, the Korean War and Desert Storm. Each of the 129 white wooden crosses bears a name and a red poppy. The powerful legacy of First World War service is everywhere apparent. On Remembrance Day 2002, the two minutes of silence leading up to 11 a.m. saw the unfurling of the Canadian and US flags and their lowering to the

ground in homage to the dead. 'The Last Post' echoed across the rain-swept sky, a wreath was laid at the foot of the memorial and afterwards John McCrae's 'In Flanders Fields' was read. (Shaw, T. 2002)

51   'Veteran's Day Poppy' appeared on one of the 1960s' most eccentric and iconic albums, Captain Beefheart and His Magic Band's *Trout Mask Replica*, released in June 1969 with writing credits to Don Van Vliet (Captain Beefheart). It was produced by the equally legendary figure Frank Zappa, and was issued on Zappa's own label, Straight Records. 'Veteran's Day Poppy' was recorded in August 1968, seven months before the rest of the album, and around the time of mass anti-war demonstrations in the United States – which may have inspired Beefheart to write the song. The year 1968 had begun with the Tet Offensive, where the North Vietnamese launched a surprise attack on American and South Vietnamese forces during the Lunar New Year ceasefire. As thousands of US casualties were reported each night on the news, many Americans turned against the war. 'Veteran's Day Poppy' is Beefheart's unique contribution to the anti-war pop music genre: the only song to focus on the Remembrance Poppy. For an account of the song's origins and recording see French, J. 'D'. 2010: 813. I would like to thank Paul Cornish for drawing my attention to this song, which I had quite forgotten since first hearing it back in 1970.

52   ALA 2009

53   Dyhouse, T. 1997: 15. Bandalos usually distributes two thousand to three thousand poppies annually – 1995 was his record year.

54   Mason Jr, H.M. 1999: 58

55   G. Parker, personal communication of 29 March 1999 to Jennifer Iles, and quoted in Iles, J. 2008: 216–7

56   R. Dunning, personal communication of 2 May 2000 to Jennifer Iles, and quoted in, Ibid.: 216

57   The ceremony at Lochnagar crater commemorating those who died at the opening of the Battle of the Somme takes place at 7.30 a.m. every 1 July. This ceremony has increased in popularity over the last decade, establishing a new landscape of commemoration which is being laid on top of the old battlefields and inter-war pilgrimages of remembrance.

58   Saunders, N.J. 2003: 224

59   The 'In Flanders Fields' museum was a victim of its own success. Within a few years it became obvious that changing ideas about exhibiting the First World War and a rapid increase in visitor numbers would require either another new

museum to be built or the old one to be enlarged (Saunders, N.J. 2010: 183–186). The decision was taken to greatly extend the existing museum space within the Cloth Hall building and to incorporate state-of-the-art audiovisual technology and a range of new exhibits that reflected the multinational nature of the war in the Ypres Salient. This new museum opened its doors in June 2012, with a redesigned poppy and barbed-wire logo, and a high-tech plastic wristband in the shape of a poppy within which an embedded microchip gives visitors access to the exhibition and activates nearby displays. One is struck by how this most modern version of the poppy echoes previous manifestations in which the opium poppy opened up a euphoric world of spirituality, and the Remembrance Poppy a realm of memory and ancestral commemoration.

60 Aaronovitch, D. 2004

61 Ibid.

62 BBC 2006b

63 Ibid.

64 Goody, J. 1994: 261

65 Ibid.: 286

66 Despite suffering terrible losses in both world wars, Italians never saw the poppy as anything other than a wild field flower. Their war graves, memorials and commemorative events have been festooned instead with laurel wreaths and chrysanthemums, the funeral flower of choice in Catholic Italy, and other scented flowers. Catholic indifference to the poppy counterpoints the Protestant (especially British) obsession with it – perhaps because of a common British aversion to so-called Catholic 'excesses', including decorating the dead with flowers. It is a peculiarity of history that the poppy was brought to British shores by a Frenchwoman who had abandoned her own country's longstanding devotion to the chrysanthemum.

67 Goody, J. 1994: 289

68 HFM n.d. The cornflower (*Centaurea cyanus*) is native to the Middle East, and, like the poppy, grows on broken ground. In folklore it is associated with young men and love, and its blue colour with healthy eyes. It can also be made into a herbal tea. When Howard Carter opened Tutankhamun's tomb in 1922, he found a small wreath of cornflowers and olive leaves placed around the sacred 'cobra and vulture' (*uraeus*) headdress of the outer golden coffin – still intact after three thousand years (Pharaoh's Flowers n.d.). In later Greek mythology, the centaur Chiron educated the young Achilles, and treated the young warrior's injuries with the cornflower.

Such early associations of the cornflower with combat reappeared during the First World War, particularly among French soldiers, who, like their British allies with the poppy, noticed how the cornflower grew amid the devastation of the battlefields. The cornflower became the French flower of remembrance in 1920, but was never as popular as the Remembrance Poppy, or the well-established Catholic funeral flower, the chrysanthemum. In 1934, the French government legalised the sale of cornflowers via the National Office of Veterans and Disabled War Veterans, and since 1957 cornflower stickers have been sold throughout France on 8 May and 11 November, the funds raised supporting the veterans, widows and orphans of war (HFM (Hazebrouck Hoflandt Météo n.d.). On 8 November 2009, BBC Radio 4 broadcast a fifteen-minute programme on the poppy and the cornflower, 'Poppies are Red, Cornflowers are Blue', in which presenter Mark Whitaker shared some of this history of the two remembrance flowers (Whitaker 2009).

69   Frisbie, R. 2008

70   Ibid.

71   Large-scale, commercially organised battlefield pilgrimages, which were such a feature of the 1920s and 1930s, were almost entirely the preserve of the former Allies. During this period, some German veterans and families did make the journey back to the old front lines, but they were generally not made welcome, either by local inhabitants or by the military authorities. Their numbers were also far smaller than those of the victorious nations, and so there was little opportunity for a Germanic commemorative tradition to develop with its own symbols of remembrance.

72   Linder, A.P. 1996: 31, 137

73   Ibid.: 52

74   Anon. 2008

7. The White Poppy

1   PPU n.d.

2   Gregory, A. 1994: 67

3   Ibid.:73

4   Ibid.:79

5   Ibid.:156

6   Nicolson, H. 1937: 57–8.

7   Gregory, A. 1994: 155

8   Ibid.:155

9   Ibid.

10   Ibid.

11   *The Times,* quoted in Ibid.

12   Ibid.: 163

13   Ibid.: 157

14   Ibid.: 158

15   PPU n.d.

16   Gregory, A. 1994: 158

17   Ibid.: 158–9

18   Quoted in Kamm, O. 2004

19   Ibid.

20   HoCd 1986

21   PPU n.d.

22   Ibid.

23   Ekklesia Staff Writers 2005

24   Ibid.

25   Ibid.

26   CBC News 2006

27   BBC 2006

28   Anon. 2001

29   Smith, L. 2008

30   Siegel, R.K. 2005: 128. Arguably more inexplicable is a recent case linking animals
     with opium poppies and crop circles. Tasmania grows the world's largest crop of
     legal opiates for the pharmaceutical industry – supplying fifty per cent of the global
     total for the production of morphine and related opiates. In 2009, Tasmania's
     attorney-general Lara Giddings said that, 'We have a problem with wallabies
     entering poppy fields, getting as high as a kite and going around in circles . . .
     Then they crash. We see crop circles in the poppy industry from wallabies that are
     high.' (Associated Press. 2009). Rick Rockliff, the field operations manager for
     Tasmanian Alkaloids, added that sheep also would graze on poppy stubble and
     'they would follow each other around in large circles'. (Tedmanson 2009). The
     media fascination with crop circles and opium-snacking wallabies has a personal
     association also as it was my uncle, David Chorley, who, together with Doug Bower
     'invented' the crop-circle phenomenon in southern England during the 1970s.

31   Fowler-Reeves, K. 2006

32   Animal Aid 2007

33   Ibid.

34   Ibid.

35   Ibid.

36   Kamm, O. 2004

37   Quoted in German, L. 2011

38   Hahn, P. 2006

8. The Narcotic Grasp on Helmand

1   VFWP 2007

2   Fergusson, J. 2008: 173; Bishop, P. 2008: 21; and see Walsh, D. 2006

3   Fergusson, J. 2008: 51–2

4   Walsh, D. 2006

5   Bishop, P. 2008: 35

6   Senlis Council 2006

7   UNODC 2007

8   Heikel, M. 1973: 306–7

9   Haley, L.I. 2006: 20

10   Macdonald, D. 2007: 143

11   Peters, G. 2009: 93. In July 2000, Mullah Omar announced the ban, which was widely observed even in non-Taliban opium-growing areas. Satellite photos and ground-level surveys showed only 8,000 hectares planted during the following spring – a fall of 82,000 hectares from the previous year.

12   Ibid.: 93–4. The poppy ban has been called the ultimate insider-trading con, with Taliban leaders buying vast quantities of opium immediately before the ban, effectively 'buying low' and later 'selling high'. Everyone associated with Mullah Omar made millions. A different view sees the short-lived ban and subsequent eradication as the major causes of Afghan farmer debt, and which in turn drives further expansion of poppy cultivation. The Taliban-inspired 'success story' against opium-poppy growing is described as 'one of the most blatant examples of a humanitarian crisis being consciously aggravated under the guidance of a UN agency.' (Jelsma, M. 2005)

13   Anon. 2006

14   Anderson, J. L. 2007

15   Anon. 2006

16   Sanderson, K. 2007

17   Walsh, D. 2008

18   UNODC 2007

19   Ibid.

20   Senlis Council 2006

21   Peters, G. 2009: 5

22   UNODC 2007

23   Bishop, P. 2008: 35

24   Evans, M. 2009; Martin, D. and M. Hickley 2009

25   Starkey, J. 2009

26   Smith, M. 2009

27   Smith, M. and S. Swinford 2009

28   Fergusson, J. 2008: 325

29   Evans, M. 2008

30   Cockburn, P. 2007

31   Tibi, S. 2006

32   Ehrenfeld, R. 2009

33   Jones, A. 2006

34   Sanderson, K. 2007

35   Fergusson, J. 2008: 144–5, 169

36   Sanderson, K. 2007

37   Bishop, P. 2008: 27

38   HoCFAC 2009

39   Walsh, D. 2008

40   Ibid.

41   Ibid.

42   Fergusson, J. 2008: 45

43   Ibid.: 168

44   Ibid.

45   Milmo, C. 2009

46   Callimachi, R. 2009

47   Ibid.

48   Ibid.

49   Fergusson, J. 2008:45

50   UNODC 2007

51   Fergusson, J. 2008: 45

52   Anon. 2007b

53   Poppy Palaces, K. Vlahos 2009; the American Conservative website; 'Poppy Palaces in Afghanistan: Delving deeper into the corruption of "narco-state"', *Payvand Iran News*, 15 May 2009, http://payvand.com/news/09/may/1156.html

54   Alternatives are not always political. In a modern biochemical twist to the millennia-old power of opium and its more recent derivatives, scientists have invented a morphine-free poppy. These mutant flowers seep a light brown sap when sliced, and which is the product of the new technique which short-cuts the morphine-producing process and yields an intermediate compound used in the manufacture of painkillers (Milius, S. 2004). Eerie echoes from the past can be heard on this twenty-first-century biochemical frontier: the compound is called thebaine and takes its name, somewhat ironically, from the high-quality, full-strength variety of sap drawn from the opium poppy grown near the ancient Egyptian city of Thebes (Luxor), where the Ebers Papyrus was discovered.

55   Senlis Council 2006

56   Farmer, B. 2008. At a recent fair sponsored by US Aid, and held on the outskirts of Kabul, the ancient relationship between the opium poppy and the pomegranate was given an ironic modern makeover. While the poppy has become the deadly emblem of the current insurgency, a US Aid spokesperson said of the pomegranate that, 'It's probably the one product in Afghanistan that is the best in the world . . . We want one product that could be the symbol of the new Afghanistan.'

57   Farmer, B. 2008

58   Senlis Council 2006: 39

59   Walsh, D. 2008

60   DFID 2009

61   Ibid.

62   Cohen, T. 2008. During the Second World War, the Australian Women's Land Army grew opium poppies at Dickson Experimental Station in the Australian Capital Territory (ACT), Victoria and Western Australia. Opium was cultivated for the war effort in an attempt to increase the amount of morphine available as a painkiller, and to compare the performance of different varieties. By 1943 Australia had become virtually self-sufficient in morphine, by producing it from dried poppy heads and poppy hay (straw). The photograph reproduced in the following source shows two very relaxed and happy Land Army workers strolling through a field of tall opium poppies. (CSIRO 2005)

63   Phillips, R. and B. Wigmore 2007

64   Oliver, S. 2009

65   It is of increasing concern to some in Wootton Bassett that their town's originally spontaneous and dignified show of respect has become too well known and organised, and that something personal has been lost. Some local people fear that too many of those who now attend are virtually 'grief tourists' (Pavia, W. 2009). The whole phenomenon of Wootton Bassett is an accident, and an example of how traditions are invented. Originally, the bodies of British servicemen were flown into RAF Brize Norton, but when that runway was being repaired, RAF Lyneham took over the role, putting Wootton Bassett on the route that the hearses took to the mortuary in Oxford. On one occasion, a repatriation occurred while there was bell-ringing practice in several of the town's churches, and a second tradition was born (Pavia, W. 2009). The tradition was ended in September 2011 when the repatriation flights returned to Brize Norton and consequently a new route bypassing Wootton Bassett was used.

66   On 2 January 2010, a storm of outrage hit the Wootton Bassett repatriations when the fundamentalist organisation 'Islam4UK' announced on the social network site YouTube that it would organise a march through the town to demonstrate on behalf of the thousands of Afghans killed during the Coalition forces' invasion and occupation. The organisation's leader, former solicitor Anjem Choudary, said that, 'It is extraordinary, that with well over 100,000 Muslims killed in Afghanistan in the last eight years, that those military servicemen who have directly contributed to their death are paraded as war heroes and moreover honoured for what is ultimately genocide' (Islam4UK. 2010). Choudary later said that Islam4UK's aims were non-violent, but that it advocated putting the United Kingdom under sharia law (anon. 2010). On 12 January 2010, the British government announced that it would ban Islam4UK within forty-eight hours (BBC). Choudary has since announced that the march was a publicity stunt which had achieved its aim of highlighting the plight of the Afghan people.

67   See OFT 2006

68   Phillips, R. and B. Wigmore 2007

69   Macfarlan Smith n.d.

70   Phillips, R. and B. Wigmore 2007

71   Anon. 2007a

72   Phillips, R. and B. Wigmore 2007

73   Van Ham, P. and J. Kamminga 2006–7

74 Huggler, J. 2007

75 Ibid.

76 Ibid. It is interesting to note that the opium poppy appears on the coat of arms of the Royal College of Anaesthetists.

77 Cappatto, M. 2007

78 The Senlis Council is now called the International Council on Security and Development (ICOS), with offices in Brussels, London, Dubai, Rio de Janeiro and Kabul. It describes itself as 'an international policy think tank working to combine grassroots research and policy innovation at the intersections of security, development, counter-narcotics and public health issues'. It can be visited online at www.icosgroup.net/home. The ICOS 'Poppy for Medicine' programme, which was started in 2005, is online at www.poppyformedicine.net/.

79 UNODC (United Nations Office on Drugs and Crime) 2007

80 Sanderson, K. 2007

81 Ibid.

82 Nikiforuk, A. 2008

83 Sanderson, K. 2007

84 Senlis Council 2006. See Mercer, D. 2007, for a counter-view. Mercer was the managing director of Johnson Matthey/Macfarlan Smith in 2007, and wrote at length rebutting what he saw as the Senlis Council's superficially attractive but in fact simplistic solution to a very complex international situation concerning global production and overproduction of opium for morphine. Some arguments are convincing, others not, and there are many 'ifs' and 'buts' involved in any analysis. Individuals can make up their own mind by consulting the report and comparing it to the Senlis Council's views available at www.poppyformedicine.net/. Mercer's report concludes, interestingly, with the view that 'Surely the best way is for the consuming country to discuss their [morphine] needs with potentially legitimate Afghan suppliers, then put in an estimate to the INCB [International Narcotics Control Board] and then create the licensing system and control systems.'

85 Farmer, B. 2009a, 2009b

86 Ibid.

87 Winfield, N. 2009

88 Ibid.

89 Lakshmanan, I.A.R. 2009

90 Winfield, N. 2009

91 Kaufman, S. 2009

92   Boone, J. 2009
93   Kaufman, S. 2009
94   Loyn, D. 2013
95   Anon. 2009
96   DeYoung, K. 2009a
97   DeYoung, K. 2009b
98   Boone, J. 2009
99   Irfan, H. 2003
100 See 'Moeders voor vrede'/Mothers for Peace, Poperinghe, Belgium. http://www.
     mothersfor peace.be
101 Hitchen, M. 2009
102 Ibid.
103 Pence, A. 2004; Irfan, H. 2003
104 Weiner, R. 2004
105 Weiner, R. 2005
106 Pence, A. 2004
107 Weiner, R. 2004
108 See images of weapons in Afghan war rugs at http://www.warrug.com/
109 O'Connell Jr, J. Barry 1997
110 RBL 2008; Anon. 2009
111 Collins, K. 2009

9. THE LIVING LEGACY

1   Anon. n.d. 'The Enniskillen Remembrance Day Massacre'
2   Spain, J. 2008
3   The practice of archaeology is often intimately tied to issues of politics and identity.
     In recent years, archaeological excavations of the front-line trenches in Thiepval
     Wood have attracted much interest in Ireland, and many relatives now visit the
     restored trench system not far from the Ulster Tower war memorial. The land
     was bought in 2004 by the Somme Association as part of its programme for the
     ninetieth anniversary of the Battle of the Somme. Archaeological data concerning
     the original trench construction and repair were used in the eventual reconstructions
     that are now part of a guided battlefield walk for visitors (Robertshaw and Kenyon
     2008: 23).
4   Graham, B. and P. Shirlow 2002: 889

5   Ibid.: 895–6

6   Longley, M. 1998

7   Brown, C.1997

8   Ibid.

9   Ibid.

10   Ibid.

11   Guy, J. 1993

12   Ibid.

13   Ibid.

14   McCashin, C. 1993

15   Ibid.

16   Ibid.

17   Day, E. 2003

18   Ibid.

19   Ibid.

20   Anon. 2005

21   Jones, M. 2009

22   Dolan, A. 2009

23   Ibid.

24   Horne, M. 2009

25   Smith, J. 2009

26   Borland, S. 2009

27   DMR 2009

28   Ibid.

29   Ibid.

30   H4H 2009

31   Ibid.

32   Hahn, P. 2008

33   Ibid.

34   Ibid.

35   Nikiforuk, A. 2008

36   RCM n.d.

37   Bridis, T. 2007

38   Ibid.

39   Ibid.

40   Ibid.

41   Ibid.

42   Hogshire, J. 2001; and see, Wilcock, J. n.d.

43   The story concerning this 'rebirth' of the VC Poppy is intriguing. In 2006 the
       design consultant Robin Ollington FRSA created a decorative sales card enclosing
       a packet of the VC Poppy seeds to publicise the 150th anniversary of the Victoria
       Cross medal and to raise funds for the Victoria Cross/George Cross Association.
       The cover of the card shows a Victoria Cross medal and the VC Poppy, and
       carries the following description: 'The Victoria Cross poppy was named in 1890
       and has been grown ever since as a reminder of outstanding courage'. Curiously,
       the flower is identified as *Papaver somniferum* on the seed packet, alongside a
       health warning. It appears that it can only be bought from Mr Fothergill's Seeds of
       Kentford, Newmarket, in Cambridgeshire. I am very grateful to Robin Ollington
       for this information provided for me on 23 December 2009.

44   Grey-Wilson, C. 2005: 127–9

45   Donald, C. 2009; Cowing, E. 2009

46   Atkinson, J. 2009: 2. The Gardening Leave programme offers similar initiatives
       elsewhere, including at London's Royal Chelsea Hospital. The main activities
       offered as therapy by the charity are fishing, restoring old buildings, planting and
       growing flowers and vegetables and maintaining the National Poppy Collection.
       Key to the success of the Gardening Leave programme is that it is exclusively
       for ex-military personnel who have had similar experiences and suffered similar
       illnesses, all of which have been identified as the main problems associated with
       the mental health of ex-service personnel: substance abuse, psychiatric disorders
       and behavioural problems. Such a common bond between individuals helps to
       break down barriers, allows them to be open about their feelings and thereby
       enhances the beneficial effects of therapy.

47   Stringer, J. 2005

48   Ibid.

49   Crombie, N. 2009

50   Ibid.

51   Boettcher, D. 2007

52   Hildebrandt, A. 2008

53   BBC 2008

54   At the time of writing, Poppy Man's blog can be found at http://whereispoppyman.
       blogspot.co.uk and the Facebook page at http://www.facebook.com/legion.
       poppyman, but neither has been active since 2008.

BIBLIOGRAPHY

Aaronovitch, David. (2004) 'Are you wearing your poppy yet? If not, why not?'. *Guardian*, 2 November, http://www.guardian.co.uk/world/2004/nov/02/uselections2004.comment

Abrams, M.H. (1993) *A Glossary of Literary Terms*. Orlando: Harcourt & Brace

Adams, George Worthington. (1952) *Doctors in Blue*. New York: Henry Schuman (see especially pp. 50–1, 116–19 and 228–9)

Albenda, Pauline, and Eleanor Guralnick. (1986) 'Some fragments of stone reliefs from Khorsabad'. *Journal of Near Eastern Studies* 45 (3): 231–42

Allingham, Philip V. (2006) 'The opium trade, seventh through nineteenth centuries', Victorian Web, http://www.victorianweb.org/history/empire/opiumwars/opiumwars1.html

American Legion Auxiliary (2009) *Celebrating the 90th Anniversary of the Auxiliary. National President's Theme: Reconnect and Energize!*, http://www.kslegionaux.org/pdf%20files/finance%20POA%2009.pdf

Anderson, Jon Lee. (2007) 'Letter from Afghanistan: The Taliban's opium war – the difficulties and dangers of the eradication program', *New Yorker*, 9 July, http://www.newyorker.com/reporting/2007/07/09/070709fa_fact_anderson

———. (2007) 'Purple poppy to commemorate animal victims', Animal Aid press release, 7 November, http://www.info@animalaid.org.uk

Anon. (1850) 'The opium trade'. *Merchants Magazine & Commercial Review* (August): 147–59

Anon. (1867) 'The reformation of prison discipline'. *North American Review* 105: 572–4

Anon. (1876) *Opium Eating, An Autobiographical Sketch by an Habituate*. Philadelphia: Claxton, Remsen, and Haffelfinger

Anon. (1919) 'Still hearts voices in protest meeting'. *New York Times*, 11 January

Anon. (1921a) 'Rival societies in war of poppies'. *New York Times*, 12 May

Anon. (1921b) 'Children do honor to Maid of Orleans'. *New York Times*, 9 May

Anon. (1921c) 'Dr. Shipman named in $200,000 action'. *New York Times*, 17 December

Anon. (1922a) 'Hylan overrules Colen on poppies'. *New York Times*, 25 May

Anon. (1922b) '"Poppy Week" suit dismissed by court'. *New York Times*, 12 December

Anon. (2001a) 'Black poppy marks poverty'. BBC News, 3 November, http://news.bbc.co.uk/1/hi/england/1636327.stm

Anon. (2001b), 'How did we get here?: History has a habit of repeating itself', *The Economist*, 26 July 2001, http://www.economist.com/node/706583?story_id=E1_SDGVRP

Anon. (2004) 'Virginia city dig finds toys, opium cache'. *Reno Gazette Journal*, 15 August

Anon. (2005). 'Poppy sellers banned from centre'. BBC News, 10 November, http://news.bbc.co.uk/1/hi/england/derbyshire/4425384.stm

Anon. (2006) 'Getting to the root of opium trade'. Zee News (India), 28 March, http://www.zeenews.com/articles.asp?aid=284447&sid=ZNS

Anon. (2007a) 'Let Afghan Poppies Bloom'. *The Times*, 20 August, http://www.thetimes.co.uk/tto/law/columnists/article2048385.ece

Anon. (2008a) 'The Suriya-Mal movement', Wikipedia, http://en.wikipedia.org/wiki/Suriya-Mal_Movement

Anon. (2008b) 'The Remembrance Poppy Stamp which contains the subtly haunting face of an unknown soldier'. *Mail on Sunday*, 3 November, http://www.dailymail.co.uk/mailonsunday/article-1082422/The-Remembrance-Poppy-stamp-contains-subtly-haunting-face-unknown-soldier.html

Anon. (2009a) 'US forces chief admits war in Afghanistan is getting harder'. *London Lite*, 24 August, p. 4

Anon. (2010) 'What is Islam4UK?'. *Daily Telegraph*, 4 January, http://www.telegraph.co.uk/news/newstopics/politics/defence/6931212/What-is-Islam4UK.html

Anon. (The Wayfarer). (n.d.a) 'Poppies: "The Thin Red Line" on the Western Front', leaflet no. 9, British Legion Appeal, London

Anon. (n.d.b) '"The Enniskillen Remembrance Day Massacre" 8th November 1987 – 11 people dead (The Poppy day bombing)', IRA Atrocities, http://www.iraatrocities.fsnet.co.uk/enniskillen.htm

ARU (Addiction Research Unit). (2001) 'Before Prohibition', Addiction Research Unit, Department of Psychology, University of Buffalo, New York, http://wings.buffalo.edu/aru/preprohibition.htm

Askitopoulou, Helen, Ioanna A. Ramoutsaki, and Eleni Konsolaki. (2002) 'Archaeological evidence on the use of opium in the Minoan world'. *International Congress Series* 1242: 23–9

Atkinson, Jacqueline. (2009) 'An evaluation of the Gardening Leave Project for ex-military personnel with PTSD and other combat related mental health problems', Pears Foundation

AWM (Australian War Memorial). (n.d.a) Online Collections database, ID number RELAWM14156, http://cas.awm.gov.au/heraldry/RELAWM14156

———. (n.d.b) 'Will Longstaff's Menin Gate at midnight (*Ghosts of Menin Gate*)', http://www.awm.gov.au/encyclopedia/menin/notes.asp

Bailey, Paul. (2000) 'From Shandong to the Somme: Chinese indenture labour in France during World War I' in Kashen, A.J. (ed.), *Language, Labour and Migration*. Aldershot: Ashgate, pp. 179–96

Balbi, Marco. (2009) 'Great War archaeology on the glaciers of the Alps' in Saunders, Nicholas J., and Paul Cornish (eds), *Contested Objects: Material Memories of the Great War*. Abingdon: Routledge, pp. 280–90

Barrett Browning, Elizabeth. (1843) Letter to her brother George Barrett. In Kelley, Philip, and Ronald Hudson (eds). (1984). *The Brownings' Correspondence: Vol. 7, March 1843–October 1843. (Winfield, KS: Wedgestone Press)*, p 242

BBC (2006a) 'Red Cross poppy "less Christian" claim'. BBC News, 9 November, http://news.bbc.co.uk/1/hi/6131464.stm

BBC (2006b) 'TV's Snow rejects poppy fascism'. BBC News, 10 November, http://news.bbc.co.uk/2/hi/uk_news/6134906.stm

BBC (2008) 'Poppy Appeal Launched from Basra'. BBC News, http://news.bbc.co.uk/2/hi/uk_news/7685840.stm

BBC (2010) 'Islam4UK Islamist group banned under terror laws'. BBC News, 12 January, http://news.bbc.co.uk/2/hi/8453560.stm

Beals, K.M. [1917] (2003) *Flower Lore and Legend*. New York: Fredonia Books.

Bellamy, Dawn. (2007) '"Others have come before you": the influence of Great War poetry on Second World War poets' in Kendall, T. (ed.), *The Oxford Handbook of British and Irish War Poetry*. Oxford: Oxford University Press, pp. 299–314

Bergonzi, Bernard. [1965] (1996) *Heroes' Twilight: A Study of the Literature of the Great War*. Manchester: Carcanet

Berridge, V. and G. Edwards. (1987) *Opium and the people: Opiate use in nineteenth century England*. London: Yale University Press

Bietak, Manfred. (2000) 'Minoan paintings in Avaris, Egypt' in Sherratt, Susan (ed.), *The Wall Paintings of Thera: Proceedings of the First International Symposium,* vol. 1. Piraeus: Thera Foundation, pp. 33–42, http://www.therafoundation. org/articles/art/minoanpaintingsinavarisegypt

Bishop, Patrick. (2008) *3Para*. London: Harper Perennial

Bisset, Norman G., Jan G. Bruhn, Silvio Curto, Bo Holmstedt, Ulf Nyman and Meinhart H. Zenk. (1994) 'Was opium known in 18th dynasty ancient Egypt? An examination of materials from the tomb of the chief royal architect Kha'. *Journal of Ethnopharmacology* 41: 99–114

Blegen, Elizabeth P. (1936) 'Excavations at Gazi, Crete'. *American Journal of Archaeology* 40: 371–3

Boettcher, Daniel. (2007) 'Poppy Man lends families a hand'. BBC News, 24 October, http://news.bbc.co.uk/2/hi/uk_news/7060556.stm

Boone, Jon. (2009) 'UN wants "flood of drugs" in Afghanistan to devalue opium'. *Guardian*, 25 May, http://www.guardian.co.uk/world/2009/may/25/drugs-united-nations-afghanistan

Booth, Martin. (1998) *Opium: A History*. New York: St. Martin's Griffin

Borland, Sophie. (2009) 'Poppycock! Remembrance Day collectors banned from shaking tins to avoid "intimidating shoppers"'. *Daily Mail*, 2 November, http://www.dailymail.co.uk/news/article-1224211/Poppycock-Remembrance-Day-collectors-banned-shaking-tins-avoid-intimidating-shoppers.html

Brazier, James. (1996) 'The First Poppy Day'. *Western Front Association Bulletin* 46: 34–5

Brecher, Edward. (1972) Chapter 8, 'The Harrison Narcotic Act (1914)' in Brecher, Edward M. (ed.), *Licit and Illicit Drugs: The Consumers Union Report on Narcotics, Stimulants, Depressants, Inhalants, Hallucinogens, and Marijuana – including Caffeine, Nicotine and Alcohol*. New York: Little Brown & Company

Brewer, E. Cobham. [1894] (1993) *The Dictionary of Phrase and Fable*. Ware: Wordsworth Reference

Bridis, Ted. (2007) 'Canada's poppy quarters caused sensational warnings of "spy coins" in U.S.' Associated Press, 7 May, http://www.militaryphotos.net/forums/showthread.php?169974-Canadian-spy-coins-spooked-U-S

Broadway, Lisa. (1992/2007) 'Some First World War poets', English Association, University of Leicester, http://www.le.ac.uk/engassoc/publications/bookmarks/12.pdf

Brooks, Stewart. (1966) *Civil War Medicine*. Springfield (IL): Charles C. Thomas

Brown, Anthony. (1971) *Red for Remembrance: British Legion 1921–71*. Heinemann: London

Brown, Colin. (1997) 'Remembrance poppy row enmeshes McAleese'. *Independent*,

6 November, http://www.independent.co.uk/news/remembrance-poppy-row-enmeshes-mcaleese-1292314.html

Bucholz, Hans-Günter, and Vassos Karageorghis. (1973) *Prehistoric Greece and Cyprus: An Archaeological Handbook*. London: Phaidon

Buckland, Augustus Robert. (1914) *The Universal Bible Dictionary*. New York: Fleming H. Revell Company

Budge, E.A. Wallis. (1926) *The Dwellers on the Nile*. London: Religious Tract Society

———. [1930] (1978). *Amulets and Superstitions*. New York: Dover

Bushaway, Bob. (1992) 'Name upon Name: The Great War and Remembrance' in Porter, Roy (ed.), *Myths of the English*. Cambridge: Polity Press, pp. 136–67

Byrne, Andrea. (2007) 'Louis's poppy love points to our blooming maturity'. Independent. ie website, 18 November, http://www.independent.ie/opinion/analysis/louiss-poppy-love-points-to-our-blooming-maturity-26332515.html

Callimachi, Rukmini. (2009) 'Opium addictions grip families in Afghanistan's remote villages'. *Boston Globe*, 9 August, http://www.boston.com/news/world/middleeast/articles/2009/08/09/opium_addictions_grip_afghan_families_villages/

Cappatto, Marco. (2007) *Report with a proposal for a European Parliament recommendation to the Council on production of opium for medical purposes in Afghanistan*. Committee on Foreign Affairs, European Parliament, (2007/2125 (INI)), Brussels, 21 September, http://www.europarl.europa.eu/sides/getDoc. do?pubRef=-//EP//NONSGML+REPORT+A6-2007-0341+0+DOC+PDF+V0// EN

CBC News. (2006) 'White poppy emblems anger Edmonton veterans'. CBC News, 8 November, http://www.cbc.ca/canada/edmonton/story/2006/11/08/white-poppy.html

Ceadel, Martin. (2000) *Semi-Detached Idealists: The British Peace Movement and International Relations, 1854–1945*. Oxford: Oxford University Press

Chambless, Stacy. (2004) 'A memorial in scarlet: The Poppy and the ritual of remembrance', Hellfire Corner, http://www.fylde.demon.co.uk/chambless.htm

Chouvy, Pierre-Arnaud. (2002) *Les territoires de l'opium*. Geneva: Olizane

———. (2006) 'Afghanistan's opium production in perspective'. *China and Eurasia Forum Quarterly* 4 (1): 21-4

Chrastina, Paul. (n.d.) 'Emperor of China declares war on drugs', Opiods.com, http://www.opioids.com/opium/opiumwar.html

Ciaraldi, M. (2000) 'Drug preparation in evidence: an unusual plant and bone assemblage from the Pompeian countryside, Italy'. *Vegetation History and Archaeobotany* 9, pp. 91–8

——. (2003) Field Archaeology Unit, University of Birmingham. Personal communication [1/16/03 & 1/19/03] quoted in M.D. Merlin (2003)

Clarke, Stephen. (2006) 'The poppy from the NZ perspective', Digger History, http://www.diggerhistory.info/pages-tributes/poppy.htm

Cockburn, Patrick. (2007) 'Opium: Iraq's deadly new export'. *Independent*, 23 May, http://www.independent.co.uk/news/world/middle-east/opium-iraqs-deadly-new-export-449962.html

Cohen, Tamara. (2008) 'The opium fields of England . . . heroin producing poppies grown to make NHS pain-relief drugs'. *Daily Mail*, 23 June, http://www.dailymail.co.uk/news/article-1028504

Collins, Katie. (2009) Photograph. *The Times*, 6 November, p. 1

Courtwright, David. (1978) 'Opiate addiction as a consequence of the Civil War'. *Civil War History* 24, pp. 101–11

——. (1982) *Dark Paradise: Opiate Addiction in America Before 1940*. Cambridge (MA): Harvard University Press

Cowing, Emma. (2009) 'Those who serve on the front line often bring back deep psychological scars . . . an Ayrshire garden is proving invaluable as a healing environment'. *Scotsman*, 2 January

Crawford, Dorothy J. (1973) 'The opium poppy: A study in Ptolemaic agriculture' in Finley, M.I. (ed.), *Problèmes de la terre en Grèce ancienne*. Paris: Mouton, pp. 223–51

Crombie, Nathan. (2009) 'Artist transforms bullets of battle into poppies of peace'. *Wairapa Times-Age*, 21 April, http://www.times-age.co.nz/localnews/storydisplay.cfm?storyid=3797234

CSIRO (Commonwealth Scientific and Research Organization) (2005) Dickson poppy fields at CSIR Dickson Experimental Station in the Australian Capital Territory. *CSIRO* website, http://www.scienceimage.csiro.au/index.cfm?event=site.image.detail&id=2780

CWM (Canadian War Museum) (n.d.) 'The poppy, symbol of remembrance', Canadian War Museum, http://www.warmuseum.ca/cwm/exhibitions/remember/poppy_e.shtml

Day, Elizabeth. (2003) 'Poppy pins banned in case people sue'. *Daily Telegraph*, 2 November, http://www.telegraph.co.uk/news/uknews/1445714/Poppy-pins-banned-in-case-people-sue.html

Day, Horace. (1868) *The Opium Habit, With Suggestions As To The Remedy*. New York: Harper Brothers

Delano, R. (2002) '"Buddy Poppies". We've seen them, what do they mean?', Roots Web, 11 November, http://archiver.rootsweb.ancestry.com/th/read/DELANO-SURNAME/2002-11/1037019715

Dendooven, D. and P. Chielens. (2008) *World War I: Five Continents in Flanders*. Tielt: Lanoo

Derez, M. (1997) 'A Belgian Salient for reconstruction: People and *patrie*, landscape and memory' in Liddle, P.H. (ed.), *Passchendaele in Perspective: The Third Battle of Ypres*. London: Leo Cooper, pp. 437–58

De Quincey, Thomas. (2003) *The Confessions of an English Opium Eater*. London: Penguin

de Sola Pinto, Vivian. [1951] (1965) *Crisis in English Poetry: 1880–1940*. London: Hutchinson University Library

de Vries, Ad. (1974) *Dictionary of Symbols and Imagery*. Amsterdam: North-Holland Publishing Company

DeYoung, Karen. (2009a) 'Taliban surprising US forces with improved tactics'. *Washington Post*, 2 September, http://articles.washingtonpost.com/2009-09-02/world/36788859_1_nato-troops-taliban-nato-forces

———. (2009b) 'Afghanistan: suicide bomber attack; Taliban exhibits improved tactics'. *Washington Post*, 2 September, http://www.washingtonpost.com/wp-dyn/content/discussion/2009/09/02/DI2009090201595.html

DFID (United Kingdom Department for International Development) (2009) 'Wheat beats opium for Afghan farmers', 17 March, http://www.dfid.gov.uk/Media-Room/Case-Studies/2009/Wheat-beats-opium-for-Afghan-farmers/

DMR (*Daily Mail* reporter) (2009) 'Villagers boycott pub after landlady refuses to sell poppies'. *Daily Mail*, 2 November, http://www.dailymail.co.uk/news/article-1224171/Villagers-boycott-pub-landlady-refuses-sell-poppies.html

Dolan, Andy. (2009) 'Libraries lift "scandalous" ban on poppies after outcry over decision not to allow collecting tins in branches'. *Daily Mail*, 3 November, http://www.dailymail.co.uk/news/article-1224811/Libraries-ban-poppies-We-favour-charity-says-manager.html#ixzz0VtRYNVV7

Donald, Caroline. (2009) 'Seeds of recovery'. *Sunday Times*. 18 October, Section 6: 'Home', pp. 24–5

Dunlop, Ian. (1972) *The Shock of the New*. London: Weidenfeld & Nicholson

Dunn, J.C. [1938] (1997) *The War the Infantry Knew 1914–1919*. London: Abacus

Dyer, Geoff. (1995) *The Missing of the Somme*. London: Penguin

Dyhouse, Tim. (1997) 'Keeping faith through the Buddy Poppy'. *VFW Magazine* May: 12–16

Eaton-Krause, M., and E. Graefe. (1985) *The Small Golden Shrine from the Tomb of Tutankhamun*. Oxford: Griffith Institute

Editorial.a. (1915) 'Mental sequelae of the Harrison Law'. *New York Medical Journal* 102 (May 15): 1014

Editorial.b. (1915) *American Medicine*, 21 (O.S.), 10 (N.S.) (November): 799–800

Ehrenfeld, Rachel 2009. 'Stop the Afghan drug trade, stop terrorism', *Forbes*, 26 February 2009, http://www.forbes.com/2009/02/26/drug-trade-afghanistan-opinions-contributors_terrorism_mycoherbicides.html

Ekklesia Staff Writers. (2005) 'Controversy over sale of white poppies', *Ekklesia*, 3 November, http://www.ekklesia.co.uk/content/news_syndication/article_05113whitepoppies.shtml

Eksteins, Modris. (1989) *Rites of Spring: The Great War and the Birth of the Modern Age*. London: Bantam Press

El-Masry, S., M. El-Ghazooly, A. Omar, S. Khafagy, and J. Phillipson. (1981) 'Alkaloids from Egyptian *Papaver rhoeas*'. *Planta Medica* 41: 61–4

Elias, Ann. (2007) 'War, flowers, and visual culture: the First World War collection of the Australian War Memorial'. *Journal of the Australian War Memorial* 40, http://www.awm.gov.au/journal/j40/elias.htm

Emboden, William A. (1979) *Narcotic Plants*. New York: Macmillan

Evans, Michael. (2008) 'Higher opium yields "will fuel Taleban insurgency".' *The Times*, 3 January

———. (2009) 'Four British soldiers die for the sake of 150 votes'. *The Times*, 27 August, p. 1

Farmer, Ben. (2008) 'Afghanistan promotes pomegranates over opium poppies in farming overhaul'. *Daily Telegraph*, 20 November, http://www.telegraph.co.uk/news/worldnews/asia/afghanistan/3491421/Afghanistan-promotes-pomegranates-over-opium-poppies-in-farming

———. (2009a) 'US attempts to eradicate opium poppies from Afghanistan have been criticised as "wasteful and ineffective", by the new US super envoy to the region'. *Daily Telegraph*, 22 March, http://www.telegraph.co.uk/news/worldnews/asia/afghanistan/5032711/Afghanistan-opium-crackdown-doing-little-says-US-envoy.html

———. (2009b) 'Afghanistan opium crackdown doing little says US envoy'. *Daily Telegraph*, 23 March, http://www.telegraph.co.uk/news/worldnews/asia/

afghanistan/5032711/Afghanistan-opium-crackdown-doing-little-says-US-envoy.html

Fausset, Andrew Robert M.A., D.D. (1878) 'Definition for "Gall".' *Fausset's Bible Dictionary* online, http://www.bible-history.com/faussets/G/Gall/

Feilding, Rowland. (1929) *War Letters to a Wife*. London: Medici Society

Fergusson, James. (2008) *A Million Bullets: The Real Story of the British Army in Afghanistan*. London: Bantam

Fowler-Reeves, Kate. (2006) *Animals: The Hidden Victims of War*. Tonbridge, Kent: Animal Aid

French, John 'Drumbo'. (2010) *Beefheart: Through the Eyes of Magic*. London: Proper Music Publishing Ltd

Friedman, D.M. (2008) *The Immortalists*. London: J R Books

Frisbie, Richard. (2008) 'The Flowers of France Commemorate WW1: Fleur de Vie, Fleur de Mal, Fleur de Liberte', TravelLady Magazine, http://www.travellady.com/Issues/July08/5143Flowers.htm

Frye, Northrop. (1957) *Anatomy of Criticism: Four Essays*. Princeton (NJ): Princeton University Press

Fussell, Paul. [1965] (1979) *Poetic Meter and Poetic Form*. New York: McGraw-Hill
———. [1975] (2000) *The Great War and Modern Memory*. New York: Oxford University Press

Gabra, Sami. (1956) 'Papaver species and opium through the ages'. *Bulletin de l'Institut d'Egypte* (Cairo) 37: 39–56

Gaddo, Randy. (2006) 'VFW Buddy Poppies: Buy 1 before Memorial Day'. *Citizen*, 16 May

Gandhi, Maneka. (2008) 'Feeling good'. *Bihar Times*, 2 July, http://www.bihartimes.com/newsbihar/2008/July/newsbihar02July1.html

Gardner, Brian (ed.). (1964) *Up the Line to Death: The War Poets 1914–1918*. London: Methuen

George Bayntum Booksellers (n.d.) *Rupert Brooke: The Collected Poems*. London: Philip Lee Warner for the Medici Society, http://www.georgebayntun.com/gallerybrooke.htm

German, Lindsey. (2011). 'How the Cenotaph and red poppies became symbols of war', Stop the War Coalition, 4 November, http://www.stopwar.org.uk/index.php/lindsey-german/904-how-the-cenotaph-and-red-poppies

Gessert, George. (1993) 'Flowers of human presence: Effects of esthetic values on the evolution of ornamental plants'. *Leonardo* 26 (1): 37–44

Gillespie, Douglas. (1916) *Letters from Flanders: With an Appreciation of Two Brothers (Alexander Douglas and Thomas Cunningham Gillespie by the Right Rev. the Bishop of Southwark*, 3rd. ed. London: n.p.

Goebel, Stefan. (2007) *The Great War and Medieval Memory: War, Remembrance and Medievalism in Britain and Germany, 1914–1940*. Cambridge: Cambridge University Press

Goodrick-Clarke, Nicholas. [1985] (2005) *The Occult Roots of Nazism*. London: Tauris Parke

Goody, Jack. (1994) *The Culture of Flowers*. Cambridge: Cambridge University Press

Gorer, Richard. (1978) *The Growth of Gardens*. London: Faber and Faber

Gow, A.S.F. (ed.) (1965) *Theocritus*, 2 vols. Cambridge: Cambridge University Press

Graham, B., and P. Shirlow. (2002) 'The Battle of the Somme in Ulster memory and identity'. *Political Geography* 21: 881–904

Graham, William. (1997) 'McAleese should not wear the poppy'. *Irish News*, 5 November, http://www.irishnews.com/pageacc.asp?tser1=ser&par=ben&s id=213614

Graves, Dianne. (1997) *Crown of Life: The World of John McCrae*. Staplehurst: Spellmount

Gregory, Adrian. (1994) *The Silence of Memory: Armistice Day 1919–1946*. Oxford: Berg

Gregson, J.M. (1976) *Poetry of the First World War*. London: Edward Arnold

Grey-Wilson, Christopher. (2005) *Poppies: The Poppy Family in the Wild and in Cultivation*. London: B. T. Batsford

Gutas, Dimitri. (1998) *Greek Thought, Arabic Culture: The Graeco-Arabic Translation Movement in Baghdad and Early Abbasid Society (2nd–4th/8th–10th centuries)*. Abingdon: Routledge

Guy, Jonathan. (1993) 'Poppy game insult to our war dead'. *Daily Star*, 26 October, http://dspace.dial.pipex.com/ap2/dissent/poppy.html

H4H (Help for Heroes). (2009) http://www.helpforheroes.org.uk/

Hahn, Phil. (2006) 'Afghanistan brings poignancy to Remembrance Day'. *Canadian* Press, 10 November, http://forums.army.ca/forums/index.php?topic=52681.20;wap2

———. (2008) 'Aboriginal veterans recall journey of healing'. *CTV News*, http://www.ctv.ca/servlet/ArticleNews/story/CTVNews/20051107/aboriginal_veterans_feature_051107/20051108/

Haley, Laura I. (2006) *The Poppy Fields of Afghanistan: Another Vietnam?* Research Report. Major Jeanine Ryder Maxwell Air Force Base, Alabama, Air Command and Staff College Air University, April

Hanlon, Michael E. (n.d.) 'Doughboy Stamp Album', WorldWar1.com, http://www.worldwar1.com/dbc/stamps.htm

Hanson, Neil. (2005) *The Unknown Soldier: The Story of the Missing of the Great War*. London: Doubleday

Harding, Brian. (2001) *Keeping Faith: The History of the Royal British Legion*. Barnsley: Leo Cooper

Hart, Linda. (2000) *Once They Lived in Gloucestershire: A Dymock Poets Anthology*. Kencot: Green Branch Press, http://www.dymockpoets.co.uk/Brooke.htm

Hasegawa, G.R. and F. Terry Hambrecht. (2003) *The Confederate Medical Laboratories*. Bethesda and Frederick (MD): Publications and Drug Information Systems Office, American Society of Health-System Pharmacists, and the National Museum of Civil War Medicine, http://www.thefreelibrary.com/The+Confederate+medical+laboratories-a0111927750

Hayter, Aleathea. (1968) *Opium and the Romantic Imagination*. London: Faber and Faber

Heikel, Mohammed Hassanein. (1973) *The Cairo Documents: The Inside Story of Nasser and His Relationship with World Leaders, Rebels, and Statesmen*. Garden City (NY): Doubleday

Heneghan, Donald A. (1979) *A Concordance to the Poems and Fragments of Wilfred Owen*. Boston: G.K. Hall & Co.

Hepper, F. Nigel. (2009). *Pharaoh's Flowers: The Botanical Treasures of Tutankhamun*. Chicago: University of Chicago Press, ch. 1

HFM (Hazebrouck Hoflandt Météo) (n.d.) 'Le coquelicot et le bleuet de la mémoire', http://www.hazebrouck-hoflandt-nature.com/HoflandtNature/coquelicot.htm

Higgins, Ian. (ed.). (1996) *Anthology of First World War French Poetry*. Glasgow: University of Glasgow French & German Publications

High, Brandon. (2005) 'Book of the month: *Confessions of an English Opium Eater*'. Information Services and Systems, King's College London, http://www.kcl.ac.uk/depsta/iss/library/speccoll/bomarch/bomjune05.html

Hildebrandt, Amber. (2008) 'Poppy Man tours war zone to launch Remembrance Day appeal'. CBC News, 23 October, http://www.cbc.ca/world/story/2008/10/23/poppy-campaign.html

Hitchen, Mike. (2009) 'Afghanistan: Demand for carpets and rugs gives rise to opium addiction', i On Global Trends, 19 July, http://www.ionglobaltrends.com/2009_07_19_archive.html#.UcGExOsTGUk

Hobbs, Joseph J. (1998) 'Troubling fields: The opium poppy in Egypt'. *The Geographical Review* 88 (1), pp. 64–85

HoCd (House of Commons debate). (1985–1986) Official Report: 13

HoCFAC (House of Commons Foreign Affairs Committee). (2009) *Global Security: Afghanistan and Pakistan. HC302.* London: HMSO

Hodges, F.J. (1988). *Men of 18 in 1918.* Ilfracombe: Arthur H. Stockwell

Hodgson, Barbara. (1999) *Opium: A Portrait of the Heavenly Demon.* London: Souvenir Press

———. (2001) *In the Arms of Morpheus: The Tragic History of Laudanum, Morphine, and Patent medicines.* Buffalo (NY): Firefly Books

Hogshire, Jim. (2001) 'Poppy Cock: Truth and Lies about Poppies, Opium, and Painkilling Drugs (an excerpt)', Drugwar.com, http://www.drugwar.com/ppoppycock.shtm

Holden, Michael. (2009) 'Remembering the dead – or "poppy fascism"?'. Reuters, 6 November, http://blogs.reuters.com/great-debate-uk/2009/11/06/remembering-the-dead-or-poppy-fascism/

Holmes, Y. Lynn. (1975) 'The foreign trade of Cyprus during the late Bronze Age' in Robertson, N. (ed.), *The Archaeology of Cyprus.* Park Ridge (NJ): Noyes Press, pp. 90–110

Hoover, Herbert. (1931) 'Message Endorsing the Annual "Buddy Poppy" Sale'. 23 April, via Peters, Gerhard, and John T. Woolley (eds), The American Presidency Project, http://www.presidency.ucsb.edu/ws/index.php?pid=22616

Horne, Marc. (2009) 'Veterans to boycott Shell after ban on forecourt poppy sales'. *Sunday Times,* 8 November, p. 18

Huggler, Justin. (2007) 'Doctors propose using Afghan opium as NHS pain-killer'. *Belfast Telegraph,* 24 January, http://www.belfasttelegraph.co.uk/news/world-news/doctors-propose-using-afghan-opium-as-nhs-painkiller-28558427.html

Hynes, Samuel. (1990) *A War Imagined: The First World War and English Culture.* London: The Bodley Head

Iles, Jennifer. (2008) 'In remembrance: The Flanders poppy'. *Mortality* 13 (3): 201–21

INAC (Indian and Northern Affairs Canada) (1996). *Report on the Royal Commission on Aboriginal People, vol. 1: Looking Forward, Looking Back.* Ottawa: Canada Communication Group, ch. 12: Veterans, http://caid.ca/RepRoyCommAborigPple.html

Inciardi, James A. (1990) *Handbook of Drug Control in the United States.* New York: Greenwood Press

Ireland, Maj. Gen. M.W. (1923) *The Medical Department of the United States Army in the World War.* vol X. *Neuropsychiatry in the American Expeditionary Forces.* Washington, DC: US Government Printing Office

————. (1927) *The Medical Department of the United States Army in the World War.* vol II, *Administration American Expeditionary Forces.* Washington, DC: US Government Printing Office

Irfan, Hwaa. (2003) 'Weaving between wars and returning to the soul'. On Islam, 6 November, https://www.onislam.net/english/culture-and-entertainment/fine-arts/446369.html

Islam4UK. (2010) 'Announcement of intention to march through Wootton Bassett'. YouTube, 2 January (video now removed as organization is banned)

Jelsma, Martin. (2005) 'Learning lessons from the Taliban opium ban'. *International Journal of Drug Policy* 6 (2): 98–103

Jenkyns, Richard. (1980) *The Victorians and Ancient Greece.* Oxford: Blackwell

Jones, Ayatollah. (2006) 'US Considering Bio-Warfare on Poppies'. Papaver Somniferum, 7 April, http://opiumpoppies.org/2006/04/07/us-considering-biowarfare-on-poppies/

Jones, Mike. (2009) 'What do you think of library ban on poppies?'. Silver Surfer Today, 3 November, http://www.silversurfertoday.co.uk/News/Story/?storyid=1070&title=What_do_you_think_of_library_ban_on_poppies-%3F&type=news_features

Kamm, Oliver. (2004) 'White-poppy wearers, then and now'. Oliver Kamm, 16 November, http://oliverkamm.typepad.com/blog/2004/11/whitepoppy_wear.html

Kapoor, L.D. (2005) *Opium Poppy: Botany, Chemistry, and Pharmacology.* Binghamton (NY): Haworth Press

Karageorghis, V. (1976) 'A twelfth-century BC opium pipe from Kition'. *Antiquity* 50: 125–9

Kaufman, Stephen. (2009) 'US scraps Afghan crop eradication in favor of interdiction'. America.gov, 29 July. http://www.america.gov/st/sca-English/2009/July/20090729184555esnamfuak0.4385187.html

Keats, John. (1970) *The Poems of John Keats* (ed. by Miriam Allott). London: Longman

Keeley, Leslie. (1881) *The Morphine Eater: or From Bondage to Freedom.* Dwight (IL): C.L. Palmer Co

Kerényi, Carl. (1967) *Eleusis: Archetypal Image of Mother and Daughter.* Princeton (NJ): Princeton University Press

Kilgour, Frederick G. (1960) 'Medicine in art'. *What's New Journal of Medicine* 216. Chicago: Abbott Laboratories

King, Rufus. (1953). 'Personal views on narcotics'. *Yale Law journal,* 62: 748–9

Knowles, Elizabeth (ed.). (2000) *The Oxford Dictionary of Phrase and Fable.* Oxford: Oxford University Press

Koznarsky, Michael. (2007) 'Anesthetics in field and general hospitals of the Confederate States of America', Civil War Interactive & BlueGray Daily, http://www.civilwarinteractive.com/ArticleAnesthetics.htm

Kramer, Samuel N. (1954) 'First pharmacopeia in man's recorded history'. *American Journal of Pharmacy* 126 (3): 76–84

Krikorian, Abraham D. (1975) 'Were the opium poppy and opium known in the ancient Near East?'. *Journal of the History of Biology* 8 (1): 95–114

Kritikos, Pan G. (1960) 'Der Mohn, das Opium und ihr Gebrauch im Spatminoicum III: Bemerkungen zu dem Gefundenen Idol der Minoischen Gottheit des Mohns'. *Praktika es Akademias Athenon* 35 (1): 55-73

———, and Stella P. Papadaki. (1967) 'The history of the poppy and opium and their expansion in antiquity in the eastern Mediterranean area'. *Bulletin on Narcotics* (a) 19 (3): 18–40; (b) 19 (4): 1–10

Kunzig, Robert. (2002) 'La Marmotta: The discovery in central Italy of a 7,800-year-old settlement reveals the dawning of Western civilization'. *Discover,* November, http://discovermagazine.com/2002/nov/cover

Lakshmanan, Indira A.R. (2009) 'Holbrooke says US end to Afghan drug eradication gets results'. *Bloomburg,* 30 July, http://www.bloomberg.com/apps/news?pid=newsarchive&sid=aqmxssVg5ji8

Lamb, Christina, and Stephen Grey. (2009). 'UN chief scorns Miliband plan for Taliban talks'. *Sunday Times,* 2 August, p. 24

Lewis, Cecil. (1994) *Sagittarius Rising.* London: Time Warner Paperbacks

Lichfield, J. (1999) 'Fields of Somme might again turn red'. *Independent,* 18 October, http://www.aftermathww1.com/picardy.asp

Liddiard, Jean. (1975) *Isaac Rosenberg: The Half Used Life.* London: Victor Gollancz

Linder, Ann P. (1996) *Princes of the Trenches: Narrating the German Experience of the First World War.* Columbia (SC): Camden House

Lloyd, David W. (1998) *Battlefield Tourism: Pilgrimage and the Commemoration of the Great War in Britain, Australia and Canada, 1919–1939.* Oxford: Berg

London, M., T. O'Reagan, P. Aust and A. Stockford. (1990) 'Poppy tea drinking in East Anglia'. *British Journal of Addiction* 85: 1345–7

Longley, Michael. (1998) *Selected Poems.* London: Jonathan Cape

Loyn, David. (2013). 'Afghan farmers return to opium as other markets fail'. BBC News, 15 April, http://www.bbc.co.uk/news/world-asia-22150482

Macdonald, David. (2007) *Drugs in Afghanistan: Opium, Outlaws and Scorpion Tales*. London: Pluto Press

Macfarlan Smith. (n.d.) 'Company milestones', Johnson Matthey/Macfarlan Smith. http://www.macsmith.com/index.php?page=history

Mandel, Jerry. (n.d.). 'The mythical roots of US drug policy: Soldier's disease and addicts in the Civil War', Schaffer Library of Drug Policy, http://www.druglibrary. org/schaffer/history/soldis.htm

Margolis, Eric. (2007) 'Remember the battle of Maiwand'. *Khaleej Times*, 15 April, http://www.khaleejtimes.com/DisplayArticleNew.asp?xfile=data/opinion/2007/ April/opinion_April49.xml&section=opinion&col=

Marks, Jeannette. (1915) 'The curse of narcoticism in America: A reveille'. *American Journal of Public Health* 5: 314–22

Martin, Daniel, and Matthew Hickley. (2009) 'Is this what they died for?: Ten British soldiers were killed in an operation to let 80,000 Afghans take part in elections'. *Daily Mail*, 27 August, pp. 1, 4

Martin, Jack. (2009) *Sapper Martin: The Secret Great War Diary of Jack Martin* (ed. by R. van Emden). London: Bloomsbury

Mason Jr., Herbert Molloy. (1999) *VFW: Our First Century 1899–1999*. Lenexa (TX): Addax Publishing Group

McCashin, Chris. (1993) 'Poppy row magazine insults old soldiers'. *Daily Star*, 23 November

McMahon, Katherine B. (1918) 'A War nurse in the fighting fields of Europe'. *American Journal of Nursing* 18 (8), May: 603–10

Mercer, David. (2007) 'Afghanistan poppies'. Letter of David Mercer, Managing Director of Johnson Matthey/Macfarlan Smith, 12 September, http://www.fco.gov.uk/ resources/en/pdf/3036656/afg-CN-Macfarlanesmithreport

Merlin, Mark David. (1984) *On the Trail of the Ancient Opium Poppy*. London: Associated University Presses

——. (2003) 'Archaeological evidence for the tradition of psychoactive plant use in the Old World'. *Economic Botany* 57 (3): 295–323

Merrillees, R.S. (1962) 'Opium Trade in the Bronze Age Levant'. *Antiquity* 36: 287–92

——. (1968) *The Cypriote Bronze Age Pottery found in Egypt*: Studies in Mediterranean Archaeology XVIII. Lund: P. Åström

——. (1974) *Trade and Transcendence in the Bronze Age Levant*: Studies in Mediterranean Archaeology 39. Goteborg: P. Åström

————. (1979) 'Opium again in antiquity'. *Levant* 11: 167–71

Michael, Moina. (1941) *The Miracle Flower: The Story of the Flanders Fields Memorial Poppy*. Philadelphia: Dorrance and Company

Milius, Susan. (2004) 'Morphine-free Mutant Poppies: Novel plants make pharmaceutical starter'. *Science News*, 25 September, http://www.opioids.com/opium/poppy-engineering.html

Milmo, Cahal. (2009) 'At least we knew what we were fighting for in 1944'. *Independent*, 7 November, http://www.independent.co.uk/news/uk/home-news/remembrance-sunday-at-least-we-knew-what-we-were-fighting-for-in-1944-1817252.html

Moore, John Hammond (ed.). (1997) *The Confederate Housewife*. Columbia (SC): Summerhouse Press

Mosse, George L. (1990) *Fallen Soldiers: Reshaping the Memory of the World Wars*. Oxford: Oxford University Press

Newall, Venetia. (1976) 'Armistice Day: Folk tradition in an English festival of remembrance'. *Folklore* 87 (2): 226–9

Newberry, P.E. (1900) 'The poppy in Egyptian art'. *Proceedings of the Society of Biblical Archaeology* XXII (CLXVIII, May): 144–6

Nicolson, Harold. 'British public opinion and foreign policy'. *Public Opinion Quarterly* 1 (1): (1937): 57–8

Nicolson, Juliet. (2009) *The Great Silence 1918–1920: Living in the Shadow of the Great War*. London: John Murray

Nikiforuk, Andrew. (2008) 'The poppy man: Peter Facchini explores the benefits of the opium poppy'. University Affairs, 6 October, http://www.universityaffairs.ca/the-poppy-man.aspx

O'Connell Jr., J. Barry. (1997) 'Afghan war rugs: If it walks like a duck . . .' *Oriental Rug Review*, March, http://www.rugreview.com/barrwar.htm

OFT (Office of Fair Trading) (2006) *Opium Derivatives: A Review of the Undertaking Given by MacFarlan Smith Ltd*. OFT 834. Crown Copyright. London: Office of Fair Trading

O'Neill, Brendan. (2008) 'Lindbergh's deranged quest for immortality'. BBC News, http://news.bbc.co.uk/2/hi/uk_news/magazine/7420026.stm

Oliver, F.E. (1872) *Massachusetts State Board of Health, Third Annual Report (For 1871)*, Boston: Wright and Potter, State Printers

Oliver, Sarah. (2009) 'Wootton Bassett – The town where Britain welcomes home her war dead'. *The Times,* 19 September, http://www.timesonline.co.uk/tol/news/uk/article6731100.ece

Parsons, I.M. (ed.). [1965] (1979) *Men Who March Away: Poems of the First World War*. London: Chatto & Windus

Pavia, Will. (2009) 'Wootton Bassett fears being in front line of "grief tourism".' *The Times*, 29 July, http://www.timesonline.co.uk/tol/news/uk/article6731100.ece

PBS/WGBH. (1998) 'Opium throughout history', *Frontline*: The Opium Kings, PBS/ WGBH, http://www.pbs.org/wgbh/pages/frontline/shows/heroin/etc/history. html

Pedley, John. (2005) *Sanctuaries and the Sacred in the Ancient Greek World*. Cambridge: Cambridge University Press

Pedlow, Gregory W. (2004) 'American Overseas Memorial Day Association – Belgium, 1923–2003: 80 years of honoring America's fallen from the Two World Wars', http://www.aomda.org

Pemble, John. (1987) *The Mediterranean Passion: Victorians and Edwardians in the South*. Oxford: Clarendon

Pence, Angélica. (2004) 'War's warp and weft: Afghan weavers incorporate battle scenes, World Trade Center attacks into tribal rugs'. *San Francisco Chronicle*, May 12, http://www.sfgate.com/homeandgarden/article/War-s-warp-and-weft-Afghan-weavers-incorporate-2759824.php

Penney, Jim. (2006) 'Memorial Day: Poppy tribute to be launched in Rome.' *Rome-News Tribune*, 28 May, http://news.mywebpal.com/news_tool_v2.cfm?sho w=localnews&pnpID=680&NewsID=722336&CategoryID=2658&on=1

Peters, Gretchen. (2009) *Seeds of Terror: How Heroin is Bankrolling the Taliban and al Qaeda*. Oxford: Oneworld

Petre, Jonathan. (2007) 'A time to remember, but should we wear a more "Christian" white poppy or a "PC" red?'. *Daily Telegraph*, 6 July, http://www.telegraph. co.uk/news/uknews/1533752/A-time-to-remember-but-should-we-wear-a-more-Christian-white-poppy-or-a-PC-red.html

Phillips, Rhodri, and Barry Wigmore. (2007) 'The painkilling fields: England's opium poppies that tackle the NHS morphine crisis'. *Daily Mail*, 14 July, http:// aftermathnews.wordpress.com/2007/07/15/the-painkilling-fields-englands-opium-poppies-that-tackle-the-nhs-morphine-crisis/

Pommerening, Tanja. (2005) 'Altägyptische Hohlmasse Metrologisch neu Interpretiert' and relevant pharmaceutical and medical knowledge, an abstract, Phillips-Universtat, Marburg, 8-11-2004, taken from 'Die Altägyptsche Hohlmasse' in studien zur Altägyptischen Kultur, Beiheft, 10. Hamburg: Buske-Verlag

Porter, E.M. (1958) 'Some folk beliefs of the Fens'. *Folklore* 69 (2): 112–22

PPU (Peace Pledge Union). (2006) 'White Poppies'. Peace Pledge Union, http://www. ppu.org.uk/whitepoppy/white-news1.html

Preminger, Alex. (ed.). [1965] (1969) *Princeton Encyclopedia of Poetry and Poetics*. Princeton (NJ): Princeton University Press

Prescott, John F. (1985) *In Flanders Fields: The Story of John McCrae*. Ontario: Boston Mills Press

RBL (Royal British Legion). (2008) *Poppy Press 1918–2008: The Great War – 90 years On, Then and Now*. London: Royal British Legion

RCL (Royal Canadian Legion) (2007) *Poppy Manual: Remembrance . . . Pass it on!*. Ottawa: Royal Canadian Legion

RCM (Royal Canadian Mint) (n.d.) 'The Royal Canadian Mint launches the world's first coloured coin commemorating the poppy – Canada's flower of remembrance', Royal Canadian Mint press release, http://www.prnewswire.co.uk/cgi/news/ release?id=132748

Ritchie, Kerri. (2008) 'War veterans angered by poppy theft'. Australian Broadcasting Corporation radio programme, 18 April, http://www.abc.net.au/pm/ content/2008/s2221399.htm

Roan, Leonard. (1941) 'Biography of Moina Michael (the Poppy Lady)' in Michael, Moina, *The Miracle Flower*. Philadelphia: Dorrance and Company

Robertshaw, Andrew, and David Kenyon. (2008) *Digging the Trenches: The Archaeology of the Western Front*. Barnsley: Pen and Sword, pp. 91–129

Robinson, Benjamin. (2000) 'Morphine as the tertium quid between war and revolution; Or, the moon gland secretes poppy sleep over the Western Front of Johannes R. Becher'. *German Quarterly* 73 (4): 387–400

Robinson, Victor. (1916) 'A symposium on drugs'. *Medical Review of Reviews* 22: 15–26

Rouse, W.H.D. (1937) *The Story of Odysseus*. New York: Modern Books

Ruskin, John. (1875) *Proserpina. Studies in Wayside Flowers Part I*. Orpington: George Allen

Russell, Ira. (1887) 'Opium inebriety'. *Medico-Legal Journal* 5: 144–50

Sanderson, Katharine. (2007) 'Special report: Opiates for the masses'. *Nature* 449, 20 September: 268–9, http://www.nature.com/nature/journal/v449/n7160/ full/449268a.html

Sassoon, Siegfried. (1940) *Poems Newly Selected 1916–1935*. London: Faber and Faber

Saunders, Nicholas J. (2001). 'Matter and memory in the landscapes of conflict: The Western Front 1914–1999', in Bender, B., and M. Winer (eds), *Contested Landscapes: Movement, Exile and Place*. Oxford: Berg, pp. 37–53

————. (2001) 'Apprehending memory: Material culture and war, 1919–1939' in Bourne, J., P.H. Liddle and H. Whitehead (eds), *The Great World War, 1914–1945*, vol. 2. London: HarperCollins, pp. 476–88

————. (2002a) *Trench Art*. Princes Risborough: Shire

————. (2002b). 'The ironic "culture of shells" in the Great War and beyond' in Schofield, J., W.G. Johnson, and C. Beck (eds), *Matériel Culture: The Archaeology of 20th Century Conflict*. London: Routledge, pp. 22–40

————. (2002c). 'Excavating memories: Archaeology and the Great War, 1914–2001'. *Antiquity* 76 (1): 101–8

————. (2003a). 'Crucifix, calvary, and cross: Materiality and spirituality in Great War landscapes'. *World Archaeology* 35 (1): 7–21

————. (2003b). *Trench Art: Materialities and Memories of War*. Oxford: Berg

Savoie, Charles. (2004) 'Silver users and opium'. Silver Investor, March, http://www.silver-investor.com/charlessavoie/cs_mar04.htm

Schiff Jr, Paul L. (2002) 'Opium and its alkaloids'. *American Journal of Pharmaceutical Education* 66 (Summer): 186–93

Scholl, Reinhold. (2002) *Der Papyrus Ebers. Die größte Buchrolle zur Heilkunde Altägyptens*. *Leipzig:* Schriften aus der Universitätsbibliothek, p. 7

Senlis Council. (2006) *Helmand at War*. The Senlis Council, http://www.icosgroup.net/

Shannon-Martin, Louise. (2007) 'Poppy anchor ceremony', *Savannah Morning News*, 6 June, http://savannahnow.com/node/299641

Shaw, Ted. (2002) 'Remembrance Day celebrated', *Ontario Birchbark*/Aboriginal Multi-Media Society of Alberta, December, http://www.ammsa.com/birchbark/topnews-Dec-2002.html

Siegel, R.K. (2005) *Intoxication: The Universal Drive for Mind-altering Substances*. Rochester (VT): Park Street Press

Silkin, Jon. (1972) *Out of Battle: The Poetry of the First World War*. London: Oxford University Press

Sjöqvist, Eric. (1940) *Problems of the Late Cypriote Bronze Age*. Stockholm: Swedish Cyprus Expedition

Smith, James. (2009) 'Shell UK Ltd endorses the Poppy Appeal collections at our retail stores across the UK', Shell UK press release, 9 November, http://www.shell.co.uk/gbr/aboutshell/media-centre/news-and-media-releases/2009/poppy-appeals.html

Smith, Len (Private). (2009) *Drawing Fire: The Diary of a Great War Soldier and Artist*. London: Collins

Smith, Lewis. (2008) 'Shrew identified as world's hardest drinking creature'. *The Times*, July 29, http://www.perthnow.com.au/news/shrew-is-worlds-biggest-boozer/story-e6frg12c-1111117059533

Smith, Michael. (2009) 'Special forces target insurgents "spectacular" death team'. *Sunday Times*, 9 August, p. 7

———, and Steven Swinford. (2009) 'Daisy chain trap kills Helmand heroes'. *Sunday Times*, 16 August, p. 7

Solecki, Ralph S. (1971) *Shanidar, the First Flower People*. New York: Knopf

Spain, John. (2008) 'Wearing the poppy for Ireland'. *Irish Abroad* website, 12 November. http://www.irishabroad.com/news/irish-voice/spain/Articles/poppy-ireland121108.aspx

Spear, Hilda D. (1979) *Remembering, We Forget: A Background Study to the Poetry of the First World War*. London: Davis-Poynter

Stallworthy, John (ed.) (1983) *Wilfred Owen: The Complete Poems and Fragments*, vol. 1: *The Poems*; vol. 2: *The Manuscripts of the Poems and the Fragments*. London: Chatto & Windus, The Hogarth Press, and Oxford University Press

Starkey, Gerald. (1971) 'The use and abuse of opiates and amphetamines' in Healy, P., and J. Manak (eds), *Drug Dependence and Abuse Resource Book*. Chicago: National District Attorney's Association, pp. 481–4

Starkey, Jerome. (2009) 'Roadside bombs made invisible'. *Sunday Times*, 2 August, p. 24

Stidger, William LeRoy. (1918) *Soldiers Silhouettes on our Front*. New York: Scribner's Sons

Stringer, John. (2005). Interviews: 10. Stephen Mulqueen Sculptor, Dunedin. *Chrysalis Seed News*, 19, January, http://www.cs.org.nz/files/docs/19%20cs%20news%20jan%2005.pdf

Stubbe, Lieven. (n.d.) *Invloeden van de Eerste Wereldoorlog op de (huidige) vegetaties binnen de frontstreek*. ('Effects of the First World War on the (current) vegetation of war front region'). Mss of October 2008, in possession of author

Sørensen, Nils Arne. (1997) *Remembering the Great War*. Pre-publications of the English Department of Odense University no. 92, October. Odense: Odense Universitets Trykkeri

Summerby, Janet. (2005) *Native Soldiers, Foreign Battlefields*. Ottawa: Veterans Affairs Canada, http://www.veterans.gc.ca/public/pages/history/other/native/natives_e.pdf

Summerscale, Kate. (1998) *The Queen of Whale Cay: The Eccentric Story of 'Joe' Carstairs, the Fastest Woman on Water*. London: Fourth Estate

Taylor, A.J.P. (1945) *The Course of German History: A Survey of the Development of Germany Since 1815*. London: Hamish Hamilton

Taylor, A.J.P. (1967) *The First World War: An Illustrated History*. Harmondsworth: Penguin

Terry, Charles E. and Mildred Pellens. [1928] (1970) *The Opium Problem*. Montclair (NJ): Patterson Smith

Thiseleton-Dyer, T.F. (1889) *The Folk-lore of Plants*. London: D. Appleton and Company

Thompson, Francis. [1913] (1965) *Poetical Works*. London: Oxford University Press

Thompson, Reginald Campbell. (1949) *A Dictionary of Assyrian Botany*. London: British Academy

Tibi, Selma. (2006) *The Medicinal Use of Opium in Ninth-century Baghdad*. Leiden: Brill

Toland, John. (1976) *Adolf Hitler*. Garden City (NY): Doubleday

Touregypt.net. (n.d.a) 'The Tutankhamun Exhibit: Jewelry – pectoral with solar and lunar emblems representing King Tutankhamun', http://www.touregypt.net/museum/tutl41.htm

Touregypt.net. (n.d.b) 'The Tutankhamun Exhibit: Jewelry – rigid udjat eye bracelet representing King Tutankhamun', http://www.touregypt.net/museum/braceletpage.htm

Touregypt.net. (n.d.c) 'The Tutankhamun Exhibit: Basic funeral equipment – golden shrine', http://www.touregypt.net/museum/tutl55.htm

UNODC (United Nations Office on Drugs and Crime) (2007) *2007 World Drug Report*. Vienna: United Nations Office on Drugs and Crime, Vienna International Centre

USWPA/FWP (US Work Projects Administration, Federal Writers' Project) (1939) 'Miss Moina Belle Michael: The Poppy Lady'. Folklore Project, Life Histories 1936–9, US Library of Congress, 8–9 February, http://files.usgwarchives.net/ga/clarke/bios/bs122michael.txt

Valencic, Ivan. (1994) 'Has the Mystery of Eleusinian Mysteries been solved?' in Rätsch, Christian, and John R. Baker, eds. *Yearbook for Ethnomedicine and the Study of Consciousness* 3, pp. 325–36. Berlin: Verlag für Wissenschaft und Bildung

Van Ham, Peter, and Jorrit Kamminga. (2006–7) 'Poppies for peace: Reforming Afghanistan's opium industry'. *Washington Quarterly* 30 (1): 69–81

Verleyen, Herwig. (2004) *In Flanders Fields: The Story of John McCrae, His Poem and the Poppy*. Koksijde: De Klaproos

VFWP (VFW Programs) (2007) 'Buddy Poppy: Remember September 11'. VFW Programs E-Newsletter 24 (1), 1 September: 1, www.vfw.org

Waldorf, Dan, Martin Orlick, Craig Reinarman. (1974) *Morphine Maintenance: The Shreveport Clinic 1919–1923*. Washington, DC: Drug Abuse Council

Walker, Winifred. (1959) *All the Plants of the Bible*. New York: Harper

Walsh, Declan. (2006) 'The wild frontier'. *Guardian*, 31 January, http://www.guardian.co.uk/g2/story/0,,1698471,00.html

———. (2007) 'British military sanctions Afghan poppy cultivation'. *Guardian*, 27 April, http://www.guardian.co.uk/world/2007/apr/27/afghanistan.declanwalsh

———. (2008) 'Hamburger Hill: Frontline base in a sea of poppies British soldiers dare not clear. War on drugs loses out to anti-Taliban fight for hearts and minds in Helmand province'. *Guardian*, 29 April, http://www.guardian.co.uk/world/2008/apr/29/afghanistan.drugstrade

Ward Fay, Peter. (1975) *The Opium War 1840–1842*. Chapel Hill: University of North Carolina Press

Weiner, Rex. (2004) 'Weaving havoc: Traditional Afghan "war rugs" tell dramatic and often violent stories, and the ones now arriving in LA Galleries have a distinctly American flavor'. 11 January, *Los Angeles Times*, http://articles.latimes.com/2004/jan/11/magazine/tm-warrug02

Wenzel, Marian, and John Cornish. (1980) Auntie Mabel's War: An Account of Her Part in the Hostilities of 1914–18. London: Allen Lane

Whitaker, Mark. (2009) *Poppies are Red, Cornflowers are Blue*. BBC Radio 4, 8 November, http://www.bbc.co.uk/programmes/b00nnqpg

Whitman, Walt. (1898) *The Wound Dresser: A Series of Letters Written from the Hospital in Washington During the War of Rebellion*, ed. by Richard Maurice Bucke, MD Boston: Small, Maynard & Company

Wilcock, John. (n.d.) 'Guilty gardeners?', Opiods.com, http://opioids.com/jh/gardening.html

Wilkinson, Alix. (1998) *The Garden in Ancient Egypt*. London: Rubicon Press

Winfield, Nicole. (2009) 'US announces shift in Afghanistan drug policy'. Associated Press, 28 June, http://www.huffingtonpost.com/2009/06/27/us-announces-shift-in-afg_n_221826.html

Wootton, Graham. (1956) *The Official History of the British Legion*. London: Macdonald & Evans

Zervos, Christian. (1956) *L'art de la Crète néolithique et minoenne*. Paris: Éditions 'Cahiers d'art'

INDEX

Note: *n* following a page number indicates an endnote with relevant number.

ABOUT THE AUTHOR

Nicholas J. Saunders is the world's leading authority on the anthropology and archaeology of the First World War. His exhibition of trench art was the centrepiece of the 'In Flanders Fields' Museum in Ypres, Belgium. The author or editor of more than twenty books and dozens of academic monographs, he has appeared in numerous documentaries for the BBC and *National Geographic*.